OUR FOOD,
OUR LAND

OUR FOOD, OUR LAND

Why contemporary farming practices must change

RICHARD BODY

RIDER
London   Sydney   Auckland   Johannesburg

Copyright © Richard Body 1991

All rights reserved

First published in the UK in 1991 by Rider
An imprint of Random Century Group Ltd
20 Vauxhall Bridge Road, London SW1V 2SA

Random Century Group Australia (Pty) Ltd
20 Alfred Street, Milsons Point,
Sydney, NSW 2061, Australia

Random Century New Zealand Ltd,
9–11 Rothwell Avenue, Albany,
Auckland 10, New Zealand

Random Century Group South Africa (Pty) Ltd,
PO Box 337, Bergvlei 2012, South Africa

Printed and bound in Great Britain by
Mackays of Chatham PLC, Chatham, Kent

British Library Cataloguing in Publication Data
Body, Richard
Our food, our land : why contemporary farming practices
must change.
1. Great Britain. Agricultural industries
I. Title
338.10941

ISBN 0–7126–4640–X
ISBN 0–7126–4641–8 pbk

This book has been printed on recycled paper

CONTENTS

INTRODUCTION

History gives many examples to show that, when a nation's agriculture goes wrong, the rest of the nation's life goes wrong too. Whether it is a simple agrarian society or a complex industrial economy seems to make no difference. For agriculture itself is more than a mere industry; its influence percolates its way, like an incoming tide, to every hidden inlet. Agriculture is a question of food and therefore of health; it affects our landscape, the pleasure it affords us and the existence it gives our wildlife; it affects our trade with other countries and therefore our good relations with millions of people across the seas. It involves, as this book tries to show, all the material things that matter most to us. And they are all going wrong.

We in the industrialized countries – and most of all in the United Kingdom – have treated our agriculture like a mechanistic industry, as if it were the process of making television sets, suits of clothes or kitchen sinks. At the end of the Second World War, the UK government decided that we should grow much more of our own food and become as self-sufficient as was practical. The reasons for this policy seemed at the time plausible, and they were fully supported by the National Farmers' Union, by the farming press and, naturally enough, by the large chemical companies which supplied our farmers. In this book I explain how the five reasons were all fallacious. Readers may judge for themselves;

if the policy was founded on false premises, logic suggests that a terrible mistake was made.

The core of the UK's agricultural policy has been, and still is, the system of guaranteed prices. Now, if a government decreed that anyone making television sets, suits of clothes or kitchen sinks would receive a guaranteed price for whatever was produced, what would happen? A guaranteed price, of course, is nothing unless it is higher than the price prevailing in the market-place, which is no more than a willing buyer and a willing seller agree upon. A guaranteed price is therefore an inducement to produce more than what the market wants. Give this happy privilege to anyone willing to make television sets, suits of clothes or kitchen sinks, and nothing very serious will result. A great glut of the things will pile up. Perhaps they will be dumped upon markets abroad at give-away prices with the aid of massive subsidies, provoking a few protests about unfair competition from manufacturers in other countries. Domestic taxpayers will be required to pay higher taxes for the policy, and consumers to pay more for the things than otherwise.

Applied to agriculture, the same policy of guaranteed prices has results that cannot be reduced only to simple cash terms. The policy is now well established in the UK – although in the 1970s, when I first published my calculations showing an annual cost to the population of some £5,000 million a year, the figure was greeted with unanimous hoots of derision.

The financial cost of the policy is not, however, to be dismissed as of little consequence. For the average family the cost of food due to guaranteed prices is £16 a week more than necessary. This represents a significant percentage of the income of millions of families, whose standard of living is manifestly lowered by what is in effect a regressive form of taxation. Multiply this £16 by the total number of families and it indicates a massive transfer of spending power away from where the British people would wish it to be, on items other than food, and devoted instead to food made artifically more expensive than it need be. This diversion of spending power, besides cutting the economic welfare of consumers, also causes a wide range of industries to have a lower demand for their goods and services. Given the many billions of pounds lost by that lower demand, a large number of businesses, once marginally profitable, have become sufficiently unprofitable to collapse; even the most profitable ones have faced some degree of contraction, so that most industries have employed fewer men and women. How far this accounts for the UK's total unemployment can only be the subject of conjecture, but the number of jobs lost must be substantial.

Where has all this money gone? Years of naïvety persuaded us that it was supporting farmers. Guaranteed prices must be to their benefit, for they receive more for their produce than the market would have allowed. Such an obvious apparent claim to truth has been belied by nearly half a century of practice. When the UK began the system, it had in round figures 500,000 farmers; today there are, again in round figures, 200,000; so it looks as if the policy has been of little help to at least half of them. The reason is found in the law of economics. It is this: if the state artificially raises the price of a product, the initial benefit to the producer in the form of higher income is nullified by a rise in the value of the asset out of which the product comes. The asset we are concerned with is our land; out of it comes our food; so the price of land rises when the price of food is increased by state action and it rises in aggregate terms as much as the aggregate increase in the price of food. This is what happened with the Corn Laws in the first half of the nineteenth century; hence the distress and starvation in the countryside which only became worse when the levies on imported corn were raised still higher.

We can calculate the cost of guaranteed prices since the Second World War, and we can calculate how much agricultural land has appreciated in value in excess of inflation in the same period. The two figures are the same. Thus the farmer as a farmer has gained nothing. If he owns his land, the advantage may have given him the delusion of benefit; and as landowning in itself has become more lucrative, there has been a vast flood of money pouring into agricultural land from financial institutions. The last consequence has given rise to a massive diversion of capital. Instead of going to other industries which could have generated more wealth and employment, it has been invested in our land, which was there anyway, but which has suffered as a result of the pressure of excessive investment.

Higher land values leading to higher rents have put the tenant under a great strain. Of the farmers who have given up farming, the overwhelming majority have been tenants. Owner-occupiers, with their main asset raised in value, have been able to borrow money on the security of their land in order to buy adjoining farms, and with their increased acreages they have managed to expand and thus survive.

When the value of land rises a great deal more than the rate of inflation (in nominal pounds, most of our land is about 100 times more expensive than it was forty years ago) the farmer is put under great pressure to get as much out of it as he can. This brings us to the appalling yet unquantified cost of the policy – to the quality and fertility of our soil, as well as to the quality and safety of our food, the welfare of our farm animals, the beauty of the landscape and the habitat of our wildlife. Much of the damage has been recorded extensively elsewhere, and this book highlights only a portion of it.

In treating our food like inert products such as television sets, suits of clothes and kitchen sinks, and our land like the factories that manufacture them, our policy-makers have committed a tragic error. Our food and our land have been lumped together. The objective of the policy has been to get as much of our food out of our land as possible, and for our land to be treated as no more than a resource for gathering our food. Our food and our land should be regarded as two separate areas of policy-making, however. A connection between the two is plain, but it is not strong enough to blur the distinction that should go to the heart of the matter, which can be stated simply. Only some of our food ought to come from our land, and only some of our land should be the source of our food. So, in a way, the theme of this book is that our food and our land should no longer be treated as one and the same by policy-makers. But we can never rid ourselves of the danger of treating them in this way until we bring to an end the system of guaranteed prices. So long as the latter exists it will be impossible to sever the two. The system is at the heart of the European Community's Common Agricultural Policy; it can almost be said to be the policy itself; and the policy itself is the coping-stone of the EEC. Take it away and, it is said, nine of the twelve member countries would lose the benefit of membership.

Here we come to a serious dilemma for the UK. The other member countries, generally speaking, have suffered few or none of the ill effects set out in this book. This is because British agriculture has been on the treadmill of ever rising food production longer than theirs has been. Indeed, in southern Europe the farmers and growers have scarcely put a foot on the treadmill. No sense of urgency prevails on the Continent; few feelings of anxiety are found, and thus no inclination to change the policy yet. To be in a minority of one may be disagreeable, but there is certainly something we can do. After West Germany, the UK has been the main paymaster of the system. Without our contribution to the Community's budget, it would be impossible for the Common Agricultural Policy to continue in its present form unless the other member countries were to pay a great deal more towards it. Nine of them are net beneficiaries; France's income from the EEC is broadly the same as its contribution, which would leave Germany the only net contributor were the UK to say it was in its urgent national interest to pursue an alternative policy.

No harsh words need be said, no recrimination; just quietly to withdraw from the CAP should be the first step. If, however, the second largest paymaster's insistence on a change of the principles of the CAP were accepted, then we might be able to agree happily on the alternative policy. The latter is not impossible, for the views in this book have found a response in the Commission of the Community. There at least it is understood well enough that the present policy not only has brought the Common Market to a state of technical bankruptcy, as it did a few years ago, but also inhibits the Commission, through a shortage of funds, from embarking upon more desirable enterprises. Besides, the Community is not so fragile as it was; a decade ago a withdrawal from the Common Agricultural Policy might have brought the downfall of the whole Common Market, but today that fragility has given way to self-confidence. If the EEC were now unable to survive one of its member countries' withdrawal from one of its policies, there would be something sorely amiss with its architecture.

What, then, should replace the CAP? By recognizing the need for our food and our land to be treated separately, we would also recognize the farmer as having a dual role: as both food producer and manager of the countryside. When I first began to argue this duality, the response from the more vocal of the farming community verged upon the apoplectic. 'Park-keepers?' they snorted. 'We are business men!' But what a dangerous thing for them to have said. If they are business men, why on earth should they be heavily subsidized? A business man should get his money out of satisfying his customers; and if he complains that they do not give him enough to live on, he should, like other business men, look for some other source of income.

At once this brings to an end the system of guaranteed prices. The consumer then regains the freedom to buy food from wherever he or she chooses, and the average family is immediately £16 a week better off. A policy of free trade follows, and the taxes on imported food are abolished.

As matters now stand, however, there is no chance whatever of the European Community bringing to an end the system of guaranteed prices. This has been made clear in the negotiations over agricultural trade under the General Agreement on Tariffs and Trade that took place in 1990. More than 100 countries participated; there was unanimous agreement that the dumping of food surpluses on the world market with the aid of taxpayers' money caused hardship and often destitution to hundreds of thousands of farmers. The EEC accepted that truth, but it refused to bring export subsidies to an end or even to make a sufficient reduction to halt the disruption of world trade.

These export subsidies are necessary only to get rid of surpluses; and surpluses arise only when demand and supply are chronically out of balance. Dismantle the system of guaranteed prices, and the engine that makes supply exceed demand will trouble us no more.

INTRODUCTION

The economic case for free trade is deployed later in the book, but ecologically the argument is crucial. There is, I believe, a correlation between the economic and the ecological cost of food production. For, in conditions of free trade, the actual monetary cost of food goes up in parallel, as a general rule, with the ecological cost. Of course, one is quantitative and the other qualitative, but both costs stem from how the factors of production are used. If these are land, labour, capital and management, the three latter tend to be much the same wherever the food is produced, while land is the main determinant of cost. This in turn depends upon soil, climate, terrain and the natural advantages or disadvantages these have for a particular form of food production. The soil for growing wheat at a comparatively low cost, for example, is not the soil for ranching beef cattle at such a cost; the climate desirable for bananas is not the one for cabbages; and the terrain for growing tea is scarcely to be recommended for soya beans. But it would be technically feasible (just) to reverse each of those six. No doubt it would be uneconomic to grow soya bean in the hills of Assam or tea on the plains of Mississippi – most people would say it would be rather silly to make the attempt. Yet that is the kind of silliness we have been practising here in the UK.

We have, for instance, ploughed up one-quarter of the North Yorkshire Moors, the natural home of the grouse and a few sheep, then drained it at great expense and fertilized it at even greater cost – some of it to grow barley and even wheat, to be sold at a price more than double the world market price, and the rest of it to graze beef and sheep, both also sold at far above the world price. Forcing one's land to do something at a high economic cost is also ecologically costly. We are paying a terrible ecological price for what we have done not just to the North Yorkshire Moors, but on almost every acre of farmland we have.

So long as we goad our farmers with the bait of guaranteed prices, the ecological cost will continue to mount. Yet if farmers are to be regarded as business men operating in conditions of free trade, are they not entitled, like any other business men, to maximize their profits? The affirmative answer then entitles them to do whatever they think profitable with their soil, their trees, their hedges, their animals and the wildlife in their charge. So much destruction has already been done to all these things that, faced with competition from 'cheap food' from overseas, few of our farmers would survive even if goaded still more along that path of destruction. The fact is now undeniable: with the exception of organic farmers (who are virtually independent of guaranteed prices), only a handful of our farmers could survive for long in conditions of free trade. Such is the state into which British agriculture has fallen. So the door should be opened for the government to strike a bargain on behalf of the British people with every farmer and grower to enter into a management agreement to produce what he wants to sell and what the consumer wants to buy in ways that protect the environment, the quality and safety of our food and the welfare of our farm animals. Numerous difficulties can be foreseen, but none are insurmountable, as Chapters 10 and 11 show.

The supreme argument for this change of policy is that the present methods of conventional agriculture cannot be sustained. They are going to collapse, and the collapse will come first in the UK, for we have been on the chemical treadmill (its driving force), if not longer than others, then more intensively. This book argues for a change to biological methods of farming. These methods are cyclical and can go on indefinitely, while chemical farming is linear and its future is finite, for at some time the end of the line will be reached. There is a limit to the number of chemical compounds that can be made into pesticides, and one by one we are using them up as the pests become resistant; so too with antibiotics, the indispensable aid to factory farming; and in the case of nitrates, upon which every conventional arable farmer depends, we no longer question that their use must be restricted, lest our water supply become undrinkable. The natural destruction of our soil is also linear; without soil there can be no human life. Some twenty civilizations have perished because the civilizing of a nation (which literally means the transfer of people from a rural to an urban existence) led to demands upon the soil which could not be met without a high standard of husbandry. Similarly today, intensive farming methods are causing our soil to lose its health, become lifeless and be depleted at an alarming rate; unless the damage is halted or reversed, great areas of the British countryside will be unfit to be cultivated at some point in the twenty-first century. What will happen then? The same process is taking place in every continent of the globe, not least of all on the prairies of the Midwest, on the steppes of the Soviet Union and – tragically – in the most poverty-stricken regions of Africa.

There is, however, an alternative. Guaranteed prices can be withdrawn, overcultivation reduced and subsidies for destructive farming methods reversed. Farmers can be encouraged and helped to irrigate the soil with care, reduce their consumption of soil-poisoning chemicals to a minimum, improve soil quality with the use of organic fertilizer and reintroduce hedgerows and trees to provide shelter against erosion and habitats for pest predators. This means a return to farming with long-term continuity, rather than maximum short-term yields, as the main goal – and probably also a transition to smaller farms.

It has taken many years to gather and distil the evidence in this book. I have had the time to do so and the opportunity to visit twenty-two other countries to study their farming methods. I have seen at first hand the effect that the selfish and short-sighted policies followed by some Western countries – above all by the EEC – have had upon their lives, dragging down hundreds of thousands of the poorest people in the world to a state of abject penury. I began with a hunch that agriculture would go through a difficult time; as the evidence piled up, the prospect became steadily worse; and before I had finished there was in front of me a bedrock of certainty. If readers see that same certainty, and are willing to fight for the alternatives, there may be some hope.

· 1 ·

SOIL AND CIVILIZATION

Until about 350 million years ago there was no soil on the planet, there being no land-based plants or living creatures; such life as the world sustained was in the oceans. Then, during the Silurian period, organic matter began to come out of the sea and with it ultramarine life. The vegetation mingled with particles of rock, and – assisted by the air, sun and rain – the first soil on earth was formed. During the following millennia, microbes and sentient creatures, having emerged from the water, evolved to hasten the process by which living soil was made out of decomposing organic matter and lifeless minerals. Eventually, we now know, the whole world above sea level, apart from the mountain ranges, was covered by good topsoil. Primitive men did nothing to hinder or reverse this, gathering and later culti-vating food and disposing of waste in accordance with natural laws of decay and regeneration. Like the Amazonian Indians today, the first human beings seem to have evolved a way of life that was in harmony with their environment. If there were some whose instincts were otherwise, they were so few in number that the trees they felled for fuel and the animals they hunted for food were more than replaced.

SOIL EROSION PAST AND PRESENT

Then came civilized man. Historians tell us that some twenty civilizations have been born, prospered and subsequently perished. In every case, so far as we can ascertain, their end has come suddenly and unexpectedly. In a fascinating book, *Topsoil and Civilization* (1974), published in the United States, Vernon Gill Carter and Tom Dale have distilled years of research into a warning for Western civilization. As a civilization progresses, more of its people move from an agrarian existence to urban life, so the proportion of the population producing food declines. The United Kingdom, in this sense, can claim to be a very civilized place, with only 2 per cent of its people engaged in agriculture, the lowest proportion in the world, unless one wishes to include Hong Kong and Macao. As the proportion of the urban population increases, so the pressure rises on the agrarian minority to increase their production of food. As the cities of each civilization grow in prosperity, the citizens are able to pay higher prices, and the farmers out in the countryside, eager to share in the wealth, are willing to take risks to meet the rising demand. Why let the land lie fallow for a year when it can grow a profitable crop? Why not graze the land with more cattle and sheep? And why not plant wheat for the fourth year in succession if the people in the towns want still more of it?

Monoculture of only the most profitable crops begins; increased areas of cultivation reduce the amount of fertilizer each crop is given; trees are cut down to make more land available. Then an impoverished soil, deprived of protection, begins to erode. But deserts are not made by man slowly, for the pace of soil erosion accelerates. The first stages may be insidious and, to all but the good husbandman, imperceptible; then prolonged rainfall will sweep away more than it would have done otherwise, because the soil lacks the weight of humus, and trees are no longer there to bind and protect it. Those twenty or so past civilizations experienced two kinds of soil erosion: winds blew away the improverished soil and with it the seeds planted for the next harvest; and rain erosion swept soil away to the sea. Too little soil means too little food; and with hunger comes disease.

Civilization depends upon the primary producers – miners, fishermen and foresters as well as farmers – producing more than they themselves need. Without such surpluses, civilization is impossible. Not in every past case did this surplus disappear altogether; sometimes, having despoiled its environment, a nation took up arms against another with territory it coveted. Nor have all deserts been made by civilized man – but the majority have.

To claim that all the ancient civilizations perished because of bad agriculture is perhaps an oversimplification. Wars fought and lost, corruption and decadence, climatic change and perhaps inbreeding or other factors have contributed to the collapse of past civilizations. Still, each had the same common feature: an environment laid waste and its soil lost through erosion or too impoverished to a desperate degree. Great areas of the Near and Middle East bear witness to the saddest examples. The Medes and Persians flourished in what is now the harsh aridity of western Iran, the Assyrians in northern Iraq. And all around the Mediterranean – in Greece, Crete, Turkey, Syria, Lebanon, Israel, Egypt, Tunisia and Algeria – where much of Western civilization was born, nations that thrived for hundreds or thousands of years were eventually brought low or destroyed. (There are, however, pockets of land in this region where there is still soil enough to cultivate. In several incidences, as in the Nile Valley and around Ephesus in Turkey, the soil is constantly replenished by river-borne silt.)

The quantity of soil can be measured, and its erosion can be seen and calculated. Its quality is another matter. One tonne of the healthiest soil may yield more than ten tonnes of the poorest kind. The failure of these earlier civilizations to detect how their soil was deteriorating in quality as a result of the methods of agriculture they were induced to adopt was also a cause of their collapse. A grain of wheat planted for next year's harvest is too small to have within it all the nutrients needed if it is to grow into a plant 100 times larger than itself, as well as to provide the nourishment in several slices of bread. The little seed is one determinant of the food value of the wheat; more important is the quality of the soil in which it is planted. A healthy soil yields healthy food, which in turn contributes to the health of those who eat it. Monoculture, overcropping and a failure to replace lost nutrients improverished a soil then as they do today. A number of minerals are required for our health – zinc, copper and iron are examples – and if any of these are missing or insufficient, physical and mental fitness suffers, leading to impotence, deformity and disease. Some historians have ascribed the fall of civilizations to what they have called a deterioration of race. Very few of them have gone on to examine why a once healthy people ceased to be so. As it can be shown that every one of these ancient civilizations, within a century or two before their demise, began to practise forms of husbandry that led to the impoverishment of their soil, we may seem justified in assuming cause and effect.

Homo sapiens, it seems, learns little from the past, and nothing at all in the matter of treating the main and indispensable source of human life. In every country and in every area of land cultivated by man, there is soil erosion on a major scale. In the world as a whole, the loss is at the rate of 1,000 tonnes a second. This comes to more than 30,000 million tonnes in a single year, or about 5 tonnes for every member of the human race; used with a little ingenuity, this much soil would be enough to prevent all hunger till the end of time.

EROSION IN THE UK

In the UK, and most particularly in the arable areas of England, the loss of soil is accelerating. For years there were only anecdotes to support the claim. In Lincolnshire, for example, elderly countrymen were heard to say that the Wolds are getting whiter, as the disappearing topsoil brought the chalk to the surface. More recently, however, Soil Survey experts have studied what is happening. Take the not untypical county of Bedfordshire; according to scientists at the government's soil research station at Rothamstead, Bedfordshire is losing its soil at an average rate of one tonne an acre every year. If this loss is allowed to continue, some time in the twenty-first century the farmland of Bedfordshire will become agriculturally useless and no longer worth cultivating. We may assume that most other counties will be affected in a similar way.

Evidence of serious soil erosion has been found in many other areas of the UK. In Scotland, R. B. Spiers and C. F. Frost, both of the Edinburgh School of Agriculture, made a special study of the problem and published the results in *Research and Development in Agriculture, 1985*. They first noted significant erosion in 1969; from then till 1979 they found thirty instances; and between 1980 and 1984 another 300 examples were found. In winter and spring of 1984–5 the number rose to 450. It is, of course, the quantity of soil lost that is important: 100 fields were examined in detail; in 42 of them 1 to 10 cubic metres of soil per acre had been eroded, in 44 fields between 10 and 100 cubic metres, and in other cases there had been a loss of soil of as much as 350, 650, 800 and even 900 cubic metres. Fields of pasture seem to have been unaffected, all the serious erosion being on the arable land.

Dr A. Harrison Reed of Wolverhampton Polytechnic is another who has done important research on this subject. In 1976 he began a trial at Hilton, Shropshire, where he divided a site into eight 25-square-metre plots and one of 3 square metres. He found that the loss of soil in each of the following years was on average 15 to 17 tonnes a hectare (=2½ acres), and in two of the years over 400 tonnes per hectare.

Further examples were given by Dr R. D. Hodges and C. Arden-Clarke in a report entitled *Soil Erosion in Britain* (1986), published by the Soil Association. The authors acknowledged that some degree of soil loss occurs naturally and cannot be avoided; it has happened for centuries and need not be a matter of concern. Any prolonged rainfall will wash away some earth into ditches and dykes and thence via rivers to the sea; so, too, will the wind have some effect. Until recently this erosion has been made good by new soil being formed. But the losses today are far in excess of what was the case thirty or forty years ago, and they are accelerating. Those fields where a loss of 40 tonnes to the hectare in a single year has recently been reported once had no erosion of any consequence.

All these studies were primarily concerned with the quantitative loss, not the qualitative. We know that deterioration in the quality of the soil was a cause of its subsequent erosion when ancient civilizations perished, and fieldworkers who have gone out to the areas of the world where the same process is occurring most alarmingly today insist that history is repeating itself.

Before we take a more detailed look at the reasons why soil erosion is accelerating in the UK, as in many other countries, let us consider what makes good healthy soil. Much has already been recorded about this, nowhere more clearly than in Lady Eve Balfour's classic, *The Living Soil* (1944). In a single saltspoon of healthy soil there may be anything from a million to 10 million micro-organisms. These living creatures keep the soil alive; they are the agents that decompose dead vegetable matter, like a leaf fallen from the tree or a blade of winter grass, as well as the remains of dead animals and the excreta of living ones. Such matter is dead yet not inorganic, for the micro-organisms are at work making the mortified into another passage of life. Nor do the micro-organisms begin when death comes, for these minute creatures are about their business on the living as well as the dead. There is, therefore, no clear-cut division in nature's world between life and death; the two fuse into one long, unending process. Birth, growth, reproduction, decline, death and decomposition are followed by another cycle of birth leading on to eventual decomposition; and the cycles have gone round and round since any form of life began. Some call the cycle nature's 'wheel of life'; others, the principle of self-sustaining life. A wheel makes a whole movement in completing its revolution. 'Wholeness' and 'health' stem from the same word, the Germanic *heil*, and the same meaning. Allow nature's wheel to revolve naturally, and natural health will be the outcome. Once we interfere with the way the wheel goes round, it is possible that nature will react unkindly.

What the vast majority of British farmers, and 99 per cent of our arable farmers, are doing is working against that principle. There is plenty of evidence to suggest that their act of defiance cannot endure for long, no more than it could when those ancient civilizations did much the same. There are, however, two distinctions between them. The first is climate. Deserts come more quickly in those areas where the sun shines more often and more fiercely. Rainfall in the UK, more frequent than in the Mediterranean region, has the effect of postponing the day of reckoning. Against this advantage must be set those of today's farming practices which contribute to the decline in both the quantity and the quality of the soil and which were unknown to previous civilizations.

The technical triumphs of modern Western agriculture – enabling British farmers to grow four times more wheat on the same land as they could forty years ago, for example – have given us bountiful harvests and massive surpluses of wheat, barley, sugar, butter and other items. The cost of subsidizing their sale to Soviet Russia and storing what cannot be sold at subsidized prices is a scandal so well recorded elsewhere that to repeat it here must be superfluous. The consequence is that a feverish debate continues about how we can bring down production. Quotas, price cuts, set-aside programmes, a tax on nitrogen and other ideas are canvassed, and it is right that some remedy be found. But the great technical triumphs have within them the seeds of their own destruction. The practices of modern farming that have been evolved during the last four decades have been conducive both to the failure of the land to replenish the loss of soil which naturally takes place and to the accelerating rate of erosion.

Although the UK's soils vary in composition, virtually any handful of our soil is capable of growing a healthy crop and contains a mix of many minerals, once part of some rock formation that rain, frost and various kinds of vegetation have caused to disintegrate over the centuries. Oxygen, iron, silicon, calcium, sodium, potassium, magnesium, aluminium, carbon, phosphorus, sulphur and titanium are some of the more common chemical elements that come from the igneous rocks, but there are many others. Once dispersed, they may be recycled in many ways, becoming soil, plants, animals, microbes and soil again. What is important is that the soil, to maintain its health, retains the right proportions of each of these many elements.

Among the ways new soil used to be created was with farmyard manure. It was applied to the land by the tonne; it both fertilized the earth, and once absorbed, became an important ingredient in the formation of new soil, increasing its mass. Arable farmers, expecially in East Anglia, kept cattle and pigs for the specific purpose of producing fertilizer, and their value as animals for the butcher was often of secondary importance. Hence the crew-yards that were built among the farm buildings; great quantities of straw were littered down, and the animals were fed on barley or root crops grown on the farm. Today almost all of those crew-yards stand empty and forlorn, their walls falling into disrepair or demolished. Why keep stock if they may lose you money? Why work seven days a week to feed them and bed them down with straw if ICI's fertilizer bags will do the job for you?

In 1950 the Ministry of Agriculture was persuaded to introduce a subsidy for farmers who used potassium as an artificial fertilizer. This was the thin end of the wedge, for soon afterwards the subsidy was extended to all artificial fertilizers. The use of farmyard manure was then doomed. Up until this time, manure used to be spread with a pitchfork. A horse and cart or tractor and trailer would take the muck from the crew-yard out into the field, where it was unloaded in heaps. Then began the laborious task of pitching the fork into the heap and distributing the manure over the ground; it was a job to keep you warm on a cold March day, but after a few minutes, after you were duly warmed up, it became sheer drudgery. Why do it at all, once a kindly ministry gave you taxpayers' money not to do it? An automatic fertilizer spreader was then put on the market, its purchase being set off against income tax, and the whole business of fertilizing the land became transformed. One man on a tractor – to which the new machine was attached – could spread all the fertilizer necessary in minutes instead of hours, and do it so much more cheaply, too!

But artificial fertilizers have only a limited number of

elements, nitrogen being the most prominent. Though they may fertilize the soil, they are totally incapable of replacing soil that has been lost, unlike farmyard manure.

The cultivation of small fields, each bounded by a hedgerow with some broad-leaved trees, was a means of protection against wind erosion, although experts seem to be in agreement that this kind of erosion has not been serious in the UK, except in parts of East Anglia, where the soil may be silt or sandy. Much more important is the effect their loss has had on replenishing the soil, for every yard of hedge and every tree would have numerous leaves which would fall in the autumn and rot into the earth. Modern machinery, especially the massive combine harvesters, has made small fields too inconvenient; hence the destruction of thousands of miles of hedgerows. Gone, too, are the cutting and laying of hedges by hand, except in a few pockets of the Midlands. Instead, a tractor driver trawls his hedge-flayer remorselessly along, and the sapling oak and the sapling ash are treated the same as the thorn and bramble. It is rare to see a new young tree rise above the hedges that are left. The effect upon new soil formation is incalculable.

Then there is the drainage of our land. This too has had a major effect on erosion. It is not suggested that there should be no drainage work done at all. Even pastureland may benefit from it, for chronically wet fields are slow to produce a crop of grass in the spring, although it is worth keeping some wet land against a very dry summer. There is, however, a major distinction to be drawn between drainage schemes paid for by the taxpayer to induce a farmer to grow a crop which would not otherwise be economic and a scheme paid for by the farmer himself to improve the land, enabling it to grow more economically a crop which it is naturally fitted to produce.

The UK's farmland is divided into five grades of quality. When the grades were introduced by the Ministry of Agriculture in 1966, only the two top grades were designated as naturally suitable for arable crops, together comprising no more than 17 per cent of our farmland. Grade III land, 48 per cent of the total, was generally pasture. Grade IV (18 per cent) was defined as land 'with severe limitations due to adverse soil, relief or climate . . . generally only suitable for low output enterprises', while the remaining Grade V land was even worse. A drainage scheme is justified for the top grades to encourage the land to fulfil its purpose of growing arable crops, and schemes for Grade III land to improve it as pasture and in some areas, where it is of better quality, to grow cereals or perhaps potatoes. Yet hundreds of thousands of acres of Grade IV and V land, even 25 per cent of the North Yorkshire Moors, have been drained at huge expense.

This cost has been borne largely by the taxpayer. Public money has been used to drain land which would otherwise have remained pasture or some form of rough grazing on the moors, downs and heaths. Having been drained, it has become capable of growing arable crops, especially wheat and barley. Drainage grants, generous though they have been, have not covered the whole cost, but most farmers would agree that they would not have had the work done unless the grants had been made available by the ministry.

Many millions of pounds have been given to British farmers in this way. It has been enough to drain for the first time 7 million acres. This is an area equivalent to Northumberland, Lancashire, Durham and Yorkshire combined, or about one-fifth of the English countryside. The main purpose has been to convert pastureland, often wet but suitable enough for growing a useful crop of grass, into land capable of yielding a crop of wheat or barley. As I showed in *Agriculture: The Triumph and the Shame* (1982), it has been a great technical triumph, but the cost has been shameful. One consequence is that we now have a huge surplus of poor-quality wheat which nobody wants to buy at an economic price. That cost is quantifiable; what cannot be calculated is the cost to our soil.

Virtually all of this land that has been drained has been either in the hills or in more undulating areas. After a drainage system has been installed, any substantial rainfall is made to flow away quickly; but the faster it is made to flow, the more the runoff changes to a muddy effluent. Precious soil is thus swept away, and rivers such as the Trent, the Ouse and the Severn can carry to the sea thousands of tonnes of soil in a single day.

It is the practice in most of the new arable fields in hilly districts of the UK to cultivate the land down the slope instead of in tiers. Dr A. Harrison Reed, whose research has been noted above, has shown that, on more than 1,000 sites where erosion was recorded over a period of seven years, 'soil compaction and down-slope cultivation lines were identified as major contributory factors in over ninety-five per cent of cases'. He adds that 'hedgerow removal, which increases the overall length of slopes, was seen to be another important factor'. In the vineyards of southern Europe, peasant farmers learned long ago that the vines should be planted laterally, following the contour of the hillside; the steeper the hill, the more important it was to do this, for once the rain came, soil was run down the hill and would eventually be lost to the vineyard. Such cultivation is difficult with machinery, and if the hill is steep it may be too dangerous to make the attempt. Most of our farmers on the new arable land realize that their fields are suffering from soil erosion caused by down-slope cultivation. They are, however, in a dilemma. Their tractors and other machinery are larger than they used to be, and for them to be used on the side of a hill can be extremely dangerous. All British farmers and farm workers know that they are in the occupation which has the nation's second highest number of accidents, and none of them wish to risk their lives more than they need.

Not only a source of danger on the hillside, the larger tractors and heavy machinery are also themselves another cause of erosion. Dr Harrison Reed has been able to show the effect this new element in farming has had. He found that an average 15 to 17 tonnes of soil was lost annually from each hectare when a lightweight hand-held rotovator was used for cultivation. From tests carried out between 1976 and 1983 it became clear that the compaction of the soil was little more than what was naturally caused by the rainfall and the system of drainage. In 1984 a tractor replaced the rotovator on one of the sites studied, and rainfall runoff was subsequently measured. From a single wheel track of 50 metres long, 50 to 85 kilograms of sediment was found in the runoff of rain following rainfall of 8.5 to 11.6 millimetres in the course of twenty-four hours. From this experiment and others, Dr Harrison Reed estimates that a tractor's wheels will cause soil loss at a rate of from 15 to more than 100 tonnes per hectare per year.

Another feature of modern farming is the growing of winter cereals. Instead of wheat and barley being planted in the spring, today it is the general rule for the new seed to be sown as soon as practical after the harvest, sometimes as early as August. This enables the cereals planted to begin growing before the onset of winter and so to take full advantage of the warmer weather once it comes in the spring. Higher yields are thus obtained, usually half a tonne per acre more, which can make the difference between a profit and a loss. The use of nitrates as the sole or principal kind of fertilizer, available for use in plastic bags at any time, has made this change easy enough. Farmyard manure, however, is not so readily at hand; and in the days when it was the chief means of fertilizing the arable fields, the stubble was left untouched until the spring to enable the manure to be spread upon it, or flocks of folded or free ranging hens were circulated to gather any grain left behind and simultaneously to add their bit to the fertilizing. The stubble and the weeds that might grow a little through the autumn served to hold the soil once the rain came.

All the scientists who have studied the problem of soil erosion in the UK are agreed about the effects of growing winter cereals. There is no doubt that a major loss of soil follows. The quantity depends upon the make-up of the soil, the terrain, the degree of drainage and other factors; but wherever the young shoots of wheat and barley emerge in the autumn to make an arable field look to the unaccustomed eye like acres of grassland, you can be certain that erosion is taking place.

The Ministry of Agriculture's demand that farmers should grow ever more wheat is to be blamed. So, too, is the ministry's policy of subsidizing ever larger flocks of sheep on our hills. One farmer known to me collected no less than £52,000 by way of hill subsidies in a single year. Every ewe on the hill earns a subsidy for her owner; and the subsidies are so high that many a flock-owner regards the subsidy as more worthwhile than the lambing percentage. Push as many ewes as you can on the hill, and the more taxpayers' money you will get.

Dr Robert Evans of Soil Erosion Research at Cambridge has become well known for his work in this area. A paragraph in a letter he wrote to me in 1986 deserves to be quoted in full:

> Erosion of moorland grazings is particularly marked in the Peak District and a major study of this was funded by Peak Park Planning Board a few years ago. This study arose from work I did in the late 1960s which showed that overgrazing by sheep of the better pastures on steep slopes had led to the exposure of bare soil and consequent erosion. On lower, more sheltered slopes the patches of bare soil became colonized by vegetation in the summer season after the hard winter of 1969 when the number of lambs born that year dropped to between one-third and one-quarter. On the higher and more exposed slopes erosion has continued, and evidence suggests that the area of bare soil is increasing by about four per cent a year. Erosion of the western side of Kinder Scout as well as other localities has started since 1945 consequent on the threefold increase in the number of sheep. It is likely other National Parks are at risk of erosion, but little work has been done in these.

Our soil, its formation and loss can thus be looked at chemically and physically. They also need to be considered biologically. Even a teaspoonful of healthy soil may contain a million living creatures. Although imperceptible to the human eye, their biological role is crucial to the formation of good-quality soil. Grave concern at the effect that pesticides have had upon these creatures has been expressed by microbiologists. The poison may or may not kill them off, but it is certain that herbicides destroy the plant life upon which they feed.

Micro-organisms apart, a healthy soil will contain plenty of earthworms and insects, which also play an important part in enriching the earth with humus. Organic farmers never have need to resort to stubble burning, still less to setting fire to tonnes of straw as it lies in the field. The straw, of course, is used for making manure, but the stubble decomposes into humus, the work being done by countless millions of living organisms inhabiting every organically farmed field. In the case of earthworms and insects, the higher and visible creatures, there can be no doubt that pesticides cause their death and the consequent loss of soil formation.

THE GLOBAL PICTURE

In some parts of the world, erosion of soil is even worse than in the UK. In the United States it is causing such anxiety that remedies are certain to be taken on a wide scale, though erosion is unlikely to be eliminated. An annual loss of 30 tonnes an acre is not uncommon. That figure was given by Dr Charles Benbrook, executive director of the Board of Agriculture of the National Research Council, in an address to the University of Wisconsin in 1985. Dr Benbrook explained to his audience the legislation needed to set up conservation reserves. The objective is to retire 25 million acres of highly erodable land that has been cultivated for not less than ten years. One-fifth of the land would be able to qualify for compensation, based on a percentage of the grower's normal crop yield. A 'sod buster' provision, as it is called, discourages the cultivation of erodable cropland by denying various kinds of federal help to growers, such as commodity support, crop insurance and credit given by official agencies. The conservation areas would be laid down to grass; and an annual payment per acre would be given. Once the area had become pasture, the erosion would decrease to some 3 tonnes per acre per year. A reserve of 20 million acres would reduce erosion by 540 million tonnes a year. The cost to the federal budget would be about $1,000 million.

The United States can afford such a remedy. Other countries, where the problem of soil erosion is worse, are neither aware of the consequences nor able to avert them with the money necessary. Huge areas of land in Africa,

China and India, for example, have been degraded by wind erosion because of the clearing of trees, overgrazing and over-intensive cultivation with agrochemicals. The Soviet Union is another country severely afflicted. In 1985 the *Observer* quoted an article in the Russian magazine *Man and Nature*: 'If we do not take rapid steps to preserve the black earth, then in fifteen to twenty years an irreversible process will begin and then there will be nothing to save.' The 'black earth' consists of no less than 320 million acres, producing four-fifths of Russia's food supply. Much of the rest now comes from Argentina, the United States and the Common Market countries. Despite the years of cajoling and exhorting by the Soviet leaders, and the hopes of economic reform under Gorbachev, there is little sign of Russia increasing its output. Neither a weary peasantry nor the soil itself has the heart to yield any more.

Scientists around the world, among them those named above, have for a good number of years been trying to alert public opinion, and especially policy-makers, to the dangers of soil erosion and the likelihood that at some stage it will suddenly accelerate and perhaps become irreversible. Given the knowledge we now have of what may happen, there seems to be a heavy duty on us to take action. To place responsibility on the farming community, expecting a change in agricultural practices to be decided by them alone, would be unfair – especially in that the changes many farmers have made in recent decades have been imposed upon them by government policies.

Nature's wheel of life on earth began in the oceans. As life emerged above the water's edge, the wheel started the infinite number of circles which eventually covered the once-barren ultramarine surface with the soil that has enabled human beings to live. The process took about 350 million years. Modern civilization is reversing the process, sending down to the oceans through the world's rivers and water courses, at the rate of 30,000 million tonnes every year, the soil upon which human life ultimately depends. Yet as the source of life gets washed away, the number of human lives increases. The world's land could probably feed many more mouths than it does today; but if the world's population doubles in size between now and some stage in the twenty-first century (as has been predicted), what will happen if soil erosion suddenly accelerates in one food-producing country after another, as misguided modern farming practices take their effect?

· 2 ·

POISON ON THE LAND

PESTICIDES AT LARGE

Biocides, by definition, destroy life, and the dozens of different kinds sprayed upon our land all do so by poisoning. A great many of the world's arable acres are regularly treated with herbicides against weeds, fungicides against fungus, aphidicides against aphids and insecticides to kill off all sorts of insects. Long ago, Rachel Carson in her classic *Silent Spring* (1962) described the effect all this has upon wildlife by poisoning the food that sustains it. Dig out a spadeful of healthy soil in any garden, and there will be many worms squirming about, just as there used to be on every farm in the United Kingdom when the plough turned over the wheat stubble; but only on an organic farm can this be seen today. The worms, good friends to farmer and gardener alike, are in number only a small fraction of what they were. What, then, has been the effect upon the teaming microbes? More resilient to poison than the worms or the birds, their ability to survive in soil that has been dosed with biocides for forty years or more must now be in doubt. As with humans, most creatures in the wild can overcome a single small act of poisoning, but when repeated over a long period of time a cumulative aggregate may be overpowering. That these microbes do not live long enough to be treated twice with a pesticide spray is not the point; their nutrients have been treated not once or twice but perhaps hundreds of times.

The tractor with its pesticide sprayer may go over a crop of wheat several times in the course of its growth, and most of the poison will fall on the soil.

It is not just arable land that is treated like this. Innocent of what goes on in the British countryside, the visitor from the town may gaze over the pastureland with a herd of cows grazing peacefully and may think it in tune with nature; but those grass meadows will almost certainly also have been dosed with herbicides. Very little (if any) of Britain's farm-land has escaped the sprayer over the last forty years.

Among the better-known examples of herbicides used in the UK is paraquat, sold as Gramoxone to farmers and Weedol to gardeners. The farmers' co-operative to which I belong once sent me a long letter urging me to use Gramox-one and naturally to buy it from them. 'Yield reductions', the letter said, 'of 1½ to 2 cwt an acre frequently occur for every week drilling is delayed after the first of March . . . Gramoxone can help save time and preserve soil moisture.' Now, any farmer growing spring barley soon sees the advantage of that extra hundredweight to the acre; and Gramoxone, he is led to believe, can produce it for him. It is a powerful herbicide and can eliminate much of the cost of cultivation. Very great is the temptation to buy it. British farmers in their tens of thousands and gardeners in their hundreds of thousands use it every year.

Because paraquat can permeate the skin, the World Health Organization recommends protective clothing and boots, overalls and gloves which are impermeable before handling it. The chronic effects are the more serious as paraquat causes scar tissues, for which there is no antidote. A single incident of paraquat being inhaled may give rise to only minor injury to the lungs, but repeated over a period of time, irreversible damage is done. Farmers and farm workers, as well as gardeners, have suffered from nosebleeds, stomach aches, vomiting, diarrhoea and muscular pains when using this pesticide. Other consequences may follow several days later in the form of liver or kidney damage as well as injury to the lungs. The USA, Israel, Turkey, New Zealand, the Philip-pines, Denmark, Finland and Sweden have placed severe restrictions upon the use of paraquat. The justification for its being deemed safe in the UK is the data from the LD50 test (which I discuss below). Yet when given orally to rats it has been found lethal at only 57 milligrams per kilogram of bodyweight.

In the case of 2,4,5-T the LD50 test result of 300 milligrams per kilogrames indicates a much lower level of toxicity. This is a herbicide that won fame for itself as 'Agent Orange', used by the USA in the Vietnam War. Almost every country in the world which controls pesticides has taken steps to protect its people against the use of 2,4,5-T. Those banning it altogether are Colombia, Cyprus, Guatemala, India, Norway, Sweden, Turkey, the United States and the USSR. In Canada, Denmark, Finland, Hungary, Israel, Japan, New Zealand and the Philippines its use is severely restricted. The ban in Sweden followed studies on railway workers exposed to its application along railway tracks and embankments; it was found that they had a twofold excess of various cancers. Among those employed in manufacturing the chemical, an abnormal incidence of liver disorders and fat metabolism disorders has also been found. Research in other countries has indicated that 2,4,5-T is indeed carcinogenic. Probably the largest manufacturer of the chemical is BASF; based in West Germany, it has become one of the leading pesticide companies in the world, with a strong presence in the UK.

Paraquat and 2,4,5-T are but two of the many highly toxic chemicals used in the business of producing food. Their residues are to be found in what we eat. Whether our health is affected may be uncertain, but it is obvious that these residues cannot make us any healthier.

That paraquat and 2,4,5-T are freely available in the UK and not in numerous other countries raises a doubt about the way their toxicological data are assessed either here or in those other countries. The data ought to be the same. Why, then, do the specialists who assess them reach different conclusions? Paraquat remains paraquat, with the same active ingredients, whether used in the UK or the United States; its toxicity does not change with the crop, the soil or the climate. Why is ICI allowed to sell it so freely? So, too, with 2,4,5-T and all the other pesticides that are either banned as unsafe or severely restricted in other countries. The UK's standards of safety are self-evidently different, and the inference must be that we have a poorer regard for our health.

As serious are the long-term consequences if farmers and growers are impelled to use ever stronger pesticides as the old ones lose their efficacy. All the major pesticide manufacturers are engaged in a never-ending programme of research to evolve new compounds to succeed where earlier ones have failed. Generally speaking, these new pesticides are more potent and more expensive than the older ones. Farmers have spent more and more of their income on them. In 1973 British farmers spend £37.7 million on pesticides; ten years later, the outlay had risen to £298.4 million. In 1986 the cost had gone up to £450 million, levelling off slightly in 1989 to £440 million. These figures suggest that the interest of the chemical industry will be well served if the treadmill keeps on turning.

We speak of pesticides as a generic term for substances that kill rodents, insects, weeds, fungi, aphids and anything else that hinders the farmer and gardener. As too much of anything can have a toxic effect, and ultimately cause the death of anything on the farm or in the garden, including humans, it can be said that any substance can turn eventually into a pesticide. To smother a field of wheat with the finest farmyard manure will destroy the crop; to overdose a dairy herd with magnesium will kill the lot; and even precious sunlight, if we are exposed to it in excess, can cause ill effects leading to death. The accepted definition does not help, therefore, and we ought to narrow it down to the chemicals and the 'naturals', like nicotine, which in measured use are an aid to production. The 'naturals', though, are scarcely used by any modern farmer; it is the synthetic manufacturers of the chemical industry that have taken over and upon which the UK farming community now spends hundreds of millions of pounds a year.

What is pesticidal can also be homicidal. That pesticides kill human beings is beyond dispute. The World Health Organization has estimated that worldwide 50,000 people die of acute pesticide poisoning every year. Some of these deaths are suicides, and many are purely accidental, but most are of farmers and farm workers in the course of their work. An immediate death as a result of acute poisoning can be, generally speaking, a statistic of some validity. The chronic long-term effects of ingesting pesticides over a period of, say, twenty years are another story. Reasonable certainty must give way to what can only be, at best, a probability. Is it probable, then, that the human body can cope with the steady, low-level ingestion of something toxic by definition? Or do the minute doses of poison probably build up over a period of time with lethal consequences? The second probability seems the more likely of the two.

The main people in the pesticides 'front line' are farmers, farm workers, groundsmen, gardeners, forestry workers and employees in pesticide manufacturing. To what extent the food consumer is also at risk of pesticide residues is harder to assess. We are all different; people with a weak central nervous system are more vulnerable to an insecticide designed to destroy an insect's nervous system than those with a stronger constitution. Some people's kidneys and liver may be unable to discharge all toxins as efficiently as those of others. The same applies to the pesticides that seep down from the soil into our drinking water supplies. In some areas of California, however, pesticides have been used so intensively that wells from which drinking water has been drawn for many years are no longer safe to use. If British farmers persist in applying ever-stronger pesticides, then at some stage some of our water supplies will also become too dangerous to use.

SAFETY TESTING

The chemical companies are able to claim that they sell no pesticide in the UK unless they have thoroughly tested it as laid down by law, and unless the Ministry of Agriculture's Advisory Committee on Pesticides has looked at the results of the tests and satisfied itself that the product is safe to be used as directed. This raises two questions. The first is whether the tests, using animals, are appropriate for assessing toxicity to humans; the second is whether the process of assessing the toxicological data by an independent authority is as satisfactory in the UK as it may be in other countries where pesticides are more readily rejected as unsafe. Both questions deserve an answer.

The whole matter of testing pesticides – the number of tests, their nature and the qualifications of those who carry them out – has been a matter of secrecy in the UK. An official in the Ministry of Agriculture who expresses anxiety to an MP, a journalist, a representative of a farmers' organization or anyone else about what is going on commits an offence under Official Secrets legislation, first introduced in 1911 to protect the British people from the German enemy. In 1984 one official in the ministry, out of what seems sheer frustration, sent anonymously some astonishing allegations about the safety of pesticides to *Private Eye*, and 'Old Muckspreader', the farming correspondent of the magazine, claimed to have got corroboration from other sources. Such secrecy surrounding pesticide testing is necessary, says the ministry, to protect the chemical companies from competition; for if others were able to see the data on toxicity testing the information could be passed on to rival companies. Critics of the clandestine system retort that in the United States, where the Freedom of Information Act prevails, anyone can examine the data; and as both the UK and the United States share a large number of pesticides, it is not difficult – though it costs the price of a transatlantic airfare – for someone in the UK to obtain the information without putting a civil servant in the dock at the Old Bailey.

Regulations under the Food and Environment Act of 1989 have done little to lessen the absurdity. The public are now allowed limited access to the data – so limited as to be of hardly any value. In any case, this extends only to new pesticides; the hundreds of existing ones will still be kept secret. When the Act was being debated in the House of Commons, it was understood that the regulation would make access to these health-and-safety data generally available, at least in summary form. But members of the British Agrochemical Association had a number of meetings with ministry officials and apparently had a persuasive effect.

What we do know is that no agency of the UK government undertakes any pesticide testing. Tests are done either by the manufacturing company at its own laboratory or under contract by a business that specializes in this work. Critics suggest that if the reason for secrecy is to prevent a competitor gaining information about a rival product, there must be a risk of that happening when an outside company engages in testing a variety of pesticides from different companies.

A *World in Action* television programme, seen by millions of viewers in December 1984, claimed that one single contract laboratory had been responsible for testing one-third of the different pesticides used in the world. This was the International Bio-Test Laboratory in the United States. It prepared the toxicological or safety data for several leading chemical companies, and they transmitted it to both the US Environmental Protection Agency, which decides whether the pesticides are safe for use in the United States, and the Ministry of Agriculture in the UK. The data purported to be the result of tests conducted in the firm's laboratory on various animals; many of them, though, were never carried out at all; and in other cases, where the animals died, the data did not reveal it. Scientists responsible for the tests manufactured evidence of safety regardless of the truth. Once the fraud was discovered, a prosecution followed, and the offenders went to prison. The pesticides none the less remained on the market to be sold freely, the Ministry of Agriculture having allowed itself to be persuaded that they could be used despite there being no honestly obtained safety data.

We can assume that this was an exceptional case and that pesticide manufacturers, when testing their own products, do so conscientiously. Generally speaking, the tests are on rats and mice; if a pesticide is shown to be carcinogenic or otherwise malign to these animals, further work on it is usually abandoned. Some toxicologists have raised two doubts about the nature of these tests. It is well established, they say, for a cancer to appear in humans many years after the initial cause. A laboratory rat has yet to live as long; and even if it did, no manufacturer could afford to wait that length of time before deciding to put its product on the market. According to this view, no pesticide can be assessed satisfactorily for chronic toxicity – that is, for the effect even very small doses may have on humans over a considerable period of time – so long as short-lived animals are used.

Secondly, although toxicologists may concede that rats and mice may be a guide to acute toxicity (generally defined as lasting up to twenty-eight days), they flatter their fellow humans by doubting whether they should be likened to rodents. Comparisons, they remind us, are odious and also misleading. The story of thalidomide comes to mind. Here was a wonder drug that was tested fully in accordance with accepted practice. Pregnant rats and mice in their thousands were dosed with the drug, and no ill effects appeared; their progeny were born with every appearance of normality. The chickens, hamsters, rabbits, cats, dogs and finally monkeys used all confirmed the safety of thalidomide. Throughout this extensive programme of vivisection, nothing could be found to place in doubt the safety of the drug – except in the case of a particular strain of rabbit, in which deformity was found and assumed to be some aberration. After the testing was over and the drug was in use, the number of children born deformed and permanently crippled was to shock the world and leave the men in white coats amazed that animals could lead them so far astray.

Thalidomide is not the only instance of a drug whose effects on animals and on people are very different. Thousands of people who suffer from diabetes are treated with insulin, and it seems that no dire consequences follow. Give the drug to mice, rabbits and chickens, however, and their progeny are likely to be deformed. Other animals are not affected. Insulin is a long-established drug; had the scientists discovered it in recent years, it would have been rejected as unsafe to use.

Then there is cortisone, so widely prescribed that many tens of thousands of human patients have benefited from it, without doctors questioning its safety. When given to mice – though not to other animals – cortisone proves to be as teratogenic (deformity-causing) as thalidomide is to humans. Meclazine is another example; countless travellers have swallowed it on their journeys to spare them from sickness, and presumably many a pregnant mother has been among them.

No instance of a child with ill effects has been known, yet when the drug is given to rats their offspring are likely to be born deformed. The simple aspirin will also cause deformities in the rat, and it is highly toxic to some animals, though not to others.

Morphine is a powerful sedative and has brought relief to hundreds of thousands of patients. The effect on a cat or a mouse is the very opposite. Far from being sedated, they are raised to a state of 'maniacal excitement', according to one published report. Streptomycin and chlorpromazine are sensitizing drugs that when tried on animals cause various ill effects. The catalogue of chemical compounds which affect humans and animals differently is a long one, and every toxicologist is aware of it. From time to time they may write a learned paper about the dangers, but their job in life is to test the toxicity in a laboratory by methods required by law.

The principal method of testing in the UK is the LD50 test, which establishes the lethal dose which kills half of the animals in the tested group. The method began, innocently enough, some sixty years ago as a means of testing the safety of various natural substances, such as digitalis extract. Gradually, when other chemicals had to be assessed, the LD50 test was adopted. That it was simple and categorically certain in its result made it comfortably acceptable to policy-makers, whether in commerce or public service, although scientists themselves have often taken a different view. Although the doubts of the latter have caused the LD50 test to be refined in several ways, essentially it remains the same. It also remains the main determinant of a pesticide's safety and is responsible for classifying how toxic it is – whether 'extremely hazardous', 'highly hazardous', 'moderately hazardous' or 'slightly hazardous'. Regulations regarding pesticide use thus depend on the LD50 test. Ordinary common salt of the kind on millions of dining-room tables is, incidentally, condemned by the LD50 test as toxic.

How is the test conducted? Initially, 80 to 100 animals of each of two species are required for the experiment, and they are dosed orally. In carrying out such tests, toxicologists have sometimes found remarkable contrasts, with some animals severely affected and caused acute pain, while others

Table 1   Toxicity of pesticides

Degree of toxicity to humans	Oral LD50 mg/kg	Lethal for humans
Extremely toxic	5–50	Up to 1 teaspoonful
Very toxic	50–500	Teaspoon to 2 tablespoons
Moderately toxic	500–5,000	1–12 fl oz
Slightly toxic	5,000–15,000	12 fl oz–½ gallon

in the same group react differently. There are, it has been said, so many biological variables within the same species, and even within the same laboratory, that it is scarcely reasonable to assume any scientific validity for the test. While one group of animals may be tested orally by being force-fed with a pesticide, others will be injected, forced to inhale the chemical or have it applied to their skin. Then comes the conversion of toxicity from animals to humans – the scale shown in Table 1 above is generally accepted.

On the face of it, the table gives quite a good guide to acute toxicity, with, for example, a lethal dose of 5 to 50 mg of pesticide to 1 kilogram of bodyweight indicating extreme toxicity. However, at a symposium on animal toxicity testing, arranged by the Association of Veterinarians in Industry in London in 1973, a paper was given which showed that there was a considerable difference in how various animals reacted to drugs. True, the paper was about drugs and not pesticides, but it none the less highlights how humans are different from animals. The paper was by Dr Brander of Beecham's Research Laboratory and it related to a given drug. The efficacy of the drug varied very considerably between humans and three species of animals as follows:

	Milligrams per kilograms of bodyweight
Human	1
Sheep	10
Monkey	15.2
Rabbit	200

As the rabbit is frequently used in the laboratory to test how a chemical will affect a human, such an enormous difference seems to make it self-evidently unreliable. Even the poor monkey shut up in the cage shows fifteen-fold less sensitivity to this drug than humans have.

Why this huge difference? Scientists are agreed that a chemical of any kind acts upon an animal, human or otherwise, at five different stages. First comes absorption, which may take place orally, nasally or dermally. Then the chemical goes through a period of distribution to some or all of the body. Next there is metabolism. In due course the substance is excreted in faeces, urine, breath or sweat. There is also the effect on the nervous system, which may be delayed until after excretion. From our everyday lives, we know how we may respond differently to the same kind of food or drink. Shellfish eaten in the evening may cause some of us to have nightmares yet provoke no apparent ill effect when consumed earlier in the day; others can eat great quantities of crab, lobster and other shellfish at any time and never suffer for it. Then there are some who can cope with crab and not lobster, and vice versa. All sorts of other food allergies are well known, and they often seem contradictory. The fact is that humans vary in the five different stages that chemicals act upon them. Even the same person may change in a period of years, finding something toxic to his or her system when it was not so previously. Port, it is said, often acts like that.

The failure to recognize these five different stages and the failure to devise a system of testing pesticides which takes account of them must cast still more doubt to the validity of animal testing. A rat may initially absorb a pesticide in a way similar to a human, but the gut flora of a rat are likely to be dissimilar to those of a human; nor do scientists claim that there is much similarity between the species at the four following stages when further reactions to the ingested pesticide may take place. (It was possibly at the point of distribution within the body that thalidomide acted differently in human mothers than it had during tests on rats.)

This brings us to the second question and to the contradictory state of pesticide control among the countries of the world. The safety data in respect of the same pesticide may condemn it in one country yet approve it elsewhere. There are numerous pesticides freely available and lawfully used with no restriction in the UK while being banned altogether or severely controlled in other countries.

Human health cannot be set apart from the health of the soil from which all our food ultimately comes. The link between the two is there for ever. No scientist has yet been bold enough to claim that great quantities of poison applied to our soil over a period of many years have a beneficial effect upon people, farm animals and the wildlife, all of which depend upon the soil for their sustenance and good health. Some scientists may assert that the effect is neither malign nor benign, but nature is never neutral. Besides, to assume that it is practical to strike a careful balance between good and bad, the two interacting in such a way as to cause no change in the health of our soil and the quality of the sustenance it affords us, is to assume that human beings as they mount the tractor to go out into the fields to spray the poison can always be sure of judging its effects to a nicety. But can they? And how necessary or effective are the pesticides anyway?

For more than forty years it has gone on, this business of treating our land with toxic chemicals. Nine out of ten arable farmers in the UK know no other way of doing their job. The Ministry of Agriculture, aided by the chemical companies, has set them upon this course and will find it difficult to contradict itself by helping farmers to change to other methods. At some point, however, whoever is responsible for Britain's agriculture will have to answer two questions: How much longer do we go on using ever stronger pesticides? And how do we enable our farmers to carry on without them?

CHEMICAL FERTILIZERS

Farmers in the UK and many other countries have also become dependent upon the use of artificial fertilizers: nitrates, phosphates and potash. In yielding any crop — whether wheat, potatoes, vegetables or even grass — the soil also yields up a mass of nutrients. A year of wheat or a single potato will have within it many trace elements, all of which have a nutritional value. The soil can go on yielding these many nutrients provided they are replaced. As Chapter 1 noted, much of this replacement is achieved through the action of countless microbes making new soil. But unless the original soil is itself replenished with these nutrients, its quality will suffer. The application of even a very limited number of nutrients by way of artificial fertilizer imperceptibly changes the nature of our soil. Two of the most commonly used chemicals can have a toxic effect. First let us take nitrogen in the form of nitrates.

A study of the nitrogen cycle, published in 1984 by the Royal Society, likened nitrogen to Doctor Jekyll and Mr Hyde. This was a neat way to sum up the paradox. Unless plants receive nitrogen they die, and so do we; but nitrogen in the wrong form will pollute and destroy any kind of life, including our own. In using nitrogen to excess, we put ourselves at risk. The individual likely to cause the most harm is the farmer, and it is primarily the arable farmer rather than the livestock producer. Such is the conclusion to be drawn from the detailed studies on the subject. In the hope of rousing public opinion, some scientists have gone so far as to speak of the 'nitrate time-bomb'. They say that the consequences of what we are doing today will not come upon us for two or three decades, as the nitrates enter our drinking water supplies. As every year goes by, however, the consequences will prove to be increasingly deadly.

In its 'Dr Jekyll' form, nitrogen has done as much as anything to bring about the triumph of British agriculture. In both dairying and cereal growing it has had a catalytic effect upon output; other factors have played a part, but without the use of nitrogen they would have been of little consequence.

Nitrogenous fertilizer was not used at all by farmers in the UK until 1937. From then until the Second World War its used increased slightly, but the total amount was of small significance. Figure 1, taken from *Nitrate in Water*, the 1986 report of the Nitrate Co-ordination Group set up by the Department of the Environment, gives a graphic illustration of the increases in recent decades. The use of nitrogen is now

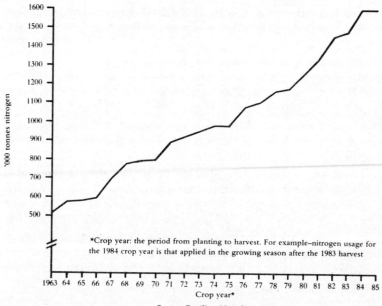

*Crop year: the period from planting to harvest. For example–nitrogen usage for the 1984 crop year is that applied in the growing season after the 1983 harvest

Source: Fertiliser Manufacturers Association, fertiliser statistics.

Figure 1   Annual use of nitrogen fertilizers in the UK.

on a plateau, but as this chapter will show, this may only be temporary.

The take-off point was in 1959. Until then land prices had been broadly constant in real terms; afterwards the price of farmland rose consistently at a rate faster than the rate of inflation. In my book *Farming in the Clouds* (1984) I suggested that land increased in market price faster than inflation because of the system of price support. The more public money is given to raise the return on the assets of any branch of our economy, the more valuable must those assets become. Thus the more a government subsidizes agriculture, the more its main asset, land, must be worth. Some may reject this thesis and point to the use of nitrates as an alternative reason. They may say that if an asset such as farmland can be made to yield more by the use of nitrates, the more valuable it will become.

In the case of dairy farming, a small herd was the norm until 1959. Twenty cows on eighty acres was perhaps the most usual size, and it was the basis of thousands of family farms. The work was done by one family with occasional help from outside for haymaking or for various jobs on contract, such as hedging and ditching. Though there were many much larger dairy farms where one or more cowmen were employed – such as were found in Cheshire and the Vale of the White Horse, both long noted for large-scale dairying – even in 1968 half the dairy herds in the UK had less than twenty cows, the average being twenty-six. Today the average farm has more than sixty.

These small farms tended to specialize in milk. Apart from a field of kale or roots, all the land was pasture. As it would have been uneconomic to grow cereals on a small scale, compound feedstuffs were purchased as a supplement to the hay, kale and roots. The cows spent most of their life out in the fields, though in winter they might be kept in yards or buildings near the milking parlour. Their manure fertilized the land, and little of anything was imported on to the farm. The usual price for an acre of pasture was £25 in 1946 and did not rise to £200 for another fifteen years, so there was no need to exploit the land intensively; one cow to two or three acres was fairly typical, a cow and an acre of land being much the same in price. Over the years, an acre has gradually become four times more expensive to buy than a cow. The number of cows to the acre has therefore had to be increased, the grassland being called upon to work harder for its owner.

Two consequences have followed. The old pastures have been ploughed up – 95 per cent of them have gone – and in their place are mainly leys of faster growing grasses, a blend of only a few varieties which offer the cow a greater quantity of feed. The old pasture contained scores of different kinds of flora (many people condemned them as weeds, though others call them wild flowers), and among them were plants that undoubtedly were beneficial to the ruminant animals, affording what we might describe today as 'herbal remedies'. The health of the cow has changed. Three lactations and she becomes a beefburger now; twenty years ago she might have had seven or eight calves. Of course, this cannot be attributed to a single factor alone; the strain upon the cow of yielding so much more milk is probably a major reason; so, too, is the way cows are concentrated together in the much larger herds of today.

The average size of the modern specialist dairy farm in England is 122 acres with fifty-five cows. Not all of this increase can be attributed to more grass being grown to the acre; a cow today yields about 50 per cent more milk than she used to, and bought-in concentrates enrich the food she is given. Still, the management of grass is recognized as being a most important element in the growth of milk output. Figures show that the UK's production of milk has more than doubled since 1947.

The Royal Society's study group on the nitrogen cycle said in its 1984 report that 'there is still substantial potential for the greater intensification of UK agricultural production. This would require, along with other inputs, the use of more fertilizer N [nitrogen] particularly on grassland.' The study group also recorded that ICI had been able to reduce the amount of energy used to produce fertilizers and this might have the effect of reducing its cost to the farmer; thus 'cost is unlikely to be a disincentive to its increased use in the near future'. Speaking of the scope for the further use of nitrogen on grassland, the study group calculated that by the year 2000 an additional 350,000 tonnes might be applied annually in England and Wales. That is an increase of about 40 per cent over what is applied now.

Quotas on milk production will not necessarily lessen use of nitrogen. The quota can only place a limit on the quantity of milk a farmer sells off the farm; it can do nothing else. His costs are still going to rise and erode his margin of profit, so instead of increasing his milk production, as he has in the past, he must turn his attention to greater productivity. More milk from fewer cows and more grass from fewer acres will be two obvious objectives. The need may be for more nitrates, not less; and if their cost is 'not a disincentive', as the Royal Society report indicates, we may see the quota system increase the use of nitrates.

In the same week as the EEC Council of Agricultural Ministers, in March 1983, agreed upon a system of quotas, a spokesman for ICI – according to a report in *Farmers' Weekly* – told a conference of dairy farmers that nitrogen was not only the key to higher production but also a means of bringing down costs. Two-thirds of dairy cows' feed energy is supplied by forage, only one-third by concentrates, he said. Fertilizer could produce forage at a cost of £80 a cow a year, while the cost of cattle cake was £300 a cow a year (£176 a tonne). Comparing it with silage and concentrates, grass was the cheapest, being 0.33 pence a megajoule of feed energy; silage was 0.67 pence and concentrates 1.55 pence. The ICI spokesman went on to chide dairy farmers in the West Country for using nitrogen at a rate of only 136 units an acre when their grassland could respond to 300 or 350 units. Assuming that his figures were correct, they are still of considerable significance. If farmers are to be enjoined to produce less milk, they can do so, yet still maintain their margin of profit. They must use much less concentrate and replace it with greater quantities of grass or silage. More nitrogen on the land, perhaps twice as much as now, will be the means of doing it. Milk yields may fall to conform to the quota, but the cost of producing the milk will fall, too.

Still, the law of diminishing returns is having its effect. When the most authoritative of all books on agriculture, Fream's *Elements of Agriculture*, had its fourteenth edition published in 1962 it gave its opinion that the application of 20 units of nitrogen per acre may be confidently expected to result in increased yield of from 6 to 10 hundredweight per acre of green herbage if the weather conditions are favourable. A unit is one-hundredth of a hundredweight, so one-fifth of a hundredweight of nitrogen yielded thirty to fifty times as much herbage. Where is the dairy farmer who can get that today? I suggest he would be lucky to be half as successful.

If nitrogen has stimulated the growing of grass, its effect on cereals and arable crops generally has been many times greater. It is a certain fact that our system of arable farming would not be possible without it. The transformation of much of the UK's landscape from pasture to plough, for better or worse, must be attributed to what nitrogen has been able to achieve for the arable farmer.

One of the earliest writers about agriculture, Hugh Platt in 1661, said that when it came to growing wheat, five or six quarters was a reasonable average for an acre. A quarter is 4½ hundredweight, so rather more than a tonne to the acre was what he would expect. In the 1930s the average was rather less than a tonne; most of our wheat was grown on Grade I and Grade II land, and only a little more than a million acres were cultivated for wheat altogether. It is plain that for some three centuries productivity at best stood still, and probably declined slightly.

Yields have climbed steadily upwards since 1945. On the Grade I and Grade II land they are at least three times and sometimes more than four times higher. Agricultural scientists are confident that in the 1990s we will grow six tonnes to the acre on such land. Improved varieties of seed are one reason; other factors are new kinds of cultivation and the use of pesticides and fungicides; but nitrogen has been the indispensable key to unlock this triumph of science.

It has also enabled a great part of the UK to go over to monoculture. With the four-year rotation, devised in the first Agricultural Revolution, where wheat was but one of the crops grown, our farming was mixed, livestock being kept on every farm, whether arable or not. Even in South Lincolnshire, Norfolk and Cambridgeshire, the traditional areas for growing wheat, cattle crew-yards were universal. Straw from the ricks was given the cattle daily to tread down and make into manure to go back to the field, the sole source of fertilizer, though on some of the land sheep might be folded to feed off root crops and so make their contribution to the soil fertility. In Victorian times some farmers, thinking themselves progressive, added guano imported from across the Atlantic, but as a rule farms were self-sufficient in the matter of fertilizer. Yields were lower, and so were costs; but it was a system that could work only if the farmer kept livestock, and this usually meant fields of pasture and roots for feeding the stock as well as fields growing cereals. A varied landscape was the outcome. Today the arable farmer can dispense with the livestock altogether, and the crew-yards in East Anglia are now mostly empty. Prairie-ization, an ugly word to mean an ugly process, is now possible.

The quantity of nitrogen going on the land has increased remorselessly. In fact, the new varieties of wheat cannot thrive unless they are given a greater dose of it than the earlier kinds. Fream's fourteenth edition speaks of wheat varieties like 'Cappelle' and 'Minister'; they are now probably unobtainable. It also advises that seventy units of nitrogen represents the average optimum rate 'provided the crop will stand such a dressing without lodging'. It goes on to add: 'Crowther and Yates originally suggested that an arbitrary upper limit of forty units per acre only should be used because the varieties in use twenty years ago were insufficiently strong in the straw to stand up to the full dressing.' That was written in 1962; today the number of units applied has more than doubled.

The trend is ever upwards. Agricultural botanists continue to develop varieties capable of responding to greater quantities of nitrogen, and the fertilizer manufacturers will be standing ready to supply whatever is needed.

So much for the work of Dr Jekyll. Now let us see what Mr Hyde has done.

The UK Department of the Environment's Nitrate Co-ordination Group published its report, *Nitrate in Water*, in 1986. The composition of the co-ordination group was subject to some criticism; two members were from the National Farmers' Union, four from the Ministry of Agriculture and even two from the Fertilizer Manufacturers' Association. Three came from the Department of the Environment itself, which might be considered more objective, and the others in the main were representatives from the water industry. The poor consumer was overlooked, nor was there anyone primarily concerned with health. The composition of the group makes its conclusions all the more significant.

After noting that the EEC Directive on Drinking Water, which came into effect in 1985, required the nitrate level in water supplies not to exceed a maximum of 50 mg per litre, the co-ordination group estimated that 912,000 people in the UK drank water polluted above that maximum. To comply with the directive an immediate expenditure of £50 million would be needed. Because the nitrate levels in our water supply are steadily increasing, the cost could be a further £120 million within twenty years. In the opinion of the group, 'in many areas of otherwise high quality, ground-water sources would have to be abandoned or blended with generally poorer quality surface sources'. It went on to say that 70 per cent of Anglian Water output and 50 per cent of Severn Trent's current groundwater sources could eventually require action to comply with the directive.

The co-ordination group concluded that modern methods of agriculture were the cause of this increasing level of pollution and made a number of recommendations that farmers should adopt to reduce the danger of nitrate leaching. These recommendations were:

- there should be no nitrogen fertilizer applied between mid-September and mid-February;
- autumn-sown crops should be planted in preference to spring-sown;
- winter cereals should be planted as early as possible;
- crop cover should be maintained in autumn and winter.

In areas where serious nitrate pollution exists, they also recommended:

- farmers should be told of steps they can take to reduce nitrate leaching;
- alternative land use, such as grassland, forestry and recreation, in place of arable crops;
- grassland to remain unploughed;
- limitation on the quantity of fertilizer.

In considering the danger to human health, the Nitrate Co-ordinating Group was influenced by a circular letter written in November 1985 by the principal medical officer of the Department of Health and Social Security, which was sent to a wide number of medical officers in the public service. It was headed 'Nitrate in Drinking Water'. However, the letter referred to only two dangers – stomach cancer and infantile methaemoglobinaemia (blue baby syndrome). There is well-established evidence that an excess of nitrates in drinking water can be a cause of both diseases, but the co-ordination group made a mistake in overlooking the other adverse effects that can result. A nitrate can become a nitrite, and this can happen once it enters the body. Nitrites can be highly toxic and inducive of cancer. When the House of Commons Select Committee on Agriculture visited the United States in 1986 it heard that experiments to this effect were carried out on thirty-six different species of animal. They all died of cancer. The World Health Organization said, in its report on *Nitrates, Nitrites and N-Nitroso Compounds* (1977): 'N-nitroso compounds are carcinogenic in a wide range of animal species . . . it is highly probable that these compounds may also be carcinogenic in man.'

In 1984 the World Health Organization urged that where a water supply reached a level of 10 mg of nitrogen per litre, advice should be sought from health authorities. This, of course, is a markedly lower level than what the EEC directive proscribes, and it indicates that even comparatively small amounts of nitrate in water should be cause for some concern.

The other artificial fertilizer which has come to be questioned is phosphate. Phosphate is indispensable to the human body, as it is to any living creature – bones consist of calcium phosphate – and most of us who are in good health will have about 700 grams within us. But as with every other element of which we are made, we can have too much phosphate; any substance upon which life depends can become toxic and dangerous in excess.

The phosphates are used extensively by food manufacturers as emulsifiers. That these are compounds different from those used as fertilizers is true, although the research undertaken on their effect does point to the danger of their use. Alexander Schauss, in his book *Diet, Crime and Delinquency* (1981), tells how the West German Minister of Health asked the university clinic at Mainz to carry out a study on whether certain food additives were a cause of erratic or unruly behaviour. Double-blind tests were conducted on a substantial number of children, and the results showed an unmistakable link.

Phosphate was found to have a definite and immediate effect. When given to children it induced hyperactivity, which in turn led to the kind of bad behaviour well known to thousands of schoolteachers. The Mainz University clinic seems to have had no difficulty in drawing the obvious conclusion that young people prone to hyperactivity should be given a diet low in added phosphates. Corroborative tests showed that once hyperactive children were fed on a phosphate-free diet their behaviour and learning ability improved significantly. Sodium phosphate, the food additive, does not have identical properties to calcium phosphate, the fertilizer; but the study at Mainz may be enough to raise a doubt, and to justify more research into the consequences of using phosphates generally.

No more work, however, is needed to establish phosphate as the cause of eutrophication. Strictly speaking, the term means 'becoming well nourished', but it has come to be used to describe the over-enrichment of water bodies, especially lakes. Too much of any chemical element, no matter how beneficial a more modest quantity may be, is as deleterious to a body of water as it is to a body in human form. Too much phosphate in still water depletes its oxygen and poisons fish and other living creatures. Algae are a visible sign of the process. These water blooms prevent light falling on to the aquatic plants beneath them, and these die; vegetation decomposes and oxygen is lost. Then the demise of the fish follows, and the body of water becomes a lifeless thing. Along with the algae there may come broad-leved aquatic plants, which also choke the open water. The consequences may reach far beyond the piece of water polluted. The Royal Commission on Environmental Pollution under the chairmanship of Sir Hans Kornberg found in its seventh report – on *Agriculture and Pollution* (1979) – that eutrophication had been accelerated 'in some water-supply reservoirs which are fed by streams draining primarily agricultural areas'.

In the United States, so many lakes with an abundance of fish have been transformed into stagnant bodies of water that eutrophication has become a major subject for scientists. As long ago as 1969 the National Academy of Sciences arranged a symposium with the title Eutrophication: Causes, Consequences, Correctives. Human sewage and industrial waste were acknowledged to be two of the causes, but inorganic fertilizers were seen to have a steadily increasing responsibility, phosphorus being the common factor in each of these three causes. Unless curbs were placed upon this agricultural pollution, all lakes and other bodies of still water in areas where the land was farmed would sooner or later become affected and eventually lose their fish-life as stagnancy took over. They would also cease to be fit for drinking water for either man or beast. In the opinion of those who took part in the symposium, correctives were urgently needed. Changes in agricultural practices were called for, including a reduction in the use of phosphates and their more careful application.

Since 1969 the evidence in the United States of phosphate having a detrimental effect on water bodies has, by general agreement, become incontrovertible. In the words of *Environmental Science and Technology*, in a feature entitled 'Water Report' published in 1978 and compiled by three scientists in this field: 'It has been recognized for many years that phosphate may be the controlling nutrient for planktonic and attached algae and macrophytes.'

Where phosphates have been withdrawn from a water body, as has been done in numerous experiments, notably in Lake Washington in Seattle, eutrophication has been reduced. Carbon and nitrogen have been shown also to play a part in stimulating aquatic plant growth, but phosphate remains the limiting element in fresh water; that is, it is phosphate, not either of the other two, which determines the degree of growth. In marine water, however, nitrogen may be a limiting element. That nitrogen contributes to the danger for our lakes and other still waters is another reason for questioning whether we should increase our use of nitrates.

The Organization for Economic Co-operation and Development has also entered the debate. Some twenty-five years ago its Water Management Sector Group set up a multi-national study on eutrophication. The study divided into four projects. There was the Alpine Project to examine what was happening to the Alpine lakes in Switzerland, Germany, France, Austria and Italy. Secondly, there was the Nordic Project to consider the Scandinavian lakes. Then the Shallow Lakes and Impoundments Project, for those of Germany, the

Netherlands, Belgium, Spain, Japan and the UK. Finally, there was the North American Project for the lakes and impoundments of the United States and Canada. In all, 200 lakes and reservoirs were studied, and eutrophication data were gathered over several years. The analyses confirmed that the accusing finger should remain pointed at phosphates.

· 3 ·

POISON IN THE MEAT

Arsenic – long used in compound feeds to quicken the growth of pigs, but in such minute quantities as to cause no anxieties – is not the kind of poison this chapter has in mind. The pressure on farmers to raise their output has extended to meat just as much as to arable crops. Intensive production of pig and poultry meat has been the most obvious case, although dairy farming is not far behind, and both beef cattle and even sheep are also reared a great deal more intensively than was the case a decade ago. Hormones and antibiotics are seen as important aids to the intensive factory production of animals. Both are poisons in the true sense of the word when put to this purpose.

To keep over 100 dairy cows in a single building throughout the winter months and 1,000 pigs or 10,000 chickens also in a single building but throughout their lives is to create serious risk of a disease spreading like wildfire. Thus antibiotics came to be used in an attempt to remove the danger; then they were found to have a remarkable side-effect; given to young pigs or chicks, it was discovered that the animals grew much faster. Antibiotics are therefore now used as a growth stimulant to make both pigs and chickens ready to slaughter much sooner than otherwise. The effect upon the health of the animals is still unknown, although the evidence so far available is giving the medical profession some concern.

POULTRY

Many medical practitioners have advised people to eat poultry meat as a healthy alternative to red meat. The leanness of the broiler is one of the reasons why demand in the United Kindom has risen to over 600 million a year. Poultry has also become cheaper for two reasons. First, labour costs have been reduced to a minimum, with one person in charge of 150,000 or more birds, although it is another question whether he or she is able to look after their welfare adequately. Secondly, the broiler birds reach a weight of 5 lb, and so are big enough to be slaughtered, within forty-nine days from the time of hatching. This amazing rate of growth would be impossible without the use of antibiotics as growth stimulants.

Despite the antibiotics, a high proportion of the broilers are riddled with disease by the time their lives are ended at seven weeks. Samples examined by the Central Public Health Laboratory over a period have indicated that a majority of all broilers are infected by salmonella – hence Edwina Currie's famous remark in 1988. The public who subsequently eat the birds may suffer the effects, but the birds themselves may know nothing of it. They are likely to suffer from a list of diseases which no creature of forty-nine days should experience. Clare Druce in her excellent book, *Chicken and Egg* (1989), described how the broiler becomes physically deformed, acquiring a body far too heavy for its legs, the latter not being able to grow as fast as the rest of it. Bones cannot be formed quickly, and the nutrients they require are not in the feed in the same proportion as those given to the birds to enable them to put on the maximum amount of meat in the shortest time feasible. Hence the brittle bones that the majority of them have. Without the growth-promoting antibiotics, scientists claim that the birds would reach only half their final weight, which means that the birds' legs are having to carry up to twice the weight that nature intended.

By enabling tens of thousands of birds to be kept in one building with limited ventilation, the use of antibiotics has also led a large proportion of them to suffer from respiratory disorders. A considerable number are also found to have fatty liver or fatty kidneys, while many others have septicaemia. More serious are two disorders which very young creatures of any species should never have, and can have only if something is inordinately wrong with their environment – that is, heart attacks and cancer. The form of the latter most prevalent among the broilers is Marek's disease, and between 5 and 10 per cent of the birds seem to suffer from it. Their excessive weight is the probable cause of their heart attacks. In the UK fourteen different drug companies between them market no less than forty-four kinds of antibiotics for use among poultry alone, according to *Poultry World*'s 'disease directory', not as growth promoters but for therapeutic purposes. What, we might ask, would happen if these drugs were not administered? To keep such vast numbers of birds close together in cramped conditions with limited ventilation and fed on a diet designed to get them to reach slaughter weight in forty-nine days must be a doubtful way to produce healthy food for humans to eat.

At the time of the salmonella scare in 1988–9, legal writs were issued by the powerful companies dominating the poultry business with the result that microbiologists and medical practitioners felt inhibited from entering the debate. None the less, salmonella poisoning is not the only risk. There is also campylobacter poisoning. This gives rise to diarrhoea, often in an acute form, and stomach pains, which may last for a week or more. Research suggests that the eating of broilers is the most likely cause of this poisoning; and according to an article in the *Journal of International Medical Research* in 1985, by Lisa Ackerley and Alan Jones, it causes at least 80,000 working days to be lost a year in the UK. The other major risk caused by broilers is of listeria. Almost the only expert in this field to brave the issue of a writ in the salmonella debate, Richard Lacey, Professor of Medical Microbiology at Leeds University, has said that listeriosis is much more common than official statistics suggest because it is not a notifiable disease and the symptoms are often attributable to something else. It gives rise to meningitis, septicaemia, miscarriages and stillbirths. Pregnant women are particularly susceptible to it, as are patients suffering from cancer, for both have weakened immune systems. To show the extent of the problem, Professor Lacey bought twenty-four items of food from a supermarket; six of these were infected with listeria, and four of those six were broiler chicken dishes for sale as ready to eat. From such a small sample, it would be unfair to the poultry industry to claim that two-thirds of its products might be infected, but the *Veterinary Record* wrote as long ago as 1976 of the dangers of listeria in broilers and the high incidence even then of these malign bacteria which seemed to infect a significant proportion of the birds.

PIGS

If the way poultry are treated is questionable, much more concern ought to arise with regard to pigs. As anyone who has kept each of the five main farm animals will agree, the pig is the most intelligent and also the most prone to stress. Several parts of its anatomy are similar to those of a human, a fact which has taken many a pig to the vivisection laboratory; in the United States pigs are used for medical research on an especially large scale. This seems to indicate that these animals should be treated humanely, also that injury to their health and well-being may affect the health of humans who eat them.

In the UK today, many hundreds of thousands of pigs are kept in conditions far removed from the old-fashioned pigsty. In the 1950s the expansion of the national herd prompted many a farmer to keep a large number of sows out of doors; and it was not uncommon to see perhaps 100 of them out in the field surrounded by their piglets. When the price of land was £100 an acre and the only other costs those of simple huts and fencing, pig keeping was usually a profitable enterprise. Then came two factors to change it. The introduction of the import levies with the Common Agricultural Policy caused the price of land to rocket upwards; and the Ministry of Agriculture brought in a series of grants, subsidies and tax allowances designed to encourage factory farming. The latter included grants to lay down concrete as well as put up buildings and tax allowances to pay for the balance of the cost as well as the fittings and equipment. The extensive system of outdoor herds, far from being subsidized, was now to be handicapped by competition from intensive systems that were highly subsidized in one form or another.

Pig husbandry, having always been a risky business, now became a monopoly for intensive factory farming. In due course about 90 per cent of the sows were placed in stalls, each one a kind of iron-bar cage only slightly longer and slightly wider than the sow herself, and in this she would be kept from the time she was served by the boar until she was removed to the farrowing pen, a period of four months. In this time she was able to stand up or lie down but unable to move forward, back or to either side except for a few inches, not once leaving the stall in all that time. Each sow would be fed the same compound feed every day with no variation of diet, although the ration might be raised or lowered depending on her condition. Come farrowing time, she would be removed to a pen where she would be held down in a crate to prevent any movement lest she injure one of the piglets.

The grants and the tax allowances to pay for this system have now been ended, and as a result these intensive systems are generally no longer being set up. The number of sows in such stalls is therefore in decline, with the figure now estimated at about 65 per cent. The minority now tend to be housed in yards or converted barns, with some going back to the fields.

While the sow has the chance of more humane treatment, the fate of her progeny has moved in the opposite direction. Eight-week weaning used to be the normal practice; earlier weaning caused stress to the sow and aggression among the piglets. However, intensive methods of production have overcome such obstacles to the objective of getting as many piglets out of a sow in her lifetime as possible. Returning the sow to the close confinement of a stall prevents her from giving vent to her stress on others. Whether in a stall or a building, it is a common practice to keep sows in darkness twenty-four hours a day as a means of 'quietening them down', as a pioneer of factory farming once put it.

As for the weaners, there are several systems in use, each with variations. The males are almost invariably castrated at the time of weaning. On our farm we carried out experiments on a large number as to the effect this had, and we found that most of them were put back three weeks in terms of growth. The stress caused must therefore have been considerable. Fortunately we were able to establish to the satisfaction of our butchers that by getting ready for slaughter earlier, 'boar taint', the dread of all pork butchers, was avoided. However, the nationwide multiples and supermarkets will take no risks, so castration without anaesthetics goes on as before.

At the same time the male piglets and their sisters are injected with iron. This is necessary because pigs are by nature a rooting animal, susceptible to anaemia unless they can have access to the variety of minerals in the soil which they can root for in their natural surroundings. Rooting is impossible in their new life, for they are now likely to be placed in wire-floored cages and kept in darkness to minimize stress and consequent fighting and cannibalism. To reduce the latter, their tails are often cut off. From the cages they will go to the fattening pens, all concrete unless with slatted floors. Again, to prevent the manifestations of stress and boredom, the weaners will probably be kept in total darkness except at feeding time. The objective is to get them up to slaughter weight in the minimum time, neither the nutritional quality of the meat nor the welfare of the animal being a consideration. The latter is denied to be a factor by apologists, on the ground that their pigs would not put on weight unless they were content. Yet this claim is an obvious fallacy. If they were content, the pigs would not require the considerable dosage of drugs which are administered and without which keeping pigs in this way would not be practical.

In the United States, although intensive pig farming has not been going on for as long as it has in the UK, there is a greater awareness of the dangers of these drugs. Sulphadimidine is commonly used against the respiratory diseases endemic in factory farming. When recently tested on rats and mice in US laboratories it was found to be a cause of cancer. The Food and Drug Administration is reported as wanting this drug to be prohibited, and legislation is likely to follow. Our own Ministry of Agriculture takes a different view. It dismisses the research on rats and mice and has made it clear that no similar ban is likely in the UK. The toxicological data in the possession of the ministry are not revealed, on the ground of commercial confidentiality. The ministry's insistence that the drug can safely be fed to our pigs and duly passed down a human gullet is not altogether supported by medical opinion. It is one of the sulphonamides. These are losing favour with doctors as they are now known to cause, according to *Medicines: A Guide* (1983) by Professor P. Parrish, rashes, loss of appetite, nausea, vomiting, fever, drowsiness, headaches, depression, diarrhoea and kidney damage.

A study carried out at the Royal Veterinary College some years ago considered whether pigs suffered more or less from a list of fourteen diseases when kept intensively. It was found that only in the case of lice was there any improvement. On our own farm, where we used to keep thousands of pigs extensively, lice used to be found occasionally, for they would breed in the barley straw. However, it is quite easy to get rid of them. Whether kept intensively or otherwise, pigs benefit from lying on straw; if barley straw is given, then in an intensive system lice are sure to be found on them just as much as elsewhere. The list of other diseases which were worse for the pigs when kept intensively included enzootic pneumonia, atrophic rhinitis and haemophilus pneumonia (the three most serious respiratory diseases for the pig), swine dysentery, *E. coli*, adenomatisis, gastric torsion, parvovirus, winter abortion, vaginal and uterine discharge, pyelonephritis and cystitis, 'greasy pig' disease, lameness, streptococcal meningitis and vitamin E deficiency. Above all, a major increase in vices arises, such as tail biting and other forms of aggression. Most of these problems can be overcome by the use of antibiotics; but resistance builds up, and new antibiotics have had to be applied.

ANTIBIOTICS AND INFECTIONS IN THE FOOD CHAIN

In 1986 doctors in various parts of England became alarmed at the spread of several strains of a germ which seemed to be impervious to all antibiotics except vancomycin. The germ is called methicillin-resistant staphylococcus aureus bacteris, MRSA for short, or Super Staph. First discovered in Essex in 1981, it then spread to London, where no less than thirty-two hospitals were affected, and through East Anglia to Nottinghamshire and Yorkshire. Patients infected by the germs had to be placed in isolation to be given the one antibiotic that is effective; even so, many died of the germ. Infected wards and intensive care units had to be closed to be made safe for use.

The gravity of the problem was highlighted by the *British Medical Journal*. According to the *BMJ*'s assistant editor, Dr Richard Smith, the potential of what can happen is frightening, and the bacteria could become resistant to the one antibiotic that can be used successfully. MRSA will reside on the skin and in the nose and do no harm until it gets into the blood stream. It then immediately becomes toxic. Many thousands of people are thus the unknowing carriers of the germ. Patients admitted for an operation may now be screened by the hospital, for even the healthiest of them are in danger once the germ contaminates the blood. According to the medical press, doctors working in the hospitals seem to be in general agreement that patients are failing to respond to antibiotics in these and other cases, when it is supremely important for them to be effective, because the patients have ingested too much of them already.

The doctors have also tried to alert public opinion to the consequences of MRSA spreading throughout the country. The *Observer* has raised the issue, recording how MRSA has also swept through hospitals in parts of Australia. In August 1986 it quoted Dr Ken Harvey, director of microbiology at the Royal Melbourne Hospital: 'We may look back on the antibiotic era as just a passing phase in the history of medicine, an era in which a great natural resource was squandered and where the bugs proved smarter than the scientists.'

Since the 1950s agriculture has used the great natural resource of antibiotics on a scale that has steadily grown. Warnings enough have been given in the past about what would happen were ever stronger antibiotics to be used on farm animals. As long ago as 1972 Christopher Smart and Pauline Marstrand of the Science Policy Research Unit at Sussex University, in a paper entitled 'Antibiotics Technology in Agriculture' published in the journal *Research Policy*, wrote these prophetic words: 'Strains of more or less harmless bacteria such as *E. coli* and staphylococcus aureus may develop resistance and then transfer it to organisms which are pathogens to stock, to humans or to both. In any case, resulting disease will be difficult to treat with antibiotics.'

As one antibiotic after another was squandered and 'the bugs proved smarter than the scientists', so more antibiotics were needed. In 1953 the drug companies were successful – aided and abetted by the farm lobby – in securing a change in the law to permit penicillin and chlortetracyclin to be used in feedstuffs as a growth stimulant, although it remained illegal for humans to have either of them except on prescription. Two years later, oxytetracyclin was also allowed. The quantity of antibiotics sold to the farmer and consumed by his animals mounted steadily from then on. Calves taken away from their dams soon after birth are very susceptible to a variety of ailments, but antibiotics enable them to be batched together in large numbers to be reared for veal or beef, and so they, too, joined the millions of farm animals regularly in receipt of various antibiotics. The drugs also started to be given to dairy cows. As herd sizes grew and the animals were grouped together on concrete rather than dispersed in open fields, the risks of disease increased; mastitis especially became a major problem.

Many doctors and scientists began to fear the consequences of the fivefold increase in antibiotics use on farm animals. Although they muttered among themselves, few of them seemed brave enough to speak out against the interests of the drug companies. Two notable exceptions were Professor E.

S. Anderson of the Enteric Reference Laboratory in London and Professor Mark Richmond of Bristol University. It was Professor Anderson who discovered strains of salmonella pyphimurium which were resistant to ampicillin. By the 1960s many outbreaks of salmonella poisoning among calves were taking place, causing the death of a huge number of them. Professor Anderson's call for a curb on the unfettered use of antibiotics received little support.

Then fourteen children in Yorkshire died of salmonella poisoning, having been unsuccessfully treated with antibiotics, which led to the subsequent inquiry by a committee under the chairmanship of Sir Michael Swann. In its report (1969) the Swann Committee accepted that salmonella pyphimurium, having become resistant to antibiotics, could prove fatal to humans, but the committee also concluded that there could be dangers with other bacteria unless the use of drugs was controlled. It recommended that antibiotics which treated humans should not be added to animal feed-stuffs as growth stimulants but should be available for prophylactic purposes when prescribed by a veterinary surgeon. Thus antibiotics were put into two classes. The therapeutic ones were those which were needed by doctors to treat humans, specifically penicillin, tetracycline and chloramphenicol; these ought only to be used on farm animals on a veterinary prescription. The remainder were to be classed as feed antibiotics, being those the doctor no longer used and which the farmers could have as growth stimulants.

Most of the Swann proposals became law, and everyone sat back content with a sensible compromise. But just over a decade later, in May 1980, the *British Medical Journal* carried the headline, 'Why has Swann failed?' It reported how two new types of salmonella, both multi-resistant, had first appeared in calves in 1977 and had been identified as causing salmonella posioning in 290 human patients; and in 1979 a third strain of salmonella had been discovered on fifty farms where calves were kept, and a further twenty people were infected. The resistant nature of the new strain was due, claimed the article, to trimethoprim being used on calves; it was resistant not only to this antibiotic but to seven others in use by doctors.

There are several reasons why the existing law, based on the Swann Report, is no safeguard. In the first place, to divide antibiotics into two watertight compartments fails to recognize how similar they are and how resistance to one may apply to another. Chloramphenicol is one of the antibiotics about which experts in this field (Professor Richmond, for example, and Dr Threlfall and his colleagues who have written papers on this for the *BMJ*) have expressed concern. The Swann Committee considered whether it should be classified as therapeutic and, though it emphasized its therapeutic importance, decided that a veterinary surgeon could be trusted not to advise excessively. Resistance to chloramphenicol, now quite pronounced, is attributed to the agricultural use of this and other antibiotics such as tetracycline and trimethoprim. Everyone in the business of keeping intensive livestock knows the great dilemma facing the veterinary profession. Inside those buildings there may be hundreds of calves, hundreds of pigs or tens of thousands of poultry; a sudden outbreak of disease could cause the financial collapse of the enterprise; and the veterinary surgeon, aware of the hazards, has to decide whether to avert the certain and immediate risk to his client, the farmer, or to consider the long-term, uncertain and less perceptible danger to other humans. He knows also that if he fails to prescribe antibiotics, another veterinary surgeon may take his place. Besides, there is also the black market.

The British drug companies spend millions of pounds a year on direct inducement to the medical and veterinary professions to promote the use of their products, as well as a far greater sum on advertisements and less questionable means of persuasion. Most medical and veterinary practices have their own dispensaries, and the companies can measure the success of their endeavours to induce them to prescribe by monitoring the volume of their purchases. The temptation for the two professions to be free with their prescriptions can be great; and it has been the subject of comment in both the medical and the veterinary press. In the case of the veterinary surgeon, it is the intensive methods of keeping farm animals that have initiated the hazard to human beings.

The Office of Health Economics, which sounds like some official agency of the government but is, in fact, a front organization for the UK pharmaceutical industry, is financed by companies like Cyanamid and Pfizer. Its booklet, *Antibiotics in Animal Husbandry* – a magnificent piece of special pleading, worthy of a place in any museum of the art – makes a plausible case for no restrictions whatsoever on the use of any antibiotics on our farms. The dangers of salmonella poisoning are brushed aside. In a very different kind of book, *Gluttons for Punishment* (1986), the *Guardian* journalist James Erlichman tells of his interview with Dr Bernard Rowe of the Public Health Service Laboratory. In 1964 there were, according to Dr Rowe, 4,500 cases of salmonella poisoning reported to the PHSL; by 1983 the number had leaped to 17,000. In his opinion, there are probably 100 cases of acute stomach upsets for every one reported. If so, 1,700,000 represents something of an epidemic. Salmonella poisoning is a disease of factory farming; its incidence is increasing, and the prospect of antibiotics being able to treat it in the future is diminishing.

Two scientists at the Center for Disease Control in the United States, Dr Mitchell Cohen and Dr Robert Tauxe, have made a special study of plasmids or the rings of genetic material characteristic of salmonella bacteria. These serve as a kind of fingerprint which enables the causes of salmonella poisoning in a human to be traced to the source of the infection, through the piece of meat eaten, back to the slaughterhouse and eventually to the very farm where it was produced. Their study showed this means of identification to be so accurate that 90 per cent of the resistant strains were traced to infected livestock which had become impervious to treatment by antibiotics as a result of their over-use as growth stimulants.

Professor Mark Richmond was one of the scientists who established beyond any reasonable doubt the link between salmonella poisoning and meat from our factory farms. He suggested in the *British Medical Journal* that even at the time he wrote, in May 1980, it might be too late to reverse the incidence of resistance to antibiotics by a change in the law to block the loopholes left inadvertently by the Swann Committee. To decide where the blame lies, one passage of the Swann Report ought to be quoted:

> Finally, we recognize that our decision may prove to have been mistaken and we consider it would be prudent to monitor the amounts of chloramphenicol used in human and veterinary medicine, and the prevalence of chloramphenicol resistance in organisms isolated from farm animals and from the intestinal flora of healthy humans, so that prompt action can be taken on reliable evidence if either increases significantly. We recommend that the Minister of Agriculture, Fisheries and Food, and the Secretary of State for Social Services, should take steps accordingly.

That, of course, was written more than twenty years ago.

Hospital doctors value antibiotics as life-savers, precious instruments to be neither abused nor over-used. The tragic deaths from MRSA and salmonellosis show they can fail to save lives when they should have succeeded. To blame the farming community for using them to speed the growth of animals for slaughter is easy, though not entirely fair. So long as we keep the farmer standing on the treadmill, it will go on revolving, around and around. He will have little choice in deciding what he is to do on his farm. The danger of over-using antibiotics, despite being well chronicled, is still not acted upon adequately by the Ministry of Agriculture. Is its relationship with the pharmaceutical lobby too harmonious?

Not only pigs and poultry, but also dairy cows receive antibiotics on a large scale when housed together in close quarters, as most of them are today in the winter months, and some all through the year. Many tens of thousands of people have become allergic to cows' milk, although the same symptoms do not appear when they drink milk from goats. Whether this can be attributed to antibiotics in the milk is yet to be proved, although it is well established that many people are allergic to some antibiotics. There are, however, a large number of doctors who recommend mothers to give babies goats' milk rather than take the risk.

As for veal and beef, the calves are removed from the dams soon after birth, apart from a small minority kept as replacements for the herd. Veal crates are now prohibited in the UK. This was recommended by the House of Commons Select Committee on Agriculture in its report on farm animal welfare in 1981. In the course of the inquiry, the select committee saw several different systems of keeping veal calves. The only one that impressed it favourably was the Volac system, whereby batches of calves were kept together on straw in pens inside buildings with good ventilation. Humane methods cost money, and the Volac system has, generally speaking, ceased to be profitable. As a result, every year about 300,000 calves are shipped across to the Continent, soon after birth, where crates are still allowed. The members of the committee who saw how they were treated resolved to give up eating veal and to this day have maintained their resolve.

Ironically, the prohibition of crates in the UK may have added to, instead of lessened, the suffering of the veal calves. If reared over here in crates they would at least be spared the crossing of the Channel and then being kept in conditions which would not be tolerated here. Calves in their natural state are licked by their mothers; taken from them, the calf's instinct is to lick itself, but this causes its hair to get into the stomach and affects the quality of the veal, so they are either kept in crates narrow enough to prevent them washing themselves or they are tied by the neck to prevent them turning their heads. The committee saw many calves in the latter positon and kept there through their lives, quite obviously in a degree of stress. That veal calves suffer from stress and stress-related ailments is acknowledged by the drug companies. It has, for instance, been the basis of the advertising campaign by Crookes Laboratories and Cyanamid for their sale of antibiotics, including chlortetracycline, erythromycin and aureomycin.

Not only are the antibiotics in our meat, they also wend their way into the water supply through the urine and faeces of both animals and humans who have eaten their meat. The water drunk by most people in a city like London has been consumed numerous times already and may have been through several human bodies. No anxiety need arise about this, provided the water has been purified. Enormous efforts are made, but so far there has been great difficulty in finding a method to remove drugs such as antibiotics. The more the water is recycled and purified for further human consumption, therefore, the more it is likely to contain antibiotics. Medical practitioners have expressed their concern about this, as they have about other drugs, such as ingredients of the contraceptive pill, persisting in the water supply.

Since writing about this danger on previous occasions, I have received letters from members of the public afflicted by conditions that we once never heard about but which appear to stem from a weakened immune system. ME (myalgic encephalomyelitis) or chronic fatigue syndrome is one example. If the immune system is supported by benign bacteria, and antibiotics indiscriminately kill all bacteria, whether benign or malign, it follows that an excess of antibiotics can have grave consequences.

HORMONES

In Chapter 6 something is said about the manipulators of farming policy. But here rather than later a few words might be said about how the pharmaceutical companies have operated with regard to hormones. Some of them have spent many millions of pounds – and dollars – to develop hormones as a means of raising output of both meat, especially beef, and milk. Public opinion, doubtful of the benefits, has led to hostility to the idea, with the result that the drug companies are in the midst of a political campaign in which further huge sums of money are being spent in the United States and the European Community in order to ensure that a favourable decision will be made for hormones.

In the UK the main body in the campaign is NOAH. The name conjures up the kindly man whose Ark saved the animal kingdom – a good name for a good cause – but it stands for the National Office of Animal Health. NOAH has for several years published a broadsheet entitled *Animal*

Health Matters; the first issue had an article headed 'Advice on Handling Pets', but all the article did was tell readers how to get a cat to swallow a pill. A much longer article was devoted to hormones and an attack upon the EEC Commission for proposing a directive to ban their use. Readers were left in no doubt about the terrible consequences if hormones were no longer to be used by farmers:

> If implants should not be considered a tool of the Common Agricultural Policy, nor should other productivity aids. Should we ban tractors or ration diesel fuel, so that there is no grain surplus? Should there be no irrigation for sugar beet so that there is no sugar surplus or no fungicide for vines to prevent a wine lake? It is obvious that all farming enterprises should be conducted as efficiently as possible and in a manner which allows the maximum flexibility of land use and capital. We view the use of implants as a more efficient method of improving productivity in beef production rather than a means of producing more beef. It is estimated that at farmer level the cash return on the use of implants is in the region of ten times the implant cost. This is obviously beneficial to the farmer and housewife in keeping prices down.

The business of manufacturing and selling hormones is a multi-million-pound affair. Milk hormones are banned worldwide, although as late as 1990 some UK consumers were still drinking milk from cows injected with the bovine somatotropin hormone as part of a government test programme. Beef hormones, which used to be allowed in the UK, have been prohibited by the EEC. The ban on their use is having a major effect upon the profits of some of the British companies involved, and they are doing their utmost to persuade the Ministry of Agriculture to oppose the decision of the EEC.

NOAH, as the article quoted above makes clear, wants all hormones to be allowed because they are safe and necessary for productivity to be increased. There is no doubt that productivity does improve when hormones are implanted.

My neighbour was able to convert week-old calves into animals ready for slaughter as beef in just twelve months by implanting hormones and feeding them barley ad lib in fairly close confinement so that they did not lose too many calories. Without hormones they would probably have taken twice as long to grow to the same size. Being cheap to produce, hormones can be sold to the farmer at an attractive price, and the claim is made by the manufacturers that for every £1 the farmer spends on hormones he will make another £10. Initially the farmer gains; but in this as in every case, when his costs of production fall, the intense competition in the business of food forces down prices and removes any gains in the profit margin. This was the experience of my neighbour, and he has given up the beef enterprise. Despite the ban imposed by the EEC, hormones are available on the black market, and many farmers are tempted to use them.

What about safety? Before the ban on the use of hormones was imposed, the EEC invited Professor Eric Lamming of Nottingham University to preside over an investigation into their safety. He considered first the naturaly occuring anabolic steroids and afterwards the two synthetic products, Ralgro and Finkplix, both of which have been in common use in the UK. His conclusion was that no scientific grounds existed for prohibiting either the natural or the synthetic hormones.

Professor Lamming's opinion was rejected by the EEC, and a ban was placed on both kinds. The Ministry of Agriculture was persuaded to take the issue to the European Court of Justice, alleging it was an improper decision as it did not pay regard to the scientific evidence. The drug industry has transferred the main thrust of its campaign to Brussels. The aim is to have as powerful a lobby to influence the decision-making as the industry possesses. The forty drug companies have set up the Animal Health Federation for Europe to speak on their behalf and work for the removal of the hormone ban. *Animal Health Matters*, in revealing this item of information, said it was 'an essential move as the consumer lobbyists prepare for their next onslaught on the livestock industry'.

The drug companies have so far made little impact on

farmers in the rest of the EEC. The other countries lack a farming press as beholden to advertisers as ours is. Week after week, whole pages of these British magazines are taken over by the drug companies to sell their products to readers, and without this revenue the farming press could not continue in its present form. On the Continent farmers have been warned of the consequences of using hormones; they have seen the sale of veal fall drastically after it was found that baby food containing veal from calves treated with synthetic hormones was the cause of cancer in children and of giving them characteristics of the opposite sex.

The Bureau of the European Consumers' Union took this up with the EEC officials, but farmers themselves had two arguments in favour of the ban. First, they realized that a fall in demand for red meat as a result of the publicity about hormones was not in their interest. Secondly, the use of hormones would not, in their view, benefit them financially, even if the demand for beef and veal were to recover. They perceived the effects of the chemical treadmill. Higher productivity inevitably forces down prices, and lower costs of production benefit the consumer, not the farmer. EEC officials, who have a better grasp of economics than they are usually credited with, understood this argument plainly enough and proceeded with their proposal to ban hormones for the advantage of both consumer and farmer. No doubt they also took into account the massive surplus of beef already occupying so much space in the cold stores that some of it had to be placed in storage outside the Community. When production has outstripped demand there seems little point in trying to increase it still more, especially when it is at great expense to the taxpaying public which has to buy up the surplus.

Professor Lamming's opinion was therefore of little importance. There is, in any event, an obvious flaw in it. Whether hormone implants are dangerous or not must depend upon the number that are made. He, it seems, was assuming that implants are done as prescribed by the drug company. Perhaps he has not visited a cattle market in recent years. If he did he would be almost sure to see some of the animals with dipped backs and distorted hips – the tell-tale signs that they have been over-drugged with hormones. In the slaughterhouse another symptom is to be seen: a rind on the skin rather like that on bacon. The fact is that there is a great temptation to implant hormones more often than one should. The law of diminishing returns may apply; yet if in the eye of the beef producer every implant seems to accelerate growth, those extra implants will be given. Besides, the advice given by the drug companies tends to vary. For example, the manufacturers of Ralgro, one of the two main synthetic hormones, declare in their advertisement: 'With Ralgro, an additional weight of 53 kg is achieved by implanting regularly.' The obvious inference is to go on using the stuff as much as one can; and, despite a warning not to implant within a certain period before slaughter, there is plenty of anecdotal evidence among farmers that it is a good idea to carry on regardless. So, although Professor Lamming may or may not have been right theoretically, practice on the farm makes his view very questionable.

Diethylstilboestrol (DES) was the hormone responsible for advancing the puberty of girls and feminizing boys when given to veal calves in Italy in 1980. This oestrogen-based drug has had similar effects in Puerto Rico. In the early 1980s Dr Carmen Saenz, an endocrinologist, carried out a study of 3,000 cases on the island of children who had eaten poultry. Chicken is generally the main form of meat there, and much of it was produced using DES, despite prohibition of the hormone. Dr Saenz found there were hundreds of instances of girls reaching puberty at the age of six and even five; once poultry meat produced with DES was withdrawn from their diet, the signs of oncoming puberty disappeared. The sheer number of cases where this happened convinced her that there could be no other reasonable explanation for the premature puberty.

Among the many members of the medical profession who have expressed concern at the use of hormones in meat and dairy production is Professor Howard Jacobs of Middlesex Hospital, where he holds the chair of reproductive endocrinology. He was reported by the *Observer* in May 1983 as saying that the decline in the sperm count of some North

American males might be attributed to their diet; for oestrogen can be found in the milk of pregnant cows, hormones being used to enable artificial insemination to be successful, as well as in beef and poultry, both popular in the American diet.

Stilboestrol (female hormone) implants were commonly given to capons – castrated cockerels – to speed their fattening. This practice has almost died out now that it is known that the drug is not necessarily ingested in the capon and is almost certainly a cause of cancer. The offal of these birds used to be sold to mink farmers, until it was found that the mink lost their fertility. Other kinds of hormones are now used in the poultry industry. Such is their speed of growth, the birds are ready for slaughter in a matter of a few weeks, and so it is not feasible to detect any long-term effects on them caused by such drugs. The chronic effects on the human who eats plenty of white meat are yet to be discovered.

Three drug companies – Monsanto, American Cyanamid and Elanco – are now trying to persuade the US Food and Drug Administration to grant a licence for them to sell hormones for dairy cows; and they have let it be known they are confident of success. The drug is the bovine growth hormone (bgH). A certain amount of it occurs naturally in all dairy cows; but experiments have shown that, when they are given a daily injection of the hormone, milk yields increase by between 20 and 40 per cent. This has been confirmed by scientists at Cornell University, where the dairy herd has been experimented upon with the drug in co-operation with Monsanto. Agricultural economists at the university, however, have pointed out some of the other likely consequences. The USA already has a massive surplus of dairy products which has cost the federal government $2,000 million a year. The use of hormones, they say, would lead either to still greater overproduction or to 25 to 30 per cent of the dairy farmers going out of business.

The hormone bgH has also been tested at the University of Minnesota, as reported in *Agraview* in January 1987. A 50 mg dose was needed, it seems, to get the most satisfactory increase in milk yield, but many of the cows then developed mastitis, and it was also found that the cows had greater difficulty in getting pregnant again. Both problems could probably be overcome: the mastitis by giving them more antibiotics, and other hormones injected to ensure pregnancy. Scientists who have observed the cows in these tests have felt concerned about their welfare, and, as with other farm animals performing intensively, signs of stress were apparent.

Scientists in both the USA and the UK have raised the further question as to whether hormones influence the behaviour of animals. Quite naturally, no drug company seems to have undertaken any research about this. However, the link between human behaviour and hormone imbalance is well established. Some of the evidence was summarized in an article in *The Times* in November 1985. A normally timid person, it said, can turn into an ambitious leader if there is the slightest increase in the hormone testosterone. Only an insignificant amount of it exists in the blood stream of a normal person – scarcely enough to smear the glass of a small wristwatch – yet it is so potent that the merest imbalance will cause personality change.

The testosterone level for men is between 10 and 35 nanomules per litre; for women it is only between 0.7 and 2.7. If, at the time of menopause, a woman has a higher proportion of testosterone, doctors say that the masculine traits of being aggressive and domineering may become apparent, often accompanied by a new ambitious drive. Just one or two nanomules will make the difference.

Unlike their UK counterparts, the farmers in the USA, having a perception of the chemical treadmill, have petitioned the Food and Drug Administration against the granting of a licence for bgH. The *Washington Post* reported in April 1986 what Mike Cannel, on behalf of the Wisconsin Family Farms Defense Fund, said about the petition: 'There is one key question: what do we want rural America to look like and what kind of society do we want functioning in rural America?' Sadly, this kind of key question is not posed in the columns of our *Farmers' Weekly*. Nor, between the many pages that advertise to the farmer the wonders of many drugs, would we see editorial opinion which echoes

Mike Cannell: 'It is legitimate to question whether techno-logical advancements are social progress.'

Such is the influence of the pharmaceutical companies over the farming press that were poor Mr Cannell to say the same thing in the UK he would be upbraided as being 'anti-farming' and perhaps even 'farmer-bashing'. However, even in the USA there is a suspicion that the Food and Drug Administration has been unduly influenced. Dr Richard Burroughs, who formerly worked for the FDA as a veterin-ary scientist, has alleged that the results of the tests on bgH were altered to make it appear safer. The tests, in his view, showed a higher level of cortisone and insulin in the cows than reported, while there was also a greater incidence of mastitis and a suppression of the immune system, neither of which was disclosed in the results.

The drug companies insist that bgH is naturally present in the cow. This is true, but it is equally true that many minerals are to be found naturally in the bovine family, yet every one of them would be toxic if its quantity exceeded a certain level. Originally, the hormones were extracted from dead cows, but as this is an expensive process and requires a lot of dead cows, the hormone is multiplied by the *E. coli* bacteria. As no veterinary scientist would claim this as a benign bug, another ground for doubt seems to arise.

BSE

Then there is BSE, bovine spongiform encephalopathy, the 'mad cow disease'. We can now be certain that it comes from cows eating the brains of infected sheep. As long ago as the 1920s, Rudolph Steiner, the apostle of biodynamic husban-dry, warned of the dangers of feeding meat to sheep. Unable to digest it, he said, it would go to their brains, like so much alcohol goes to the head; and if fed continually in this way, some mental disorder would be caused, just as an habitual drunkard becomes permanently befuddled. This proved to be the case: a scrapie-infected sheep behaves like an inebriate.

Fishmeal and soya bean used to be the two main proteins added to compound feeds for pigs, poultry, cattle and, sometimes, sheep. Dwindling fish stocks made the first too expensive, and the import levies imposed by the Common Agricultural Policy had the same effect upon soya bean, which was imported from outside the Common Market. Fierce competition between the companies manufacturing compound feeds forced them to look elsewhere for a cheaper form of protein. What could be cheaper than dead livestock which was unfit for human consumption? Thus dead sheep, duly minced up and processed, found their way into live animals (only in the UK – although sheep offal is used in Germany). Cows had never been known to suffer from scrapie; the disease made a species leap; and now the question is asked, can it make another species leap to humans who eat beef? More than 10,000 cows have been infected and slaughtered, and many of them had not themselves eaten sheep's brains, so it seems the disease may be transmitted by a healthy cow. It is also believed to be able to lurk for twenty years before manifesting itself.

As mice, pet cats and animals in the zoos have been afflicted by mad cow disease, it is evident that further species leaps are possible. In fact, as long ago as 1962, experiments on mice established that scrapie could be transmitted to them. This should have been warning enough of the dangers of eating infected meat. According to medical opinion, Creutzfeldt-Jacob disease is the human equivalent of BSE. Although there has been a marked increase in its incidence in the last few years, a link with eating infected beef has yet to be established. We may have a good number of years to wait before we can be sure that human beings are safe.

OFFAL, BOTULISM AND LISTERIA

The public's concern about salmonella and mad cow disease led the Ministry of Agriculture to place a ban upon recycling dead animals for sheep and cattle to eat, but not pigs and poultry. The former being nature's vegetarians, it was agreed that they should not be required to eat meat. Bits and pieces of dead animals would still be given to pigs and poultry, however, as they were considered to be carnivores. Yet whether this is a zoological truth has been questioned. In their natural state the pig and the hen are foragers; they may incidentally or accidentally eat some sort of meat – and under acute stress they may attack their own kind – but there is no evidence that either ever chooses to eat animal flesh in preference to its normal diet. The animal feed industry was able to tell the ministry that unless it continued to use offal from the slaughterhouses in its feed compounds for pigs and poultry, millions of tonnes of it would have to be disposed of in some other way. Dumping such vast quantities in pits would arouse great public anger; the rat population would multiply, principles of public hygiene would be thrown out of the window, and the stench would be awful. Hence millions of tonnes of bits and pieces of dead animals, including much that has been condemned as unfit for human consumption, is retained in the food chain as it gets recycled.

There is an alternative use for this offal. Two of my constituents, Mr and Mrs Twelftree of Surfleet, near Spalding, Lincolnshire, having only three acres on which to make a livelihood, decided to specialize and grow lettuces of the highest quality. This they did, consistently obtaining the best prices at Covent Garden. They attributed much of their success to the use of offal from a nearby slaughterhouse to enrich the soil. Such organic growers are far too few to use up all the animal waste now available and they will remain too few until the ministry ends its disdain for them. The other factor making this alternative less feasible than it ought to be is that a host of ministry regulations has brought the demise of hundreds of local slaughterhouses. Now that more than 90 per cent of the UK's stock are slaughtered in central abattoirs, far from the farms and market gardens, the cost of taking the offal to farms many miles away would make this kind of fertilizer too expensive. So the feed compounders have gained their concession, while the pigs and poultry were eating an inordinate amount of sheep and cattle as well as their own kind, until public opinion forced the ministry to change its mind in 1990.

That vegetarian cattle are no longer eating animal protein is not, in fact, true. They are eating poultry. In the huge broiler houses where tens of thousands of chicks reach slaughter weight of 5 lb in forty-nine days, the mortality rate is very high. The birds are so crammed together that the stockman is unable to move among them to pick up those that have died. The carcasses are trodden into the litter; as soon as the remaining birds are taken away to be slaughtered, tractors move in to scoop up the litter, which is sent off to be processed into cattle feed.

In 1988 sixty-eight beef cattle out of a herd of eighty died of botulism (invariably caused by bacteria from putrid meat); the remainder were also infected but managed to recover. According to the government's veterinary laboratory in Belfast, the outbreak of the disease was due to poultry litter in their feed. The *Veterinary Record* said that poultry carcasses should be removed from the litter before being processed into cattle feed. But the modern intensive units make this impractical; all the stockman can do is remove carcasses that are visible after the building is emptied of birds, but by this time many of the birds that die in the earlier stages will have been incorporated in the litter.

One comment by the *Veterinary Record* may be repeated: 'The meat from suspect cases of botulism, or from healthy animals which have been exposed to a source of botulism toxins, should . . . be considered to be a potential health risk to human beings or animals if it has not been cooked properly.' The *Record* also urged farmers to vaccinate all cattle that are eating feed containing poultry litter. As experts say that botulism toxin is not destroyed by heat, this may be the only effective precaution. But how can farmers take this advice unless the compounders are required to disclose the ingredients of the feed? As Chapter 6 shows, these compounders have been among the most adroit manipulators of the system.

A further risk to both animal and human health has arisen from a new practice on livestock farms – big bale silage, it is called. Grass is conserved by wrapping it in plastic sheeting with the object of keeping out all air. But no fermentation of sugars takes place and very little acid is produced, unlike in silage-making proper. With the absence of acid and the lowering of pH, listeria multiply, each bale becoming a 'factory' for the mass production of listeria. Botulism toxins are also multiplied, which will lead to botulism itself. Many thousands of cattle are being fed this so-called silage; and although it has expressed concern at the probable consequences, the UK ministry has so far shown no inclination for action.

FOOD IRRADIATION

Can toxic food be converted by animals into meat safe for humans to eat? Up to a point it probably can be, for otherwise the meat-eating majority would not be as healthy as they are. But can this kind of meat with its interacting hormones, antibiotics and toxins enable the majority to be in such good health as they would enjoy were it produced humanely, without either the toxins or the chemicals?

The EEC Commission is aware of the dangers and to overcome them is willing to approve irradiation. Our own Ministry of Agriculture is enthusiastic. Microbiologists are generally of the view that the risks of both listeria and salmonella can never be reduced unless the kind of food, poultry meat especially, most prone to infection is irradiated. Despite strong opposition from the Consumers' Association, the National Federation of Women's Institutes and other bodies, the principle of permitting irradiation was approved by the House of Commons in 1989, giving the Minister of Agriculture authority to introduce statutory regulations governing its use. All the supermarket chains, except Sainsbury, which has its own factory farms, have indicated that they do not wish to supply their customers with irradiated food. Irradiation will kill the bugs, but in doing so will destroy the vitamins. Besides, the bugs are not all detrimental to our health; the very opposite is the case. For healthy food is full of benign bacteria which we need inside us to beat off hostile germs. Irradiated meat and other foods may be safe to eat, but in positive terms they will have little or no nutritional value. As it will be incapable of maintaining our health, a diet with more than a small proportion of irradiated food will lead to malnutrition.

The intensive methods of the factory farms also affect our water supply – water not only that we drink but that food processers use in numerous ways. A government-appointed committee under the chairmanship of Sir John Badenoch has found that some 9,000 British people a year are affected by a parasite called cryptosporidium, of whom about 20 per cent require treatment in hospital. The parasite, which comes from ordinary tap-water, causes acute diarrhoea, usually persisting for a fortnight. The parasite is impervious to any drug or any remedy. Considerable suffering can be caused to elderly people, children and anyone in a poor state of health. The parasite comes from slurry, the inevitable product of farms where too many animals are kept. One infected pig can produce 10,000 million of these parasites in a day. Once its slurry finds its way into a watercourse and through to the main water supply, nothing can stop the infection of the water when it comes out of the tap. Even chlorine, reported to kill off all parasites, fails to destroy cryptosporidium. Only boiling the water for an adequate length of time will have the desired effect.

In a sense, all livestock farming is unnatural. Human beings have acquired domination over cows, pigs, sheep and hens and changed the way they live, eat, reproduce and die. For people to eat meat, butter, cheese and eggs as well as to drink milk, the necessity for this conversion from their original pattern of life is self-evident. But we can go too far in doing anything. Have we, then, gone too far in making demands upon our farm animals? For hens to lay twice the number of eggs, cows to yield twice the quantity of milk or pigs to be reared to slaughter weight in half the time may be scientifically a triumph. All triumphs have consequences, however, often unexpected and disagreeable. Perhaps in forcing our animals to yield us so much we have 'gone against nature', a phrase countrymen used to murmur.

To go against nature – or to go too far against nature – is always dangerous. Is the poison in the meat a signal sent by nature of greater dangers ahead?

· 4 ·

THE VANISHING COUNTRYSIDE

SUBSIDIZING DESTRUCTION

I have been a daily witness of one way in which our farming and its impact on the landscape have gone wrong. I live beside the River Pang, between Reading and Newbury, the river Kenneth Grahame wrote about in *The Wind in the Willows* (1908). The river is different now.

A few years ago the Thames Water Authority, as agent of the Minister of Agriculture in drainage matters, was ordered to spend a further £800,000 on top of the £5 million its own experts considered was enough for drainage to lower the local water table. The gentleman in Whitehall knows best, we are told, and the water authority had to comply with the ministerial decree. First the trees were felled, including willows that Kenneth Grahame might have known. Then came the dredgers to straighten some of the bends, making some stretches look more like a scaled–down version of the Grand Union Canal than a meandering chalk stream. It was thought necessary to lower the water table because arable crops like wheat, barley and oilseed rape cannot grow in this valley unless the wet lowland is dried out by drainage. The larger farmers here have been goaded by grants, subsidies and import levies into growing such crops, instead of keeping cattle and sheep.

A few of us with smallholdings continue to breed and fatten cattle, and three have dairy herds; we need a *high* water table to enable the grass to grow well all through the dry summer months. Also, the great variety of grasses and flora that make our cattle fatten into top-quality meat cannot flourish on dried-out land. Now some of the flora has died out and disappeared, and the beef is the poorer for it. Beef from these fields has been, according to the wholesale butchers, the best in a radius of many miles. Our interests are thus, by public policy, put in conflict with those of the other farmers. Many of the wild flowers have gone or are markedly fewer. Of the birds, the snipe, the peewit and the kingfisher are seen no more, and the mallard and the moor-hen have become rarer. Removal of the cover along the river bank has taken away the habitat of the otter and the water-vole – Kenneth Grahame's 'Ratty'.

All this has come about because public money has been spent for the benefit of one-half of the landowners and farmers to the detriment of the other half. The farmers for whose benefit it was done would be the first to admit that they would never have spent their own money in this way. As it is, much of the wheat they have grown has gone down to the docks, then to Cuba or the Soviet Union with the aid of export subsidies. I calculate that in one year alone the subsidies to export this surplus wheat from our part of the Pang Valley cost us not less than £120,000. The value of the subsidies alone – quite apart from other grants, subsidies and tax allowances – has exceeded the personal income received by these farmers.

To make one poor-quality field at the top of the hill capable of growing wheat, the owner drained it with a grant of public money. The water was drained on to the public highway, so that, whenever there was a sudden downpour, the road at the bottom of the hill would flood and become almost impassable. So the county council closed the road for a month, much to the inconvenience of the public who used it every day, and set about spending a lot more public money on a scheme to cope with the floodwater. The true cost to us of growing wheat in that rubbishy field at the top of the hill, and the true cost of getting rid of it to Cuba or the USSR, must add up to quite a sum. Examples like this, of lane widening, of sewerage schemes for intensive farms and of purifying the water supply polluted by excess fertilizers – of extra public money having to be spent as a result of the present policy – are probably to be found in most parishes in the countryside.

Here at home, then, my wife and I can witness the constant and contrived change in the wildlife and landscape, and reflect on how much it costs. Then constituents write to me, complaining about the cuts in public expenditure that fall upon our schools and hospitals and that postpone yet again the building of a bypass. As I look out of the window, up the Pang Valley, I find it difficult to write back a sensible answer.

Ought we to blame the farmer for what he is doing to the landscape? When we had the system of deficiency payments given to the farmer to make up the difference between the world price and his guaranteed price, he was able to buy his wheat, maize and barley to feed his cattle, pigs and poultry at world prices. The emphasis of agriculture in the United Kingdom was therefore on livestock, and because of our climate and the poor soil that covers more than half our land, this was economically sensible. It also made our country green and pleasant. Then came the preparations to join the Common Market, and we had to abandon deficiency payments and go over to the system of import levies and duties.

The main purpose of the new system was to keep out cheap wheat, maize and barley from countries outside the Common Market, especialy Canada and the United States. From then on the farmer has been induced to grow those arable crops rather than keep livestock, and a great change has come over our countryside.

The more intensively an area has been farmed, the more the local countryside has changed. Sturdy souls who stride across Dartmoor, Exmoor and even Snowdonia discover sights and sounds which would never have been there in the late 1940s and early 1950s. The Forestry Commission – state-controlled and heavily subsidized by the long-suffering tax-payer – has acquired many thousands of acres and planted upon them a dark green vastness of conifers. Sheep have also multiplied since import duties have been imposed on lamb from New Zealand, and substantial grants to pay for drainage, fencing and the reclamation of marginal land have had the effect of reducing the area of moorland. Yet the visitor returning after thirty years still recognizes the scene; he knows it remains Dartmoor or Allendale.

But what of the visitor to the village of his birth anywhere south of the River Trent? The more agriculture has 'prospered', the more far-reaching the change that the visitor will see after an absence of thirty years. As he approaches the village he will notice fewer hedgerows; many have been uprooted and have disappeared altogether, while many others have been replaced by barbed-wire fencing. Millions of pounds of public money have been responsible for this: grants to pay for the removal of hedgerows and further grants to pay for the barbed-wire fencing for which the farmer has received 25 per cent of the cost. Such fencing is 'economic'; it enables livestock to be kept in more effectively; it does not need many man-hours to be spent cutting it once a year; it enables every square inch to be grazed; and the plough gains another two feet around the field.

Our observant friend will also see many fewer trees and scarcely any within the field itself. Such trees were useful when stock farming predominated, but are a nuisance to the arable farmer. It is likely that more than half the fields will now be arable, at least twice as many as before the war when the policy of minimal state control tilted the balance in favour of livestock.

Then the visitor drives past the farmhouse. The old barns are gone. Some were built of local stone, others of elm and thatch; but only a few survive now. They were large enough for the old farmer, but government grants have subsidized the amalgamation of farms, so now it is necessary to have new buildings erected two or three times the size of the old ones. These new structures are made of concrete; they are efficient and sensible, but scarcely objects of beauty. Two companies specialize in erecting them throughout the country; so wherever our visitor goes he will see the same uniform buildings and the same standardized materials. Again, substantial grants and generous tax allowances have speeded up the process of replacing the old with the new.

The eye of our observant friend will catch sight of a pond where he used to stalk the newts, but now it seems to have a different shape. No wonder. The owner was given a government grant to fill it in, but later the scheme was reversed and the owner took advantage of the help that was made available to dig the pond out again and to restore its previous usefulness.

Next our visitor will be surprised to see a huge factory beside one of the farms. How was planning permission granted? It has to be explained to him that planning laws are quite different for the farmers; they are, in the real sense of the word, privileged. Although this building looks identical to a factory on an industrial estate, it is, in fact, called a cowtel. Inside, a herd of some 200 dairy cows live their lives. Some are upstairs and some down. Much of their food is stored under the same roof, and their milk is treated and pasteurized there as well. Our visitor may gaze in awe at its massive size and, if he is eccentric enough, at its beauty, too. Should he be a taxpayer he might also contemplate how much he has contributed to its cost.

Yet it is in the country village itself that the greatest transformation has come about. The village where I live is said to be the least changed in the whole county; its population is now 135, while thirty years ago it was 125. Only a few new houses have been built in those years. The main difference is that forty years ago there were fourteen farm workers employed upon the farms in the parish – now there is one. There are eight farms in all and, apart from that single exception, each is worked by the farmer himself assisted only by his family or occasional part-time help.

The size of the farms has not changed much, but what they produce has. The emphasis used to be on dairying. Six of the farmers were almost wholly dependent upon a monthly cheque from the Milk Marketing Board for their incomes, and each of them did quite well. None of them could now. Some twenty years ago a dairy farm of 80 acres could support a milking herd of twenty cows, and the farmer could afford to employ a full-time herdsman. The pastures were not overstocked, and feedstuffs were bought in on only a small scale. In a short space of time, such farming has been made quite unprofitable. It is not because wages have risen disproportionately; farm workers' incomes have not, in fact, kept pace with those of industrial workers. Nor can it be because of 'cheap imports'. None of the usual explanations can point to the reason why our farms have been denuded of men who used to work on them. The finger must be pointed at the system that has made it worthwhile for the farmer to replace his men with machines.

Of course, the movement to the towns from the land has been going on for centuries, but now the picture is a different one. Former farm workers have tended to remain living in the villages and hamlets, and either new jobs have been brought to the country areas or the men have gone by the day to work in the country towns. It is this that has utterly transformed the scene in our old market towns and country villages.

As work was lost on the land, so it was found in hundreds of new small industries – and some not so small – that have been established in our country towns and villages. Anyone travelling through counties such as Wiltshire and Suffolk, whose fortunes were once entirely wrapped up in agriculture, can see how many new factories have been built since the war, on the outskirts of the towns, and every one on what used to be farming land. In Wiltshire, for example, the towns of Marlborough, Devizes, Melksham, Bradford-on-Avon, Chippenham, Calne, Warminster and Westbury were, some thirty years ago, redolent of rurality. Any customer in a shop was as likely as not to be a farmer or his wife or a farm worker or his wife. The townspeople felt themselves to be part of the agricultural scene, for most of them had jobs that in one way or another served agriculture. They talked farming.

Today, not one in twenty of the customers in the shops in any of those towns would be a farmer or farm worker or the wife of one. In fact, of Wiltshire's half-million population, only 2 per cent are now in agriculture.

Physically and outwardly all these old market towns have changed as industry has largely replaced agriculture. Market squares are taken over by supermarkets and chain stores, the corn exchanges by bingo halls; scarcely a single cattle market survives in the centre of any town. Each one of them, without exception, is larger than it used to be; many of them are twice or three times their previous size. As they have sprawled out, gobbling up green pastures and rural lanes, they have done nothing to enhance the beauty that used to be there.

There need be no mystery as to why this has happened. Business men wanting to expand or begin a new venture have sought out the place where labour costs were comparatively low. When an industry sheds as many of its employees as agriculture has done, there is a vacuum to be filled. In the conditions of full urban employment that prevailed in the UK for more than two decades, business men had little choice but to move out into these country towns, and often into the villages as well.

The new industries needed wider, straighter, faster roads to connect the old country towns and villages with railheads and motorways and directly with the cities and conurbations. Many a country lane has had to change to accommodate this new traffic. This demand for speedy communication and heavy goods vehicles has brought changes to the countryside that conservationists have had to accept with regret. Villages on the main traffic routes have suffered in obvious ways, but so far it has not been clear to what extent the fabric and structure of many ancient cottages and manor houses have been damaged by the vibrations of these heavy lorries. If my reasoning as to why these new industries have come to the countryside is even partially right, it will be quite impossible to calculate how much of the beauty of our countryside, of our country towns and of our villages, has been lost by a policy that has caused so many men to lose their jobs on the land and to be replaced by machines subsidized by the taxpayer.

SHOULD WE BLAME THE FARMER?

The people most obviously affected by these changes are, of course, the farmers. Their way of life has been largely transformed, and it is they who have been the instruments of change in the agricultural landscape. Faced with growing public hostility on that count, they have naturally defended themselves, claiming that they are still the custodians of the countryside. Farmers, they point out, have an interest in protecting the landscape. They live as well as work in it; it is their home, and they have every reason to cherish the sights and sounds they have known since childhood. Like most self-evident truths about agriculture, there is need now to question this one.

At one time, it would indeed have been difficult to find a single British farmer without a feel for the countryside. Life for him, his wife and children was not quite so idyllic as some writers have portrayed. Unless he had the instincts of a countryman and desired his recreation as well as his work to be rooted in rural life – being content for his children to have the same upbringing, with a wife who shared his feelings – it was better for him to head for the town.

All this was a generation or more ago, and while it is true that the majority of farmers are still countrymen in the sense that they want to protect the environment in which they live, the present system has enticed many thousands of others to take up farming primarily for the financial gain. Chief among the sources of this gain are the tax privileges available for the rich individual who thinks he is paying too much income tax or who would like his children to inherit more of his wealth than they otherwise would. In some parts of the southern half of England, such a man is to be found in nearly every parish. When he has made his money in the City or some other form of business, the idea of a farm with its amenities and opportunity for some sporting recreation is very agreeable.

This trend has existed since time immemorial. Even in Tudor times, wool merchants bought their country estates as evidence of their success, but for them the social and sporting advantages were reasons enough for buying farm-land. They never damaged the countryside; rather, by bring-ing their purchasing power into the country they sustained its prosperity; and because they wanted to be proud of what they had acquired, the beauty of the countryside was invariably enhanced. They often toyed with farming. The larger estate would have what was called the 'home farm', usually the farm on the estate nearest to the owner's house, and this was kept in hand and run by a bailiff. Whether or not it paid its way did not matter very much; its owner would take his thumb-stick and stump over its acres or stand in the yard with the bailiff debating whether to buy a new bull.

Townsmen they may have been, and their efforts at playing the country squire may have sometimes been the subject of ridicule. But they never did any positive harm to the countryside; and in their favour it must be said that most of the advances made by agriculture for over two centuries were due to their willingness to risk their money doing things which the ordinary farmer could not afford to do. These men could afford to experiment and to try out new ideas. Some were disastrous financially; others came to be copied by neighbours and later further afield.

Jethro Tull is usually cited as the farmer who did more than anyone else to further the Agricultural Revolution, being portrayed as some kind of honest John Bull. Honest I am sure he was, but the portrait is otherwise false. He was my kinsman and, like me, he was a barrister for many years, taking to farming the family acres only because ill health required him to spend his days in the fresh air instead of at the Inns of Court. Tull's motives, ambitions and way of life were not untypical of many hundreds of others who took up farming, though not born to do so. Everything they did enhanced the self-evident truth that the farmer's well-being and that of the countryside were one and the same.

What has happened in the last twenty years or so is a challenge to what all of us concerned with the good name of agriculture would wish to believe. Two kinds of farmer have destroyed much of our countryside. One is the agribusiness man (or is he the aggro-business man?) who has moved into farming because of the financial and fiscal gains which he sees to be greater there than elsewhere. The other is the farmer standing on the treadmill, feverishly trying to keep pace with the demands upon him. Typically, he is a tenant whose rent is higher in real terms than ever, or an owner-occupier who has borrowed heavily for the purchase of his

only. No accurate figure exists for Scotland, but as much of the lowlands and a significant part of the east coast have also been subject to the same pressures as in England, it would be reasonable to add several thousand more miles to the total destroyed.

There has often been some justification for what has happened. I have myself been responsible for about 200 yards, for that was the length of a boundary between two small fields which, once amalgamated, made one that was still only two acres in size. (In this case, might I be permitted to add, the work was done entirely without any subsidy.) From time to time, as farming practices change, there is a need to change the shape of a field or to make an enlargement or a division. When we had tens of thousands of dairy farms with herds of ten or fifteen cows, always kept out in the fields, it was sensible to rotate them among several fields, to prevent poaching of the grass and worm infestation. Such fields of three or four acres make life unreasonably difficult for a combine moving in to harvest a crop of wheat.

It would be wrong, therefore, to condemn the disappearance of all those 130,000 miles of hedgerow. The point is that the destruction has gone much further than it need have done, and much further than economic and practical considerations alone would have taken it. In 1957 the Minister of Agriculture decided to ask the Treasury for public money to subsidize the cost of removing hedges; the Treasury was persuaded to agree to a scheme that was to cost the taxpayer many millions of pounds. Such a subsidy can have only one purpose – to induce a farmer to do something that he would not otherwise do, because it would not be financially worth his while.

Hedgerows can cost money to retain and look after. Once a year they should be cut. Ideally, they ought to be cut and laid, but that can be done only by a highly paid and skilled craftsman, and it is now rare outside the counties of Leicestershire and Warwickshire where the leaping of fences in pursuit of the fox has done much for the conservation of our hedgerows. Elsewhere, a hedge-cutting machine is set to work, which, by always cutting off the top, weakens the bottom of the hedge and thus diminishes still more the habitat of the wildlife.

The Institute of Terrestrial Ecology (a body which obtains most of its funds from the Department of the Environment, the Nature Conservancy Council and the European Commission) published a report entitled *Landscape Changes in Britain* in 1986, which spoke of 'derelict' and 'relic' hedgerows. The former resemble hedgerows as we know them, but neglect has made them useless for the purpose of keeping in stock. Often they may avoid being grubbed up because they are the boundaries between one farm where stock used to be kept and another; in other cases they are allowed to continue as they afford cover for pheasants and other game. The Institute calculated that there were 58,000 kilometres (36,250 miles) of these hedgerows. Common sense suggests that they, too, are in danger of being lost in the event of boundaries changing, especially if the owner is no longer in pursusit of pheasants.

'Relic' hedgerows are the remains of what was once a hedgerow but has become little more than a line of trees and a few shrubs – a sight quite common now in the South-West. The Institute estimated in 1986 that there were 48,600 kilometres (30,375 miles) of them. The strong demand for fuel to be used in wood–burning stoves may well be a factor in their demise; and, as they are also anathema to many a farmer who likes to keep his land 'tidy', their future can only be uncertain.

Stone walls have also gone. The Institute of Terrestrial Ecology found that, in the period 1978–84, 1,400 kilometres (875 miles) of these field boundaries had been removed. The total may now be substantially more, despite the efforts of volunteers to restore the walls. As with derelict hedges, once livestock give way to arable crops the need to maintain stone walls disappears, and many of them now have a woefully neglected look about them, with many a gap beside a heap of fallen stones. Maintaining this part of our landscape demands time, money and a skill which few possess. We cannot wonder that farmers have allowed their walls to deteriorate.

This cost of maintaining the hedges and stone walls has

been avoided by many thousands of farmers taking advantage of another scheme of the Ministry of Agriculture: replacing hedges and stone walls with barbed-wire fencing. When the Minister of Agriculture persuaded the Treasury to take money from the taxpayer in order to pay farmers to put up thousands of miles of barbed wire, the aim of this subsidy was the same as that for removing hedges. Thousands of farmers accordingly put up the barbed-wire fences when they would not have done so unless there had been a subsidy. The subsidy transformed an uneconomic activity which the farmer could not afford into one that was economic, but artificially so.

For some mysterious reason, the Ministry of Agriculture has no record of the amount of money it has given to farmers for the removal of hedges. When asked for this information in a parliamentary question in April 1987, the minister said he regretted that it was not available. He was also asked, at the same time, to tell the House of Commons how much money had been given for the erection of fences. He was able to give the figures only for the years since 1980, and only for England, Wales and Northern Ireland. This subsidy added up to no less than £41.2 million. In the case of Scotland a further £17.5 million had been given away, but this figure included payments for hedges, walls and dikes as well as for fencing, and presumably separate records are not kept. That no records for the years before 1980 exist seems rather surprising. Assuming the payments were much the same before 1980 as since, I calculate that the total amount of money given away for fencing must be enough to pay for at least 125,000 miles – the length of hedgerows lost.

The essential purpose of the two subsidies demonstrates how very perverse has been the thinking of the ministry, for it is the opposite of what it should be. If a farmer wants to make his business more profitable – that is, to make more money for himself – it seems odd that the taxpayer should be coerced into paying for this to be done; but if a farmer decides not to damage the landscape so that both he and the taxpayers can enjoy it, he is penalized in that he has to continue running a business with a financial handicap. Ministers have failed to perceive that it might be less unjust if the farmer who sacrificed some part of his profits to protect our landscape should have some modest recompense.

A further supply of UK taxpayers' money has gone to the owners of wetlands to tempt them into drainage schemes and to grow wheat and other arable crops. The wetlands, as most of us know, provide a habitat for a range of flora that is unlikely to flourish elsewhere and they have traditionally provided some of our richest grazing pastures; but an artificially high price for wheat makes for a more profitable alternative. So again the Ministry of Agriculture has goaded farmers to go into what was already a more financially rewarding form of husbandry by giving them the additional inducement of a subsidy. The sums have been very substantial. The Minister of Agriculture has admitted to the House of Commons (Hansard, 9 April 1987 and 18 July 1990) that the subsidies between 1980 and 1989 came to £358 million. Since it costs only a few thousand pounds to drain quite a large field, the total represents a huge acreage – millions of acres, even just since 1980.

The result is that our wetlands, once a distinctive feature of the landscape, offering a scene scarcely found anywhere else on our planet, have mostly disappeared. But for the memorable rearguard action for the Halvergate Marshes (one of the earliest victories for the conservationists) there would have been a botanical disaster there.

The Farming and Wildlife Advisory Group estimated in the mid-1980s that no less than 20,000 acres of wetland were still being drained in the UK for the first time every year. In the ten years 1971–80 more than 180,000 acres were drained for the first time. It is not easy to comprehend the magnitude of what has happened; it means that every four years an area of wetland the size of the Isle of Wight has been lost.

Then there is the loss of southern England's downlands, a loss for us in terms of recreation and a loss ecologically. The latter has been well explained by Dr Bryn Green in his admirable book, *Countryside Conservation* (1985). Conservation, he has argued there and on many platforms, is about diversity. Diverse soils, climates and other conditions are needed; what will suit one species will be death to another. The poor impoverished soil of the downs of Berkshire,

Hampshire, Sussex and elsewhere favoured a list of flora that perishes in conditions where others flourish. The downs were quite wilfully impoverished by their owners with flocks of sheep which used to be taken up to the hillside to feed by day and return in the evening to be folded on the meadows below; and the sheep were bred to defecate on their return, thus enriching the lower land at the expense of the downs in a unique way. Tens of thousands of these acres have now been transformed into land suitable for cereal and other crops; indeed, the downs of southern England have gone, except on some steep hillsides, as in Sussex, where the tractor is not safe to use. Gone is the distinctive flora that was there before the surplus wheat; and none of the wheat would have been planted but for the artificially high prices of the Common Agricultural Policy, and for the new varieties, capable of absorbing huge doses of nitrates, that have been evolved. Truly a case of Science plus Subsidies doing their damage. Some of this land has changed hands at more than £2,000 an acre; in 1939 it could have been bought for £10 an acre.

Before the Second World War the downs were not 'farmed'. Some sheep or cattle might be seen and perhaps too many rabbits. The downlands were treated then as such land would be treated in Germany or France today – as a place for human recreation. The downs of southern England are within reach of millions of people; it is a paradox that, as the number of people looking for recreation in the countryside increases, so the area available to them diminishes. The pensioner of 1939 may have sat about in slippered feet; today he joins Saga to sail up the Nile, and there are at least twenty recreations he may pursue, each requiring access to open countryside. Then there are the early retired and the many jobless; they, too, ought to have the opportunity that an open countryside can afford. Thanks to VAT, let alone the other taxes, everyone, even the unemployed, is a taxpayer. The paradox becomes an irony when we realize that it is the taxpayer who has paid for what has been done to the downs of southern England.

The heathlands have not been lost to the same degree, but only because many were common land. Those that were not have almost gone in the cause of agricultural improvement. Gone, too, in those areas is the particular flora that flourishes on the kind of poor soil (poor in a farming sense, that is) that is the feature of our heathlands. Again, it is the coalition of Science plus Subsidies that has done the deed.

Then there is the story of Britain's moorlands. From 1950 through to the 1980s we lost on average 1 per cent of our moorland each year in mid-Wales, Exmoor, North Yorkshire, Northumberland and the Brecon Beacons. One per cent may seem insignificant, but an annual loss of that amount over a period of thirty years represents many tens of thousands of acres.

All that was said about taxpayers losing their recreational lungs on the downs of southern England can be multiplied three or four times over for the moorlands of the North, Wales and Exmoor. Over 25 per cent of the North Yorkshire moors gone! Some of it has been reseeded to grow grass for cattle to add to the mountain of surplus beef. Other acres now grow barley, though we have a surplus of 5 million tonnes of feed grain for our cattle. The total cost to the taxpayer of converting all these acres to arable land by means of grants and subsidies runs into the equivalent of millions of people's income tax for the whole period it has been done. The total acreage of moorland that has been taken away with public money has been estimated by the Council for the Protection of Rural England to be 188,000 acres.

For many years the Ministry of Agriculture gave away money to farmers to get rid of their ponds. Again a parliamentary question asked in April 1987 showed that the ministry had no account of how much money it was. The minister's reply was: 'I regret that the information requested is not available.' However, we know that it was enough to make what was once an integral part of the English landscape become something of a rarity. It also destroyed the habitat of millions of creatures, causing such concern to naturalists that the plan to get rid of ponds came to an end and was replaced by the Save the Ponds Campaign. Thousands of pounds then began to be spent to restore the ponds destroyed. However, on that occasion it was not public money that was used.

THE VANISHING COUNTRYSIDE

Much of the UK was once forested; and even in quite recent times a substantial proportion of our lowlands were ancient woodlands – wooded since time immemorial. Today, however, ours has become one of the least afforested countries. The following figures (from Hansard, 9 April 1987) tell the story:

	Percentage of land surface afforested
Greece	45
Portugal	35
France	28
Italy	27
Spain	25
Belgium	20
Denmark	11
Netherlands	10
United Kingdom	9
Ireland	6

The study by Hunting Technical Services, referred to earlier in this chapter, contained some gloomy facts about our woodlands. It showed that in the last forty years there has been a sharp acceleration in the loss of our broad-leaved trees. In 1947 there were 2,748 square miles of these woodlands, and since then more than 1,099 of them have been destroyed – 40 percent. There has admittedly been new planting, but not enough to avoid a large net loss.

The system of grants and tax privileges has encouraged the conifers to be established, and there is general agreement that they are ecologically damaging. That they add to the acidity of our rivers, causing death to the fish and other life, is no longer in dispute. Unfortunately, the acreage of conifers in the UK has increased fourfold in the last forty years, from 402 to 1,644 square miles.

The controversy about acid rain has prompted research into whether the demise of so much of our broad-leaved woodlands has had the effect of increasing its incidence. The broad leaves of our oaks and ashes, limes and maples can soak up and detoxify at least some of the acid in the atmosphere, so there may be a link between the loss of a high proportion of our broad-leaved trees in recent years and the way acid rain has now become such a serious problem. After all, the apparent cause of acid rain has been with us for many years without this perceptible damage to our forests, rivers and lakes. The scientists who are gathering the evidence are yet to give their opinion, but it looks as if this part of the destruction of our landscape is at least a factor in the acid rain story.

There has been a further loss of trees to be found in our hedgerows and open fields, once a common feature of the English landscape. Most hedges that survive are now cut annually by mechanical means; a hedge cutter attached to a tractor is moved along, and saplings, whether oak, ash or any other, get cut down to the same height as the hawthorn and bramble. Except where the tractor driver has marked down a sapling to be saved, there is no chance of new trees being allowed to grow. Besides, trees in the hedgerow require a cutter to pause and be raised up and directed around the tree – a process that takes time. Trees in hedges cost money.

Trees in the midst of arable fields also cost money, for they take up space, and several square yards around them will give a poor yield of any arable crop. The temptation to cut them down is very great. In thousands of meadows that were once pasture, the trees that were a useful shade to both stock and grass have been felled.

The Countryside Commission in its paper *A Second Look* (1984) has told how dramatic has been the loss of these trees. The commission took seven counties as being representative of England and compared how the number of trees in hedgerows and fields for every 100 acres fell between 1947 and 1983. In Cambridgeshire there were 4 trees instead of 39 per 100 acres, in Huntingdonshire 6 instead of 59, in Dorset 9 instead of 17, in Somerset 15 instead of 50, in Herefordshire 32 instead of 49, in Yorkshire 27 instead of 51 and in Warwickshire 29 instead of 69. These figures show that the loss of our broad-leaved trees has been greater in our hedgerows and fields than in the woodlands themselves.

Lastly, but importantly, there is the loss of pastureland that used to be an important home for wildlife, as well as a beautiful part of the landscape. Seven million acres (an area the size of Northumberland and Durham, Yorkshire and Lancashire combined) have been changed from pasture to arable land. Economically, the cost has been very high – and so has the ecological cost. Not only our flora, but hundreds of thousands of birds and other wildlife, their habitat gone, have disappeared. So often the remaining areas of pasture are too small to avoid inbreeding and the consequences that follow. Not for some years yet will it be feasible to estimate the extent of this destruction. Some scientists believe that it could prove the gravest count in the indictment against the engine of destruction that our agricultural policy has become.

· 5 ·

VANISHING FARMERS

British farmers are on a treadmill. They have been standing on it ever since the Agriculture Act was passed in 1947. All political parties then agreed that farmers should receive guaranteed prices for what they produced – price support, as it came to be called. Undoubtedly the Act was passed in good faith. There was abundant goodwill towards the farming community born of a recognition that it had worked hard throughout the Second World War to produce a large proportion of our food, and it did not deserve to return to the low prices and insecurity of pre-war days.

On the face of it, a guaranteed price *should* afford security. In the short term this may be the case, but the evidence shows that any benefit is soon nullified, and then it progressively increases the farmer's insecurity.

If a policy of guaranteed prices had the effect of supporting farmers, the number of people dependent upon agriculture for their livelihood today should, we might suppose, be no less than the number when the policy began. Just after the war there were 500,000 farmers in the United Kingdom. Since then the definition used by the Ministry of Agriculture has slightly changed, and an exact comparison cannot be made. However, even on the ministry's present definition a remorseless fall in the number of farmers is beyond dispute. According to the ministry there were 350,000 in 1960, 233,000 in 1970 and 185,200 in 1980 (Hansard, 22 January 1986). Since then, according to the ministry's *Annual Review of Agriculture* and its successor, *Agriculture in the United Kingdom*, the number continues to decrease by several thousand every year.

THE 'BAD OLD DAYS'

It is of some interest to compare this exodus from the land with the figures before the war when farmers were said to be so insecure. Although there was no census return to make an exact comparison, there were the Decadal Censuses of the whole population which recorded the occupation of everyone. Farming and fishing were put together; and looking at the censuses prepared for this century – in 1901, 1911, 1921 and 1931 – they show very little variation. If it can be assumed that the number engaged in fishing remained fairly constant, the same can be said for farming, for the number of people who described themselves as being engaged full time in either agriculture or fishing was about 1,300,000 for each period.

Undoubtedly many thousands left the land between the wars, but a more or less equal number took their place. Of course, those times were hard for farmers. But they were hard for everyone. Those who defend the system of price support since 1947 persist in comparing the standard of living of a farmer then with what it is today. The comparison has caused a lot of harm and led to a false conclusion. The fact that a typical farmer of today is better off than his father before the war is meaningless. The same can be said of 99 per cent of the population.

The proper comparison is between a farmer of the 1930s and someone else of a similar walk of life. If two brothers went to seek their fortunes then, one in farming and the other in some trade or profession in a nearby market town, both would have found it difficult, because times were difficult for virtually everyone. The inter-war years were marked by an almost continuous slump with a high level of unemployment and low incomes for most people. Two pounds a week was the normal wage and 10 shillings the dole money. With this kind of income no one could afford to be a good customer of the farmer or of anyone else. Those of us who remember the 1930s, if we are honest with ourselves, would admit that the farmer and his wife had a few worthwhile advantages over their cousins in the towns. Most farms in those days had 'a bit of everything': potatoes from the fields, fruit from the orchard, vegetables from a well-manured garden, a pig in the sty and milk from the cowshed, which a wife could make into butter; with cartridges only a penny each, it did not cost much to bag a pheasant, a hare or even a humble rabbit. None of that could be done by the cousins who lived, as most shopkeepers did, above the shop, which had debts piling up.

None of this is intended to be a reason for going back to pre-war policies. The purpose of this book is the opposite – to urge that we go forward to another and quite different system. Yet it is necessary to show that any special hardship of the farmer before the war is a myth; farm-gate prices before the war were higher than they are today, despite all the support of guaranteed prices. This may be difficult to believe, but because it is central to the argument, let us look at what has happened to two main items in our agriculture, wheat and milk.

Almost any arable farmer will swear he would be ruined without price support. He will tell you how before the war his father faced ruin, how he humbled himself before the corn merchant, how the landlord of the farm next door could not find a tenant and was driven to paying someone to take it in hand and how his best crop of wheat fetched only £3 a ton. Desperately bleak years they are painted. Yet the records show that, on average and in real terms, wheat prices were higher then than they are today. It is true that they varied considerably from year to year and from market to market in any one week. They were often lower in parts of East Anglia where large quantities were grown far away from the places where they were needed, when the cost of transport was higher than it is today. In contrast, there is little variation in price nowadays, no matter where in the UK the crop is produced.

To underline the point, let us take wheat prices in the ten-year period between the repeal of the Corn Protection Act in 1921 and the introduction of the Wheat Act in 1932. In this period there was no support for wheat at all, and no form of protection shielded the British farmer from the chilly winds of competition from low-cost producers of Canada and the United States who had unfettered access to our markets. The prices are set out in *Agricultural Records AD 220–1977* (1978), a fascinating book edited by the distinguished writer about farming, Ralph Whitlock. The following figures are taken from it:

Year	Price of wheat per hundredweight	
	s.	d.
1922	11	2
1923	9	10
1924	11	6
1925	12	2
1926	12	5
1927	11	6
1928	10	0
1929	9	10
1930	8	0
1931	5	9

The average price worked out at 10s. 2½d. a hundredweight. That is £10. 4s. 2d. a ton. It does not sound very much. However, when we translate it into the money terms of today, it is very different. There was very little inflation, and to some extent there was deflation, in those years. Since 1931 the pound has fallen to one-thirtieth of its former value. To multiply pre-war wheat prices by that factor of thirty would give us a reasonably accurate idea of what the pre-war price was worth. It works out at £306. That is nearly three times more than what our farmers receive today. In fact, the pre-war figure was more favourable than that. Expensive combines were not in use; horses were as numerous as tractors; muck from the yard went on to the land more than bought-in fertilizers, and pesticides were scarcely used. The farmer's main costs were labour and rent. Wages were as little as £2 a week and in East Anglia less than that (£60 a week in today's money instead of about £150 as they may be now), and rents were considerably lower than today.

So the pre-war farmer enjoyed both lower real costs and higher real prices, which should have made him a much more prosperous man than the present generation.

In fact, however, it must be acknowledged that this was not the case. The reason is that the farmer's yields are now much greater. A huge increase in the inputs of fertilizer and pesticides, introducing a new technology of fertilization and cultivation, and a succession of new varieties of seed have brought about an amazing rise in productivity. On land that grew 17 hundredweight before the war – usually the average crop – 3 tonnes are likely to be harvested today. Yields are still on a rising trend, and agricultural scientists speak of 6 tonnes to the acre in the 1990s. It is the fourfold increase in the yield of the land that has brought the farmer prosperity. To grow 4 tonnes at £100 a tonne is likely to be more profitable than 1 tonne at £150. Agricultural research, not the system of price support in itself, has raised the farmer's income. He should give his thanks to the scientist, not to the politician.

A similar story can be told of milk. After the Milk Marketing Board was set up in 1936 all milk producers in the UK received a common price; before then there were such considerable variations that a comparison with today is not easy. Cows walked the streets of London, being milked by hand beside the pavement, so that householders could buy what they wanted, fresh and unpasteurized. The price the cowkeeper received in St James's Street was a great deal more than his cousin got in Carmarthenshire.

The price the dairy farmer received for his milk before the MMB took over was pitiful, so we are led to believe. The board was set up following two official reports, one produced in 1933 and the other in 1936 by the Reorganization Commission on Milk (HMSO Economic Series nos. 38 and 44), and both of them assessed producers' returns in some detail. The average monthly price for each year from 1923 to 1936 varied only a little; in 1934 and 1935 it was 1s. 0¼d. a gallon. Allowing again for the pound's decline in value, this is equivalent to about £1.50 in today's money. More than half a century's effort by what is meant to be a producer-controlled monopoly has ended with the dairy farmer receiving about half that price of the bad old days! What other producer of anything has had a cut of 50 per cent?

Over the last fifty years great strides have been made by cattle breeders to evolve a more prolific cow. Instead of the Dairy Shorthorn fed mainly with grass or hay, we see Friesians and Holsteins, able to convert rich compounds of cattle cake into many more gallons of milk. In the place of the small herds of ten or fifteen cows, once the average, now there are many with more than 300. The use of antibiotics has enabled dairy farming to be intensified, and herds to be kept in conditions which would have been fatal half a century ago. All this has raised yields. The average-sized dairy farmer of today will send away ten to twenty times the quantity of milk that was the case when the MMB paid out its first monthly cheques.

The increased yields of everything that our farms produce have verged upon the miraculous. One can go through each commodity in turn and the same can be said of each. Even our shepherds, who have changed their ways the least, now have lambing percentages almost twice those of before the Second World War; two lambs a year for every ewe is not uncommon for our leading flocks.

The picture is one of increasing productivity and falling farm-gate prices. We also see a steady decline in the number of farms and an inexorable increase in the size of those that remain. The treadmill can be shown graphically, as in Figure 2 (p. 102).

THE PROFITS OF RESEARCH

The treadmill begins with agricultural research. Why? Only an insignificant amount of public money was spent on agricultural research in the UK before the Second World War, mainly by the universities. ICI was almost alone among commercial concerns in devoting any of its resources to it. The total sum in both the public and private sectors was a bagatelle. Yet since 1947 the total has run to thousands of millions of pounds. To spend such a vast amount and not make some remarkable advances is scarcely possible.

This great programme began in the public sector because

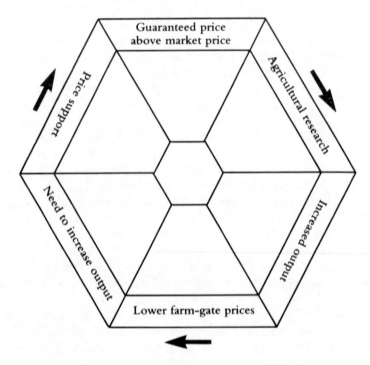

Price support

Guaranteed price
above market price

Agricultural research

Need to increase output

Increased output

Lower farm-gate prices

Figure 2   The farming treadmill.

of the policy of successive UK governments to pursue the goal of self-sufficiency. If they were to will the end, they had also to will the means. The National Agricultural Advisory Service, an arm of the Ministry of Agriculture, was represented in every county to spread the word about new methods of husbandry and to give advice on how to increase production and to reduce costs. From the beginning the advisory service received news of what was being done on university farms and at research institutes funded by the government. Through the 1950s and 1960s there was steady progress in pushing out the frontiers of knowledge in every area of agriculture; at the same time an increasing flow of the most talented of the students in the faculties of agriculture, as soon as they graduated, found a niche in the new empires of research which were established. There was no shortage of money both to pay their salaries and to provide the far greater sums for their resources. If President Nixon was right to say 'throw enough money at a problem, and it will go away', then, by spending such vast sums, British governments were justified in hoping that they could achieve food self-sufficiency.

The private sector was happy to join in with a massive agricultural research programme of its own costing hundreds of millions of pounds as soon as it could be sure that it would pay off. The signal it needed was given by the Labour government immediately after the war, in its decision to introduce a system of price support. That the decision was also agreed by the Conservative and Liberal parties made the policy bipartisan and gave the private sector the confidence to believe it would endure for a long time. A system of price support implied that farmers would receive higher prices for what they produced than would otherwise be the case. Such a distortion of the price mechanism could have only one outcome; farmers would take advantage of higher prices by producing more.

Companies like ICI, Shell, Unilever and Boots could begin to look upon their farmer customers with a happier eye. There were 500,000 of them: all privileged (literally so, because they were placed above the law of supply and demand), all favoured by a guarantee of the government that what they produced would be assured of a sale at a higher price than before. For those not blessed with such favouritism, it was natural to see how they could share in the blessing. Any company stood to gain that was able to supply the farmer with some sort of input. Fertilizers and pesticides are obvious examples, but the whole range of agricultural machinery can also be included, as well as feed compounds from the mill, new kinds of farm buildings, plant and equipment. The modern farm with its concrete yards, purpose-built sheds and high-powered machinery bears little resemblance to what it was like forty-five years ago, with its mud, its manure heap in the corner, hens scratching about and an elderly Fordson in a century-old barn with clapperboards awry. The transformation has brought prosperity to some famous names in the world of commerce. Accordingly, the programme of agricultural research was directed towards maximizing production by the use of all the various inputs that the world of agribusiness was capable of supplying.

The treadmill started to revolve. Over half a million farmers stood on it, and with them nearly a million farm workers. The more they used the new inputs, the more output was raised. From 1950 until today, as each year goes by, farmers have used more inputs, and what they have produced has tended also to increase. A few figures culled from *Agriculture in the United Kingdom* for 1989 can be cited to show how remarkable has been the expansion. In 1947 the UK's farms yielded 1,967,000 tons of wheat; in 1989 the total was 13,843,000 tonnes (1 tonne = 0.984 ton). Milk production was 1,653 million gallons in 1947, and by 1986 it had risen to 3,470 million gallons (but was reduced by quotas by 1989). For the same years (1947 and 1986), barley production rose from 1,963,000 tons to 10,015,000 tonnes, eggs from 451 million dozen to 1,021 million dozen, beef from 550,000 tons to 1,018,000 tonnes, pork from 15,000 tons to 760,000 tonnes, sugar from 593,000 tons to 762,000 tonnes and oilseed rape from *nil* to 971,000 tonnes.

As output has increased, farm incomes have fallen in real terms. Table 2 (p. 105) and Figure 3 (p. 106) come from *Agriculture in the UK 1989*. As it is real and not nominal changes in income that matter, the bottom half of the table is the more significant. It shows a drastic fall in income that cannot have been matched by any other occupation in the UK. This fall in real income is illustrated graphically in the figure (p. 106).

Those who defend the system will say that this downward trend is attributable to the curb on increased production imposed by milk quotas, co-responsibility levies and the set-aside scheme. They are wrong. The trend has continued ever since the UK adhered to the Common Agricultural Policy, despite the initial bonanza given to the arable sector.

To prove cause and effect, between higher output and lower farm-gate prices, need hardly be necessary. As farm-gate prices are the main determinant of their income, farmers have to choose between (a) accepting a lower standard of living, (b) cutting the costs of their operations or (c) increasing their production. Many smaller farmers, unable to cut costs any further or increase production because of the

Table 2   *UK farm incomes, nominal and in real terms*

Year	Farming income (of farmers and spouses) (£ million)	Cash flow from farming (of farmers and spouses) (£ million)
1978	1,253	1,266
1979	1,161	1,258
1980	1,060	1,361
1981	1,420	1,801
1982	1,809	1,982
1983	1,422	1,572
1984	2,197	2,300
1985	1,160	1,714
1986	1,557	1,955
1987	1,623	2,402
1988	1,240	1,913
1989 (forecast)	1,441	1,930
Indices in real terms (deflated by RPI: 1985 = 100)		
1978	204.2	139.6
1979	167.1	122.5
1980	129.5	112.5
1981	154.7	132.8
1982	181.7	134.7
1983	136.7	102.2
1984	200.8	142.3
1985	100.0	100.0
1986	129.8	110.3
1987	129.9	130.1
1988	94.6	98.7
1989 (forecast)	101.9	92.4

limited size of their farm, took the first course and continued to do so until they were forced to give up farming altogether. Cutting some costs was feasible for all farmers, but costs were increased as a rule in that more inputs were used because this was the way to increase production; and the balance of advantage lay in forcing up yields to keep pace with inflation. Fertilizers, pesticides, agricultural machinery and the new methods of intensive animal husbandry were all

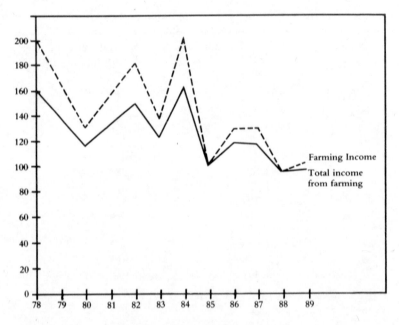

Figure 3   Farm incomes, in real terms (1985 = 100).

improving as a means of increasing productivity – this was the inevitable result of the research being carried out. The new technologies gave farmers the means of meeting their higher costs by raising production.

MEASURING FARM EFFICIENCY

To import new technology into agriculture sounds exciting, especially when it suggests a thrust away from the old order of 'dog and stick'. Put into practice, however, this change has shown several disagreeable symptoms. Many demurred from what they saw as undesirable husbandry. As one example, there were once tens of thousands of poultry farmers, and many of them succeeded in earning a livelihood in keeping no more than 500 or so Rhode Island Reds, all given their liberty on a few acres. When the deep litter system was introduced, whereby the same number could be kept indoors, making their competitors with a free-range system no longer profitable, a large number of these poultry-men so disliked the idea that they preferred to give up keeping hens altogether. Then came the battery cages; these in turn made the deep litter houses uneconomic; and a whole legion of poultry farmers recoiled from keeping their birds in such places.

Others have disapproved of rearing beef cattle indoors all the year round and making them ready for slaughter in less than half the normal time with the aid of hormone implants. Sow stalls have made it possible to keep hundreds of sows on less than an acre of concrete, preventing them from turning round or doing anything except standing up and lying down again for four months at a time – the period between serving and farrowing. Repugnance at such a system has made thousands of pig farmers look elsewhere to earn a livelihood. Arable farmers have also faltered; the need to force ever more out of the soil, while a challenge to many, has seemed to some a self-defeating task.

Latter-day Luddites they have been called. Such scorn is out of place. No doubt they have included the chronically inefficient, often charming as they stand in their yard with time to talk rather aimlessly about the crops and the weather with mud and muddle visible all around. But to dismiss them all as incompetent would be a cruel calumny. Many tens of thousands of them were intelligent, long-sighted and successful in running an efficient farm. The treadmill was not for them, however; they saw no future on it and turned away from doing things to their stock or their soil which they believed to be wrong. The word 'husbandman' has dropped out of our vocabulary; parish registers confirm that there was a time, several generations ago, when farmers were so called. Those who have left agriculture in the last thirty years include many thousands whose farming practices could fitly have been described as good husbandry.

Well, this is a pity, admit the supporters of the present system, but it is a price we had to pay for the splendid rise we have achieved in agricultural production. The UK's gross agricultural output in 1970–1 was £2,644 million; in 1989 it is estimated at £12,698 million. This is virtually a fivefold increase and, on the face of it, most impressive. It looks too good to be true – and it is too good to be true, because it does not take account of inflation and also because output figures are meaningless unless one takes into account inputs. The cost of the inputs has, in fact, risen at a faster rate than the value of the outputs, and this is one more commentary on why agriculture has taken a wrong turning. Anyone can increase output to dazzling heights, provided he pays no heed to inputs. To gauge the true value of what any branch of our economy has achieved, we must subtract the cost of inputs from the value of the outputs, then subtract depreciation of plant, machinery and buildings. Having done so, we may arrive at the net product.

Fortunately, the *Annual Review of Agriculture* and its successor *Agriculture in the UK* do these sums for us. They define net product as 'a measure of the value added by the agricultural industry to all the goods and services purchased from outside agriculture after provision has been made for depreciation'. First, let us see what effect the Common Agricultural Policy has had upon net product; has it gone up or down? The *Review* for 1987 takes 1980 as the base year, giving the net product for that year the index of 100; and it goes back to 1970 – very conveniently for us, for that was a full year before the import levies began. Allowing for inflation, the index for 1970 is 119. This means, of course, that UK agriculture's net product was substantially more in 1970 than it was in 1980.

Since 1987 the ministry has been overcome by statistical coyness. However, one can glean from the 1989 edition of *Agriculture in the UK* the net product for the last four available years; the figures are:

1986	£4,469 million
1987	£4,487 million
1988	£4,227 million
1989	£4,735 million

Each is at current, not constant, prices; and once we allow for inflation, we see a big drop in net product within just a few years.

What about improvements in productivity? Let us see

what has happened on one particular farm, say one of 400 acres. Back in 1946 its owner or tenant would have been fully engaged in managing it, and four men would have been employed. Today it would be one man. Where have the other three gone? One is a lorry driver employed by a firm of agricultural merchants, founded since 1946 to supply local farmers with fertilizers, herbicides and suchlike. Another has left the district, unable to find other employment, and is now living in the Midlands making agricultural machinery of a kind that was not invented in 1946. The third may have joined the pool of permanently unemployed or perhaps he has been recruited by one of the companies that specialize in putting up new buildings for farmers, or possibly one of the firms of agricultural contractors that are expert at draining and other well-subsidized land-improvement schemes.

Fewer people are engaged on the farm itself all the year round, but many more are engaged in supplying or servicing agriculture. The National Farmers' Union admits in its publicity leaflets that agriculture employs indirectly hundreds of thousands of men and women. Thus there has been a transfer from one sphere to another; and it is questionable whether the total number of people employed in and for agriculture has become smaller than it was in 1946.

Our agriculture's productivity is based upon a fallacy. A few generations ago, a farm was virtually self-sufficient. The cart-horse was the main source of power; he was bred on the farm or in the neighbourhood by another farmer. His source of energy was hay and oats, both produced from the acres he spent his life upon. Such machinery as existed on the farm was simple and made in the neighbourhood or on the farm itself, for the larger farm had its own smithy. Muck from the farmyard fertilized the land; home-grown barley and beans fed the stock.

Even in 1946 many of our farms were still being run on not very different principles, especially the ones in the remoter parts of the country. Up in the North, they used to speak of a 'statesman' – a farmer with his own freehold, living in independent state, buying in very little of anything, being an island to himself and his family. There is no farm like that now. The cart-horse has long since left, and the tractor made in the Midlands or, as likely, somewhere abroad has taken his place. A quantity of advanced machinery is there; bag upon bag of artificial fertilizer is piled up in the barn; canisters of herbicide stand ready for use. A hundred operations may still be performed on the same farm, but there is not a single one among them that can be undertaken without some outside help or the supply of something from off the farm.

So when we claim that productivity has increased in agriculture since, say, 1946, we are not comparing like with like. The figures that are quoted ('one man on the farm now produces enough food for sixty people', for example) are specious and lead to false conclusions. We must stop treating agriculture as the only part of food production. What we should be asking ourselves is how many people were engaged in the whole business of food production in any base year and comparing that number with the equivalent number for today. Whatever base year is selected, it is unlikely that there will be sufficient difference to support the argument of productivity.

Productivity is sometimes related to acreage instead of to labour, a higher yield from an acre being made the touch-stone. Again the record in the UK appears to be impressive and a triumph for applied technology. More tonnes of wheat grown to the acre (most farms have trebled their yields) or more cows kept on the same field may seem to be worth-while achievements; but again, is this a true test of efficiency?

The fact is that these high yields have been achieved by uneconomic means. The big machines that have replaced farm labour have been written off 100 per cent against tax for the year. The fertilizers and toxic chemicals that are poured on to the land have side-effects that other people pay for. Stripping of the landscape to prepare it for this type of cultivation has been heavily subsidized. High yields do not indicate efficiency if producing them costs more than the food is worth.

In the United States and Canada, where the kind of land costing £2,000 an acre in the UK can be bought for £350, the farmer is under no such pressure. He can make his farm pay by growing wheat at half the yields – 1.5 tonnes to the acre compared with the 3 tonnes of his British counterpart. Does the comparison make him half as efficient? Or does it show to what lengths British agriculture has been driven by (among other things) the crazy overvaluation of our land that is one of the chief effects of subsidizing output and one of the main features of the treadmill on which farmers now stand?

How much longer do they want to keep standing on it? Do we let it continue revolving all through the 1990s or indefinitely? Until recently, the question never seemed to enter the heads of the agricultural establishment. One Minister of Agriculture after another failed to see the dangers and gave the treadmill an extra turn. The National Farmers' Union never even attempted to examine the matter, let alone offer an answer. *Farmers' Weekly*, under its former editor, used to be remarkably scathing about anyone who raised this issue. The reason, it seems, is that these two founts of farming opinion were of the view that there was no treadmill – or, if there was, it could go on turning without much worry. Now at last it begins to dawn on a few of the NFU leaders and even on *Farmers' Weekly* that the treadmill does exist and that it cannot go on revolving. Great surplus food mountains make admirable visual aids and are beginning to have a persuasive effect.

There have been several years recently when the UK has grown so little wheat good enough for human consumption that 2 or 3 million tonnes have had to be imported, yet in the same years there have been surpluses of twice as much low-quality wheat fit only for animal feed. Because there are not enough farm animals in the country for such vast quantities, the grain has had to go into the intervention stores at great expense to the taxpayer, who has been called upon to pay £13 a year for every tonne. Most of it has become, in the word of an Intervention Board official, 'valueless', so a large proportion has gone over the years to the Soviet Union to feed its pigs and poultry, with an export subsidy of about £80 a tonne. The opportunities for fraud have been immense, and the European Community's Court of Auditors has estimated losses to the taxpayer at as much as £6,000 million in a single year in consequence. The Common Agricultural

Policy has made the EEC insolvent on more than one occasion, being unable to play the debts incurred by these surpluses. So some changes have had to be made. A 'set-aside' programme has been introduced whereby a British farmer may be paid £80 an acre for it to grow nothing, although he can put it down to grass and keep horses on it. (Some farmers find this a congenial way of getting their family's recreation subsidized, while others rear horsemeat for the French market.) A co-responsibility levy has also been introduced which requires the wheat producer to make a contribution to the cost of the export subsidies.

Such modest reforms are no solution. They fail to go to the root of what is wrong. As long as any system of guaranteed prices exists there will be an inducement to increase production and to raise the input–output ratio.

Previous chapters have set out some of the reasons why high–input agriculture is dangerous to all of us, and later we examine the economic fallacies in the arguments used to support the system that has given it such an artificial impetus. The point to emphasize here is that if anyone thinks farmers have benefited from it they are sadly wrong. The more output has been pushed up, the lower prices have fallen – and the fall will be all the steeper as the public grows impatient with the taxes and restraints that now support the overpricing of its food. The farmer can never catch up – barring, perhaps, a few rich agribusiness men who can play the system. For the ordinary farmer it must mean higher inputs, greater costs, probably greater debts, harder work and, at the end of it all, a smaller reward. The time has come for him to realize how he has been misled and to demand an end to the system that forces him on to such a treadmill.

FEWER WORKERS, FEWER FARMS

The efficient farmer is the major victim of the present agricultural policy, which has forced many thousands of them off the land. They are to be found as lorry drivers, milk roundsmen, in the hotel trade and in journalism, mostly far removed from what they used to do well. Those who remain are among the ones having greatest difficulty in holding on to their farms.

I would define the efficient farmer in quite simple terms. He is the man who can make a livelihood out of his farm without asking the taxpayer to subsidize him. It is a yardstick which provides a scale of efficiency. The very efficient will be running a very profitable enterprise, but even the less efficient will lead an independent life, able to give his customers at least some degree of satisfaction and to support himself and his family. The usefulness of such farmers is self-evident, yet they are the very kind of farmer the system now liquidates. This is a strong word to use; let us see whether it is deserved.

Efficiency is a word often on the lips of the farming establishment. When pressed to explain what is meant, they carefully avoid any definition like mine and instead talk about productivity. Now, productivity is about the relationship of labour and output; an increase in productivity means reducing the number of people needed to do the same job. Even at a time of large-scale unemployment, this is deemed to be desirable in itself and a measure of increased efficiency. The figures for agriculture are, indeed, impressive, and they are set out in Table 3 (p. 114).

British agriculture has lost no less than two-thirds of its labour force in the period of price support. Furthermore, these figures are for all farm workers, male and female, full-time, seasonal and casual. If only full-time farm workers are considered, the fall has been still greater; and in the last nineteen years, since the UK went over to import levies, their decline has been at an even faster rate, from 250,000 to 98,000.

This decline in the number of people working on farms is taken as an index of increased efficiency. Here is a typical example of this viewpoint:

Farm incomes have been maintained only because of increased efficiency. This is a fact that must be heavily emphasized. One valid yardstick of efficiency is how much food can be produced on average by each individual who is engaged in the nation's farming. In the

Table 3   Decline in the number of farm workers in the UK

Year	Total number of farm workers	Year	Total number of farm workers
1950	918,000	1970	425,000
1951	882,000	1971	418,000
1952	869,000	1972	413,000
1953	842,000	1973	416,000
1954	815,000	1974	398,000
1955	788,000	1975	395,000
1956	754,000	1976	383,000
1957	750,000	1977	379,000
1958	730,000	1978	374,000
1959	719,000	1979	358,000
1960	693,000	1980	353,000
1961	662,000	1981	342,000
1962	633,000	1982	338,000
1963	611,000	1983	334,000
1964	584,000	1984	329,000
1965	551,000	1985	324,000
1966	522,000	1986	315,000
1967	485,000	1987	306,000
1968	450,000	1988	298,000
1969	433,000	1989	285,000

United Kindgom one man produces food enough for 23 people. In Denmark, it is 17; Federal Germany, 9; France, 8; and Italy, 7.

I wrote that myself in a booklet about agricultural policy in 1965. Since then, apparent productivity has improved still more. Now one man is said to produce enough for 60 people. The other countries have also 'gone ahead', but they have remained 'behind' the UK to the same extent as in 1965.

There is a fallacy in these figures that is very relevant when we examine the way a heavily subsidized system of agriculture diverts manpower from efficient enterprises (those that can prosper without government help) to those that are inefficient (those that cannot). The fallacy lies in the fact that there is not a single man left in British farming who produces an ounce of food without the aid of people outside agriculture. The man in Coventry who works on the assembly line making a tractor is not, statistically speaking, engaged in agriculture, although he is as much in the process of food production as the man who drives the machine in the field. So, too, are the many thousands who manufacture or transport the artificial fertilizers that have taken the place of farmyard manure. While the number of British people directly employed as farmers or farm workers has fallen drastically in the years since the war, the number indirectly employed by agriculture has increased just as much. Whole new industries have come into being with the sole object of supplying and servicing our farms. Had they not come into existence our countryside would not have been blighted by the social evil of rural depopulation.

The fall in the number of farm workers in the UK is matched by a decreasing number of farms. *Agriculture in the UK* tells us that in 1989 the total number of holdings was about 257,000. The corresponding figure for 1953 was 454,000. Overwhelmingly, the exit of those 197,000 has been among smaller farmers. To dismiss them as 'unviable' would be a cruel calumny; it would be nearer the truth to say that they were made unprofitable by the way the support system has been operated. It has been the policy of successive governments since 1953 to encourage farm amalgamations, and the encouragement has been provided by a whole range of grants and tax allowances being tilted in favour of the large farmer. As the small farmer is being driven out, the large farmer is becoming larger.

'UP CORN, DOWN HORN'

As a broad generalization, the smaller farmer tended to be dependent on livestock and the larger farmer upon arable crops. What has happened over most of England is that the small livestock holdings that were predominantly given over to pasture have been amalgamated into substantial farms, and the pasture ploughed up to grow corn. These farms are generally owner-occupied rather than tenanted, so the typical farmer of today is likely to possess assets worth half a million pounds and to employ only one or two men. He may have borrowed heavily from the bank, but he remains a rich man, having become probably twice as well off in terms of both capital and income. Yet it should not be overlooked that most new entrants to farming in recent years have not been young men beginning their career with limited resources. The opportunities that used to be theirs are lost – destroyed by the present system. Instead, when a farm of any substantial size comes on to the market, it is likely to be sold to a middle-aged man who has made his money in some other walk of life. Is this really to the advantage of farming? Perhaps it is time for the leaders of the NFU to pause a while and to contemplate what the future holds should this process continue much longer.

The alternative policy advocated in this book will not make it tougher for farming. It may indeed be tougher for those who have benefited from ploughing up pasture to grow wheat at inordinate cost, but not for arable farmers with Grade I and II land, and certainly not for the many thousands of young men and women who would like to have a small farm of their own, doing what the small farmer can do best – producing livestock.

It is true that there are livestock farmers, especially in Scotland, Wales and the upland parts of England, who have survived upon marginal, Grade IV and V land, and they would not have done so without some kind of support from the taxpayer. The countryside would be, and look, the poorer for their departure from the land. There is, however, an alternative policy which would give them the assistance they need and which the taxpayer would be unlikely to resent. In short, it would mean paying them to farm as custodians of the countryside. I have set out some details of this policy in Chapter 11.

As things are, most livestock farmers are seriously damaged by the way the support system discriminates against them. 'Up corn, down horn' is an old saying; when the growing of corn becomes more profitable, the return on keeping cattle and other stock goes down. That is what is happening today. High import levies on wheat and maize keep prices artificially high. And as cereals such as wheat and maize form the greater part of the feed compounds, the obvious truth is that artificially supported arable farming has undermined the profitability of the livestock sector, which historically has always been the largest branch of British agriculture. In the process, many thousands of farmers have been driven out of business. One statistic highlights the exodus; in 1964 there were 250,000 farmers with less than 100 acres, on which, not so long ago, a reasonable livelihood could be made with livestock. Less than twenty years later their number had been halved. When about 70 per cent of the expenditure of a typical pig or poultry farmer is likely to be on feeding compounds, high cereal prices are bound to make it difficult for them to balance the books.

The process of artificially stimulating arable farming on Grade III land did not begin with the introduction of import levies. It began when other forms of government support were given, such as guaranteed prices, grants, subsidies and tax allowances. But the effect was the same. High-cost farming on unsuitable land was made marginally profitable. This was done at the expense of the taxpayers, importers, consumers and, above all, livestock farmers. The enterprises of the latter became, as each year went by, marginally less profitable. As the profitability of arable farming increased artificially, year by year, so the profitability of livestock farming decreased artificially. If successive governments had not intervened, arable farming would not have expanded; livestock farmers would not have been forced out of business; and those that survived would not have been forced into ever fewer and ever larger units.

To some extent it is understandable that pig and poultry farmers have been victims of the policy, for the Common Agricultural Policy itself has made no attempt to support and protect them as it has the other farming sectors. The British dairy farmer seems to have been the most cushioned of them all. He has had a guaranteed price for every drop of milk his cows produce, import levies to tax cheap New Zealand butter, a prohibition on imports of other butter from abroad and subsidies to make our own butter artificially cheaper, besides grants and other kinds of financial support to help him along. In fact, it has been of little avail. The same trend is to be seen as in other kinds of farming: the small men squeezed out and the large ones made larger still.

In 1950 I went off to learn about dairy farming. Fifteen cows – no more, no less – was the size of the herd on an eighty-acre holding, and in those days a dairy farmer of that size could earn a living. Today he would need seventy-five cows to earn the same income in real terms. The story of that change holds the essence of what has gone wrong with British agriculture, so let it be told.

In the first place, dairy farming in those days was very efficient. By that I mean its owner made a good livelihood without collecting a penny's worth of government aid. In many ways the small dairy farmer led a very comfortable life. Fifteen cows did not take up much of his time; he was never in a hurry when callers came, and he never grudged spending the time of day with them. (How different it is now, when a farm entrance so often sports a board saying 'No callers without appointment' or 'Representatives must telephone first'. In the 1950s we never saw such notices in the countryside.) Nor did he have any worries that I can remember. He certainly never had an overdraft.

The milk yields would have been about two-thirds of today's average, perhaps less. In the months when the herd were out on the summer grass, the yield would be higher; in winter the yield would fall because hay was the principal feed and bought-in compounds were scarcely used. Thus the eighty acres fed the cows with most of their needs. There was one elderly tractor that might have fetched £10 at a sale; it was good enough for the harrowing and rolling and the haymaking. All the machinery used in the course of the year could not have been worth much above £100. No fertilizers went on the land, except the manure from the cows and hunters; no herbicides either – just the swish of the scythe or, if the weeds were really bad (which I do not remember them ever being), the tractor and grass-cutter could be brought into use.

The dairy farmer's expenses were trifling. There was very little he needed to purchase, and it was a shamelessly low-cost system. Every month a cheque for the milk came in;

this was his gross income, and his net taxable income was not much less. He paid his income tax and he took nothing out from Treasury funds. Judged as a business man, he was successful, making a profit every year.

No animal welfarist could have complained at the way his cows were kept. No environmentalist or conservationist could have demurred at his hedgerows and the hundreds of birds living on his acres, or at the absence of sprays and chemicals. Neighbouring farmers considered him perfectly normal − just like themselves. In fact, there were tens of thousands of dairy farmers running their farms as he did.

Even in the 1960s this was still true. By then, one cow to the acre was seen as a sensible aim. Since then, stocking densities have risen sharply and productivity per person involved has quadrupled. To achieve such an increase, a very different system of husbandry was needed. To begin with, another breed of cow would have to be bought. Off to slaughter would go the low-cost Dairy Shorthorns, Red Polls and Ayrshires, and in their place would come the Friesians. The old pastures had to be ploughed up and reseeded, and the new kinds of grass heavily fertilized and sprayed with chemicals. The high stocking density made the new grass too valuable to be poached when the rain fell, so the cattle had to spend much of the year indoors. This meant that expensive new buildings had to go up, and yards had to be concreted; and as the risk of disease was then made considerably greater, the animals had frequently to be dosed with antibiotics and other drugs. This last element has given birth to a substantial sub-industry, whose sales to farmers have reached many millions of pounds. To maintain the high stocking rate and to gain the extra high yields of milk, expensive feedstuffs had also to be purchased. Finally, to have one man employed looking after fifteen or twenty cows was now totally unprofitable, so expensive machinery was introduced to enable one man to look after seventy-five cows or more. Thus jobs were lost in the countryside and gained in the cities where the machinery is made, as often as not in some other country.

If enough has not already been said to question whether the dairy farmer has benefited from protection, perhaps a few hard figures will suffice. In 1967 there were 131,600 dairy farmers in the UK, and more than half of them (71,300) had fewer than twenty cows. In the following five years the number of dairy farmers fell to 98,700, and only 41,000 of them had herds of less than twenty. For several years there have been so few herds of that size that their numbers have ceased to be recorded separately in the ministry's annual surveys. Still, we are told that 22,000 herds of fewer than fifty cows exist, that altogether there are only 46,000 dairy farmers and that the average size of herd has risen to sixty-two animals.

None of this is to suggest that we ought to revert to herds of less than twenty, though that would soon get rid of the milk surplus. But it does establish that in 1967 there were more than twice as many dairy farmers able to make a livelihood as there are today. Moreover, they were economically efficient, and common sense suggests that many of them have been driven out of dairying because perhaps the largest item in their budget – feeds – is now heavily taxed.

MISUSING THE LAND

But – the apologist will say – all this is about the livestock farmer; what about the arable sector? Here we are assured that all would be darkness and gloom if the price mechanism were to take charge and the present system of support were taken away. Indeed, there *would* be trouble for all those farmers who have abandoned stock and gone over to arable crops at the behest of the policy-makers, because they have been diverted from efficient to inefficient farming. But the day of reckoning must come for them sooner or later. It will come when the kindly taxpayer decides that to go on subsidizing, at increasing cost, the production of food we do not want to eat is a silly waste of public money at a time when restrictions must be imposed upon schools, hospitals, road-building and other forms of public expenditure that most rational people believe to be more worthwhile. Enough is enough, the taxpayer may say; with that one puff of wind, the castle of cards falls down.

The inefficiency arises largely from the way in which

farmers have been persuaded to use their land for unsuitable purposes. It would be totally absurd to grow bananas on the side of Ben Nevis, but technically it could be done; and no doubt if it were achieved, it would be hailed as a triumph. The earth on the slopes of Ben Nevis, such as it is, would have to be considerably improved; probably many tonnes of good soil would need to be dragged up and then heavily fertilized. Huge glasshouses would be necessary, constructed with elaborate support to withstand storms and snow, and then heated to an inordinate degree. Special varieties of bananas would have to be evolved. It would all cost vast sums of money. No one in their right mind would spend their own savings on such foolery, but there would be others who would be willing to learn the skills if offered enough public money to do so.

When the bananas came to be sold, the economic price might be £3 or £4 each, and then the special pleading would begin. 'Buy British', we would be told; every pound spent on a home-grown banana is a pound saved on the balance of payments. We need 'secure supplies' of bananas and we cannot be sure that Jamaica or the Windward Islands would continue to supply us with 'essential fruits' in a hostile world. 'The Banana Industry of Ben Nevis is needed to provide jobs for Highlanders who would otherwise be out of work.' The NFU would call for a massive injection of fresh capital to enable this valuable new industry to reach its full potential; and in the columns of the farming press it would all be written up, with bated breath, as 'a triumph for Britain'.

Absurdity is only a matter of degree. Not so very far down the scale is the growing of wheat on what was, a few years ago, the heather-strewn moorland of North Yorkshire. A banana grown on the slopes of Ben Nevis might cost fifty times more than one produced in Jamaica; to grow a tonne of wheat in North Yorkshire costs about three times more than one in Manitoba; both are the fruits of absurdity.

To understand what is happening, we need to recall that all the UK's agricultural land has been graded into five qualities by a Ministry of Agriculture Study Group on Agricultural Classification. Only 2.8 per cent of the farmland qualifies as Grade I, and a very large part of this is in my constituency, the Parts of Holland (Lincolnshire), being largely formed by deposits of rich alluvial silt. This is 'land of exceptional quality', as good as any on our planet, and capable of growing any temperate crop in an efficient and profitable way. Not far behind is Grade II, and 14.6 per cent of our agricultural land comes within this definition of 'land of high quality'. It also can produce all temperate crops efficiently and profitably, the margin between it and Grade I being of little significance except to the experienced eye. Using either grade of land for any purpose other than the growing of food verges upon sacrilege. Those fortunate enough to farm such land, assuming a modest competence and a little luck, should earn a fair return from any crop they cultivate.

'Should', however, is the operative word. The present system works against the small farmer regardless of the high-quality land he may have, and in the longer term it provides unfair competition for even the largest farmer with such land. Taking the latter first, the present policy has caused most of our Grade III land to grow arable crops, especially wheat, barley and oilseed rape; 48.9 per cent of our farmland is so classified. It was defined by the ministry's study group as 'land of average quality with limitations due to the soil, relief or climate'. After describing its defects, the experts concluded that 'in fact, some of the best quality permanent grassland may be placed in this grade, where the physical characteristics of the land make arable cropping inadvisable'.

Nothing could be plainer. Between our good land in Grades I and II and the land in Grade III there is a clear distinction; the quality of the first makes it wholly suitable for arable crops, but the average nature of the latter renders it more appropriate for pasture. Of course, there are variations in Grade III. Much of it has been drained thoroughly (with public money), and as long as the draining remains effective, and plenty of fertilizers are applied, such crops as wheat, barley, potatoes and sugar beet can be produced with moderate success. Generally speaking, however, it is simply not possible for an arable farmer to earn a reasonable income out of Grade III land unless the taxpayer helps him.

Grades IV and V are even worse. Yet one can see wheat and barley growing on both. The ministry study group defined Grade IV land as 'land with severe limitations due to adverse soil, relief or climate . . . Generally only suitable for low output enterprises'; 19.7 per cent of our farmland is so classified. The remaining 14 per cent is Grade V and should, at best, carry a few sheep or perhaps some of those splendid Highland cattle. Yet I have heard even the former president of the NFU claim with pride that he was growing barley on such land. One wonders how much has been paid out by way of grants, subsidies and tax allowances to enable that miserable soil of his to produce yet more tonnes of surplus barley.

It is unfair competition of the grossest kind. We need a certain quantity of barley every year for malting and animal feed; and a sensible policy would try to make sure that it was made available at the lowest cost, and grown by the most efficient producers. In other words, if home-grown barley is to be used, our farmers with Grade I and Grade II land should come first in the market. Instead a kind of handicap race has emerged, those who would otherwise be hopelessly behind in the race being given so much support that they are able to keep alongside the natural winners. So long as we actually need these arable crops to be grown, no particular damage is done to the efficient; but come a system of quotas to curb the surpluses, and the unfairness would be plain enough for even council members of the NFU to see.

Forty or fifty acres of rented land of Grade I or Grade II quality used to afford a good livelihood. That was before the present policy came about. In my constituency there were hundreds of farmers with no more land than this, and many with less than half as much; and though they may never have been rich, they were certainly not poor. They were also efficient; that is, they were able to make a livelihood from the land without public money.

Not many of them survive today. Apart from the import levies to protect those growing wheat and barley, not a single one of the many other forms of support has served their interests. They would fail to qualify for the grants and subsidies because they were deemed too small, because they were tenants or because their forms of farming were ineligible; or the sum of money, being related to the size of the holding, would not be worth the paperwork involved in applying for it. The tax allowances have positively worked against them. Because they entitled a farmer to write off 100 per cent of the cost of his machinery against one year's income tax, the manufacturers have been able to increase their prices far beyond the rate of inflation, and the cost of even the smallest new tractor has exceeded the taxable income of a small farmer.

Thus hundreds of efficient small arable farmers in my constituency, and many others elsewhere with Grade I and Grade II land, have gone out of business. Instead they may be driving a lorry or helping to make diesel engines in Peterborough, or they may have joined the swelling ranks of local government. Is the nation's economy the better for the change? The victims' opinion seems to be that they themselves are not.

Our arable farmers with Grade I and Grade II land are a diminishing band. Only a few thousand of them exist. Technically they are extremely competent, and given world prices they would be efficient. But even those of them prospering under the present system are now getting near to a danger point. In 1939 the average yield of wheat was 18.3 hundredweight to the acre. On this good land it has become 3 or 4 tonnes, and it is rising year by year. What will happen when it reaches 6 tonnes to the acre, as predicted, at the end of the century? New varieties of wheat and new advances in cultivation are on the way, and the continental farmer will not be so far behind.

The scandal of the grain surpluses has been well recorded. With several million tonnes of unwanted wheat stored in aircraft hangars and elsewhere, every tonne deteriorating and many infested with weevils and other vermin, the massive surplus had to be got rid of on almost any terms. In the end, vast quantities were sold to the Soviet Union for £19 a tonne, having been bought from the farmer for more than £100. Most of the wheat was unfit for humans and was fed to the Russians' pigs.

VANISHING FARMERS

Some kind of control over production had to be introduced, and several have been canvassed. An obvious remedy was – and still is – a reduction in farm-gate prices. Of all the alternatives, this would suit our efficient farmers the most. Lower prices would not drive them out of business, but it would mean the end of many of the smaller arable farmers on the Continent. The remedy would be 'efficient', but the Common Agricultural Policy is meant to be about keeping farmers on the land, and the other eleven agriculture ministers would almost certainly oppose this step. Electorally it would be disastrous for some of them.

It is for this reason that a system of quotas has been mooted in Brussels as a suitable brake on increasing production. There are two major objections for our efficient arable farmers. The first concerns how quotas can be supervised. Whether the quota is on acreages or tonnage, the opportunity for a grower to be less than totally honest will be at hand. The possibilities for cheating are so many that it is difficult to believe that the temptations will be resisted. I have a suspicion that a few of our own farmers would cheat with a clear conscience; they would be utterly convinced that the French were cheating, so why shouldn't they?

The second objection to quotas is particularly serious for those with Grade I or Grade II land. Quotas will be intended to restrict all those who grow wheat today. This includes tens of thousands of British farmers with Grade III, IV or even V land who have gone over from keeping livestock to growing wheat only because the system of import levies makes it more profitable. The efficient farmer on Grade I and Grade II land will be required by law to grow less of what he can grow efficiently, and the inefficient farmer will be allowed to go on growing what he can grow only inefficiently. Both must look for alternative crops. The only fair quota system would be one that allowed the farmer with Grade I and Grade II land to grow as much as before and required the great majority with the lower grades to grow a great deal less. Then it would have the same effect as the price mechanism, but that of course would clash with the objectives of the Common Agricultural Policy.

A tax on nitrogen has also been considered. Although

ecologically attractive, it has not been successful when tried in Sweden. To pay for the higher cost of the nitrogen, Swedish farmers decided to increase yields and so use more nitrogen for the purpose. In the end, the EEC decided on two forms of control. A co-responsibility levy was brought in, whereby a reduced price was guaranteed for wheat when the sale of surpluses had to be paid for. This works unfairly for the efficient farmer who produces wheat of a quality that is in demand. The other control has been the set-aside programme, for which nobody has a good word except the idle farmer happy to be paid to do nothing. He can receive £80 an acre for letting his land grow nothing, although he can produce grass on it for horses. This helps to reduce the cost of keeping a hunter or ponies for the children; it has also induced some farmers to go into the horse meat trade for the French.

The plain fact is that there is no fair and satisfactory way of holding down output within a system dedicated to subsidizing it. Sooner or later the farmer is bound to suffer, and if one examines farm incomes one can see that he is already doing so. The consumer and taxpayer will suffer rather more.

THE LEAKING PIPELINE

One significant pointer to the inefficiency of the present system is that, as more and more public money is pumped in, a smaller and smaller proportion of it reaches the farmers it is supposed to help.

Peter Walker is almost forgotten as Minister of Agriculture. He was appointed in 1979, and the consequences live with us still. He poured public money into agriculture with great gusto and zeal. Not only was production to be pushed up; farmers' incomes were to be raised, too. He did not realize that, if the high-input/high-output path has been followed for a long time, the law of diminishing returns applies. Proportionately, you must then put in a great deal more money for the farmer to receive a higher net income. When the price support system began, in the years 1947–50, a given input of public money had the effect of raising farm incomes by almost the same amount. For every £1 put in, about 90p went into the total income earned by all British farmers. Today their net income does not seem to rise at all when subsidies are increased.

In 1978 (the last full year before Mr Walker became responsible) British farmers' incomes were £1,238 million. To obtain the figure for price support, one has to take the nearest fiscal year (1977–8), and it totalled £1,061 million. By 1981, despite price support going up to £1,928 million, farm incomes actually fell to £1,209 million. In real terms, the reduction was much worse, of course. Still, farmers' incomes rose considerably in the following year to £1,800 million, but to secure that increase it was necessary to raise total taxpayers' support to £3,200 million. So, to get farm incomes increased by less than £600 million above their 1978 level, support had to go up by over £2,000 million, giving an 'effectiveness ratio' of almost 4 to 1. The policy-makers have had nearly a decade to digest the significance of Mr Walker's attempt to boost the prosperity of agriculture by pumping in enormous sums of public money. There is no evidence yet that a lesson has been learned.

There are two explanations for this growing ineffectiveness. One is the recurring theme of this book: that the more the government expands agricultural output, the more economically inefficient it becomes. The other is that when large sums of public money are spent to distort the price mechanism, with the avowed intention of trying to help the farmer relative to people in other jobs, it is natural for people with capital to invest to divert part of it into the favoured field. Agriculture becomes a good investment, with unearned public money going to swell the return. Farming used to be only for farmers; a price support system has brought in purely financial interests.

The new system was established by about 1950 and was seen to be benefiting agriculture. City institutions (which employ clever people to spot these things) calculated that a modest investment in agricultural land was desirable. From then on, the more public money went into agriculture, the more financial interests invested in agricultural land. They now know that the party is nearly over, and the interest in further investment is beginning to wane. Meanwhile, they have forced up the price of land; and as I show in Chapter 8, during the 1980s the value of all Britain's farmland reached a level £70,000 million higher than it should have been. Rents have risen accordingly and are two or three times more than they ought to be; and people who have bought land to farm have been hit just as hard as the tenants. Farmers have gone to the banks in their thousands and borrowed millions of pounds, and their total indebtedness to the banks and other mortgagees has risen enormously. All of them have had to force high yields out of their soil and stock to pay the first charge upon their income. Their net return has thus failed to rise as fast or as far as their higher input costs, and the need to force more money out of the same acreage has been a prime factor in locking farmers on to the treadmill that we looked at earlier in this chapter.

WHAT HAPPENED UNDER FREE TRADE

Despite all this, there are still some defenders of the present system. All very well, they say, but what would happen if we dismantled it? There would be an agricultural slump, just as there was in the bad old days of unprotected farming between the wars.

I have already showed that this argument does not stand up. In a bad time of slump and unemployment, the farmer was no worse off than others and in some ways better off. At the very least, he was able to stay on the land.

The classic test of how free trade affects agriculture was, of course, the repeal of the Corn Laws in 1846. The opponents of repeal believed that without the protection of import duties on cereals British farmers would be ruined. The great Lord Melbourne summed up the views of many landowners and farmers in words that would be echoed today: 'To leave the whole agricultural interest without protection, I declare before God that I think it the wildest and maddest scheme that has ever entered into the imagination of men to conceive.'

Thus he thundered, no doubt in profound sincerity, but how mistaken he was proved to be! Those who speak in the same language as Lord Melbourne in this century are also mistaken, but for rather different reasons. The facts of today are the foundation for fresh arguments as to why farmers should give their support to a free trade policy.

The Act repealing the Corn Laws was passed in 1846, but there was a three-year period of transition in which the duties were gradually reduced, with the result that from February 1849 there was only a nominal duty of one shilling a quarter imposed upon imported corn. Then followed thirty years of prosperity for British agriculture. Thousands of farmhouses were demolished to make way for larger and more opulent homes; the children were sent away for a private education; the daughters were given piano lessons and the sons ponies to ride. The farmers themselves were now to be seen riding in the hunting field or trotting off in dog-carts for a day's shooting; the wives went to the most expensive dressmakers in the market towns and, at home, left the kitchen to the servants so that they might spend their hours in the new drawing-room entertaining friends and neighbours. A social gap developed between farmer and farm worker; the latter now ceased to live in and eat his meals as one of the family. Instead he had a home of his own, married young and was given a substantially higher wage.

All this is chronicled and is not to be gainsaid. Many a Victorian novel conveys an accurate picture of this prosperity. So do the Probate Records that tell us how much money farmers left compared with their fathers. So do the local newspapers of the time in giving the details of farm sales and market prices. These and other annals have been drawn upon by historians who have all reached the same conclusion about the state of British agriculture after thirty years of free trade. Let one quotation suffice, from an article in the *Encyclopaedia Britannica*, written in 1875: 'In closing this review of British agriculture it is gratifying and cheering to reflect that never was this branch of national industry in a healthier condition, and never was there such solid ground for anticipating for it a steady and rapid progress.'

The reason for this great prosperity in conditions of free trade is relevant to the present situation. The repeal of the Corn Laws brought down the price of bread – an item that comprised the greatest part of the diet of the industrial worker and his family. His wage did not diminish, so he had more money to spend than before. It is significant that he and his family then became meat eaters. Meat consumption rose rapidly in this period and reached a level, per head of the population, higher than it is today. The meat that was now in demand had to be produced on British farms, for it was not practical to import it on any scale, unlike corn. Producing meat was more profitable than growing corn, and any loss that was borne by harvesting less corn was more than made good by the gain of grazing cattle and sheep for the butcher together with the rearing of pigs. Arable farming in East Anglia continued as before, but elsewhere it gave way to an emphasis on livestock production.

Arable farming was hit by the agricultural recession towards the end of the century, and 1879 was the year when it went into decline. Throughout the summer and autumn of that year the rain persisted; harvesting was impossible, and by November the arable fields were covered with rotten corn. In 1880 it again rained continuously, although this time some of the crops were gathered in.

These two disastrous years coincided with an agricultural revolution in the United States, Canada and Australia. Their great wheat-growing areas were being opened up by the railways, and steamships were now available to transport the corn across the ocean in large quantities, speedily and cheaply. The tractor was soon to follow; Messrs Massey-Harris and McCormick were in due course to bring to the farmers of North America and Australia machines that would transform the whole process of harvesting, making it possible to reap and thresh at a fraction of what it had cost before.

The British farmer, especially in England, still held fast to mixed farming, with most of his land under plough. The four-year rotation was the alpha and omega of what he considered to be the right use of his land. His father had believed it to be so, and so had his grandfather. All his neighbours were of the same mind; and the pundits who sat at their desks, as they do today, and wrote their books on the science of agriculture, did not deviate from this accepted wisdom.

As the 1880s gave way to the 1890s the incomes of these farmers, in countless cases, were transformed into losses and bankruptcies. Farms came up for sale, fetching less than they had done since the days of the Corn Laws. This was the situation throughout most of England; in the West Country and in counties like Northumberland, where the emphasis tended to be on livestock farming, the prosperity continued. So, for the same reason, it did in Wales and Scotland.

Quite a movement of farmers and of farmers' sons was now to be seen. As the farms of central and southern England came on to the market, livestock-rearing Scotsmen, Welshmen, Northcountrymen and Westcountrymen arrived on the scene to take advantage of the opportunity to buy up these holdings and adapt them to the skills they brought with them. Many a parish in central and southern England still has a Davies or a Jones, a Graham or a Stewart, whose forebears made such a journey.

Having bought these farms, they put them down to grass: perhaps a few fields of oats or beans for feed, but the rest stayed green the whole year through. These were the men who survived the depression. The others gradually sold up, unless they followed the example of their new neighbours or had other sources of income. The depression did not descend on all agriculture, but upon the old-style arable farming – that agreeable, gentlemanly way of earning a livelihood that carried on despite the repeal of the Corn Laws, until others, with the advantage of a more favourable soil and climate, were able to provide the consumer with a supply of cheaper wheat. The other branch of agriculture, concerned with producing livestock, continued to expand, although not to such an extent as to prevent the total level of agricultural production from falling.

The First World War went a long way to reverse the trend. The price of wheat rose from 31 shillings a quarter to over 80 shillings; in other words, it was back to the price prevailing at the time of the Corn Laws, in the first half of the previous century. Thus, the enemy U-boat achieved the same result as the Corn Laws had.

Once the war was over, the price fell again, and this time it gradually slithered down, reaching 20 shillings a quarter in 1934. By this time the combine harvester was in general use in the great wheat-growing countries; their wheat did not have to be dried by any expensive process as it did in the UK. The vast prairies enabled economies of scale to be practised, not only in every facet of production but equally in marketing.

The Wheat Act and the Import Duty Act, both passed in 1932, went some way to slow down the decline in our arable farming. Yet despite these restrictions upon the free trade in wheat, so few farmers returned to this crop that by 1939 there were, throughout the whole of the UK, no more than 150 combine harvesters in use. This fact seems to indicate the small part wheat was able to play in our economy. Regionally, wheat was important in those areas of East Anglia where the good-quality land will always make its growing sensible and profitable, whatever agricultural policy is pursued; and it was in East Anglia that nearly all those combine harvesters were to be found. Nationally, it was a different story.

It is none the less a myth that British agriculture was in a state of depression by the time the Second World War began. Arable farming was indeed depressed; but in terms of capital investment, labour employed and production, it had been for many years of considerably less significance than the livestock sector. The latter flourished before the war, and flourished as much as any branch of our nation's trade and industry.

Despite the fall in arable production, total agricultural output increased. O. J. Beilby of the Agricultural Economic Research Institute of Oxford published an index of production that included every agricultural commodity. The years taken were from 1885 to 1936, and he made the years 1927–9 the base of 100. The startling result of his research is:

1885–9	94
1890–4	93
1895–9	85
1900–4	82

1905–9	89
1910–14	87
1915–19	91
1922–4	83
1925–7	94
1927–9	100
1928–30	99
1931–3	104
1934–6	110

According to figures published subsequently by the Ministry of Agriculture, farming continued to expand, and in 1939–40 production was 4.8 per cent more than in 1936. Mr Beilby's index shows that 1900–4 was the lowest period of output; by 1936 it had risen from that point by no less than 34 per cent. While critics of our pre-war policy point to the 'black years' from 1919 to 1939, Mr Beilby's index totally rebuts their argument. For the period of 1915–19, agricultural production was 9 per cent lower than it was in 1927–9, yet the former were the war years when farmers were goaded and coerced to grow the maximum their land would yield. Reaching 110 by 1934–6, the index actually gained nineteen points in the inter-war period. This represents a 20 per cent increase in production! No other industry of any significant size in the UK found it possible to increase output by 20 per cent during these years.

Mr Beilby's index has been confirmed by all subsequent research. In a book entitled *British Agriculture* (1938), Viscount Astor and B. Seebohm Rowntree produced an alternative index, taking gross output instead of Mr Beilby's net output, and using the figures published by the Ministry of Agriculture. Making 1923 their base year, they found that by 1936–7 gross agricultural production had increased by 22 per cent. Again, this compares favourably with any other trade or industry.

The Ministry's statistics show that a remarkable expansion took place in all forms of livestock rearing between the wars. Between 1923 and 1939 the population of our herds increased as follows:

Cattle	up by	1,108,000	or	14 per cent
Sheep	up by	5,802,000	or	27 per cent
Pigs	up by	1,401,000	or	45 per cent
Poultry	up by	21,982,000	or	63 per cent

The increase in the number of pigs and poultry is particularly remarkable. Both have been called 'walking cereals', for both consume considerable quantities of corn in one form or another. Low cereal prices were undoubtedly the reason why their numbers rose so dramatically. If the price of cereals had been kept artificially high after the First World War, at the same level as it had reached during the war as a consequence of enemy action, there would never have been the expansion of the pig herds and poultry flocks. Nor could the cattle and the sheep have been able to return to the fields that had been ploughed up.

Both the consumer and the farmer gained in the process. The British people were able to eat meat more cheaply than people in any other industrialized country. Moreover, they were given a variety of choice that was not available anywhere else in the world at comparable prices. As to the farmer, he became the most successful and prosperous in Europe. Sir John Russell, author of *English Farming* (1942), produced a table to prove the point – see Table 4 (p. 135).

Two facts stand out in this table. The first is that farm wages were far higher in Britain than in Germany – how the tables have turned today! A paper published by the Low Pay Unit in 1981 showed that 35.5 per cent of British farm workers were paid badly enough to entitle them to Family Income Supplement, three times the average for manual workers in general.

The second fact that emerges from the table is that there is a correlation between the value of output and the quantity of livestock. France and Germany, then as now, believed in growing their own arable crops regardless of the supply in the world market. They deliberately shut out of their own market wheat and other cereals that could have been exported to them at lower prices. The result was that, unlike Britain, they were unable to produce meat at a low cost.

Arable farming is for the larger farmer, livestock for the

Table 4   Comparison of British and continental farming in the 1930s

| | Output per worker per year | | Wages in shillings per week | Livestock units per worker |
	Gross (£)	Net (£)		
Great Britain	240	200	30.36	10.3
Denmark	180	135	23.26	8.4
Netherlands	150	120	23.30	4.9
Belgium	110	100	18.22	3.4
Switzerland	110	100	27.29	4.3
France	90	90	20.28	2.8
Germany	70	70	18.23	2.8

small farmer. The proposition is almost self-evident. In south Lincolnshire and the Isle of Ely there are some owners of arable smallholdings, but they produce mainly specialist non-cereal crops, and when they do grow corn they find it necessary to bring in a contractor for harvesting, and even for drilling. Modern machinery for arable farming, not least the combine harvester, now costs so much that a man of few acres cannot make profitable use of it. On the other hand, livestock benefits from the intensive management and individual care that the smallholder can provide.

The present-day structure of farming in the UK militates against livestock and favours the arable sector. Throughout most of the country a general picture can be seen. It is that the average farm is the result of two, three or four pre-war farms having been amalgamated in the last thirty-five years, probably with the aid of a government subsidy. This larger unit is economic for the growing of cereals; and most, perhaps nearly all, of its acres will be under plough. It will employ one or two men in the place of five times that number who worked there before the amalgamations took place. There is, of course, one farmer in the place of the several who presided over the separate farms.

What pressures caused those others to leave agriculture?

Some retired, perhaps content with the price their farm fetched. I suspect that they were in the minority. The others were likely to be men skilled with livestock, perhaps in dairying or with pigs or poultry; some were in beef, but a high proportion had several kinds of stock on their farm. They were not specialists, but they were good with animals generally. How many of them still survive? Very few. And how many would have survived if we had pursued a policy enabling them to buy cereals for their feedstuffs in the world market free of import duties or levies? The answer must be, very many of them.

In that area of central and southern England that went over to the different kinds of livestock farming in the last 100 years, this new structure is everywhere apparent. By previous standards, the farms tend to be large, some 500 acres upwards. Each is predominantly arable, heavily mechanized and capital intensive, having received numerous grants and tax allowances; and in consequence each employs the minimum labour force. Wheat is the favourite crop, being sold by the farmer at 50, 75 or 100 per cent above the price in the market outside the European Community.

The Corn Laws were oppressive, we are told in the history books. Yet today we submit to a tax on corn that is twice as high as it ever was under the Corn Laws! The housewife, in paying more for her bread than she should, does not suffer to the same degree as the livestock farmer. Ever since the Wheat Act and the Import Duties Act of 1932, he has been squeezed. As a result, hundreds of thousands have ceased to be either farmers or farm workers.

The evidence points to one conclusion. If the state had not interfered by restricting and taxing cereals from abroad, and if it had not further spent taxpayers' money on a policy that has had the effect of inducing farmers to grow arable crops rather than produce livestock, there would today be more and smaller farms, and more farmers and farm workers. Almost certainly, all but the largest would be better rewarded.

· 6 ·

THE MANIPULATORS

The management of our land – and with land we must include the creatures that live on it – should be oriented towards three goals: health, beauty and permanence. Food then comes naturally from it. This view was put forward by the late Dr E. F. Schumacher in his book *Small Is Beautiful* (1973), and it is one which I hope pervades the present book. It is also the opposite of what the United Kingdom's agricultural policy has sought to achieve in the last two or three decades.

The origins of this sorry distortion of good economics and good sense can be traced back to the post-war period and the determination to make the UK as near self-sufficient in food as possible. Various arguments were put forward to show why this was necessary, and at the time they seemed convincing to most people. More than forty years later, things look very different, and Chapter 7 examines the fallacies in those arguments.

In the pursuit of self-sufficiency, vast sums of taxpayers' money have been spent by the government to goad farmers into getting more food out of the same number of acres. In the early days of price support, after the Agriculture Act of 1947 was passed, farmers were found to be spending their higher incomes upon improving their standard of living; public money was going into their pockets and being spent by them on making their farmhouses more comfortable or buying new cars and in other sensible ways. But this did not suit the policy-makers, and after 1951 most of the financial aids to agriculture were direct inducements to increase food production. We then had subsidies to use phosphate fertilizers, and in the following years the principle of subsidizing fertilizers was extended to all artificials, much to the benefit of certain chemical companies. A ploughing-up grant was also made available to encourage permanent pasture to be ploughed and reseeded with temporary grasses, which again benefited some chemical companies, because farmers were strongly advised to apply their particular fertilizers on to the new varieties of grass. Another new grant at that time was for rearing beef calves. As the years went by, new subsidies were devised to force up the production of food: grants for the removal of hedges, grants to uproot old orchards, grants to plough up hill land (£12 an acre, while on the low land it was £7 an acre), grants for winter keep, grants for land drainage, grants for numerous other things.

All this public money – and hundreds of millions of pounds were made available – did very little to help the farmer lead a more contented life, and it was not intended to do so. As production rose, farm incomes tended to go down. Far from attaining Schumacher's three goals, the policy had precisely the opposite effect. The health of our soil and our stock, and our own health too, was impaired; and the beauty and permanence of our landscape were diminished. Permanence is about conservation; and while the conservationist believes that there are certain features of the landscape that are so naturally in their proper place that they should remain there permanently, he also believes that there are lots of places where the bulldozer should move in. The trouble is that any system that blindly subsidizes increased production makes it certain that the bulldozer will move in far too often, and usually in the wrong place.

It also makes sure that the impact on the farming community will be the opposite of what it should. It does nothing for the small farmer, who needs help, or the responsible custodian of the countryside, who deserves it. Instead, it pours additional money into the bank accounts of the big, prosperous exploiters of the land who neither need nor deserve any help from the rest of us.

PLAYERS IN THE GAME

Unfortunately these distortions made it not less but more likely that the policy of subsidizing increased production would become entrenched. Those who benefited were those best placed to exert a subtle but powerful influence on government policy, and the game of manipulation was played with great skill.

First came the big farmers – the agribusiness men. Their chosen instrument was the National Farmers' Union. Now, you might suppose that a *national* union of farmers would speak up for farmers of all kinds, and particularly for the small farmers who form the large majority. In reality, no one has any significant influence in the NFU unless he is a member of its council. To serve on the council, a member must leave his farm to travel down to London most weeks in the year and there sit on committees and perform other duties which are likely to take two or three days a week. Small farmers cannot do that; they are too busy sitting on their tractor or milking their cows. Others who enjoy farming and have made it a career because they want both to live and to work in the countryside (and they tend to be the best farmers) are loath to turn their back upon their farm to sleep their nights in a London hotel and take their place in interminable debates and discussions.

So the NFU Council has gathered to itself men less aware of the day-to-day realities than most farmers, and less sympathetic to them. Being the larger farmers – having 1,000 acres or more is not unusual for an NFU Council member – they have, almost by definition, been the beneficiaries of the system which has amalgamated tens of thousands of small farms. These are the men who have enjoyed the lion's share of the grants, subsidies and tax allowances; they have worked the system; and they have prospered. Prosperity has blurred their vision.

Over the years, cosy meetings between the Minister of Agriculture and the NFU, with the Country Landowners' Association tagging along behind, became a regular, almost a weekly, event. So began the way our farmers submitted to state control. More strictly, it was corporativist control; for the public, whether as taxpayers or consumers, had little influence over their deliberations. According to corporativist philosophy, just two should decide what ought to be done: the government and the industry in question. Considering how soon after the Second World War this began, it is surprising how much the process of consultation resembled the way our erstwhile enemies had managed their own agriculture.

Of course, in all these consultations no word is said that the consumer is to be prejudiced. On the contrary, protectionist measures are always couched in terms that suggest the opposite: help us to help our customers. In this way the thin end of the wedge is inserted; a little protection leads to a request for more; and there is never a stage when those protected sit back in a state of contentment. The present-day lobbying by the NFU illustrates it only too well. Despite all the massive help given to agriculture (and it has been insidiously increasing year by year for over half a century) the NFU is far from satisfied. Not a single day goes by – as the NFU admits – without it making some representations to the Ministry of Agriculture or the Treasury or some other government department for still more help.

An article in *Farmers' Weekly* in January 1984 was quite frank. After describing more conventional forms of lobbying it went on:

> [T]here is the more undercover style of lobbying which the NFU does so well. This means knowing who the most powerful people are on a certain issue and bringing them round to the farmers' point of view. It is the kind of lobbying which goes on at lunchtimes, in bars and at private dinner parties where Cabinet Ministers are mellowed by good claret and port. It's expensive and exclusive but it works. . .
>
> Ask one of the NFU staff men who unashamedly revel in their ability to play the game – or manipulate others into playing it – whether the system is just, and he will just shrug his shoulders. It's the way the world goes round.

The Treasury occasionally disagreed with the level of spending by the Minister of Agriculture, and from time to time this inhibited him from giving away to the farmers all the money he would have liked. Success or popularity was measured by the largesse distributed, so he had a natural interest in getting as much as he could out of the Treasury; and when he failed to do so, the NFU obliged with some criticism of the minister himself. Nothing too severe was spoken – the comfortable relationship must not be disturbed – but it was strong enough to convince the rank-and-file farmer that the NFU was fighting his case, and strong enough also to enable the minister to tell the Treasury that the farmers' anger had to be abated. A game was being played: not quite collusion, but each side knew the other's difficulties as well as its own, and both found it served their purpose to be accommodating. When the minister of the day called for more food to be grown, an echo came from the NFU.

Backing up the NFU was another powerful interest, the agrochemical industry. One day the political activities of this industry will come under closer scrutiny, and the story will be told of the influence it has wielded. There is no big money to be made out of low-geared farming; but the more highly geared it becomes, the more the industry can sell. Its sales to farmers were but a few million pounds in 1946, but since then they have climbed steadily upwards, despite the use of nitrates having now reached a plateau. Indeed, receipts from farmers for nitrates actually rose from £671 million in 1988 to £757 million in 1989. The UK's chemical companies received no less than £1,197 million from farmers in 1989, which is almost as much as total farm income! In real terms this is about a tenfold increase on their sales since the introduction of guaranteed prices.

Pesticides have afforded the greater growth area for the chemical companies. In the 1970s their cost was so small – and their use so insignificant – that the Ministry of Agriculture did not record pesticides as a separate item in the farmer's budget. Over the last decade they have become a major cost. In 1980 £147 million was spent by British farmers on pesticides; in 1989, £440 million. Parallel with this increase in use and cost has been a rise in public concern about pesticide safety, which has in turn led the agrochemical industry to intensify its lobbying of MPs and the media, especially the farming press. Two of the pesticide manufacturers have winkled officials out of the ministry to act as their consultants.

No company has been more politically minded than ICI, which has seen the advantage of maintaining strong links with government ministers, MPs and officials in all the departments which have responsibilities touching its activities. ICI began to give special attention to the Ministry of Agriculture immediately after the principle of guaranteed farm prices was established at the end of the Second World War; and its 'government affairs department', under the redoubtable C. F. Thring (known as Peter Thring in Westminster and Whitehall), acquired considerable influence. Once the ministry had begun to subsidize the use of artificial fertilizers, ICI's sales embarked on a period of substantial growth, rising to more than £1,300 million a year. With the company investing hundreds of millions of pounds of capital in developing its agricultural interests, agrochemicals became its largest and – until recently – its most profitable branch of activity.

Contacts at high level have been of inestimable value to the agrochemical industry. To watch one of its 'government affairs officers' enter a party where the farming establishment was present was enough to open one's eyes to the regard the establishment had for him and the influence he wielded: the warmest shake of the hand, even an embrace or two, genial smiles, followed by close attention to what he said. As he went about the room, heads would turn, and in each knot he joined he became its centre. A stranger to the scene would have assumed he was the most important man in British agriculture present.

The third major player in the game of manipulation is the small handful of compound-feed manufacturers, which, with their ranks of nutritionists and batteries of computers, supply most livestock farmers with feeds for pigs, poultry, cattle and sheep. One by one the smaller firms that used to exist in nearly every market town have been gobbled up by these major concerns. To the farmer they have become household names; and half of the UK's ten largest and most powerful industrial companies have an interest in the business. Feed-compound sales to farmers now add up to almost 16 million tonnes annually and have climbed to £2,900 million a year, making up the biggest item in many a farm budget. This dependency on bought-in feed is – like other forms of farmers' dependency on outside assistance – a post-war phenomenon as the British livestock sector has become as intensive as any in the world.

The cost of feeds to the farmer has risen by 12 per cent since 1985. This may seem fair enough, given the rate of inflation. Yet when the arable farmer sells his wheat or barley to the compounder he receives 3 per cent less than in 1985. The feed companies assure us that the costs of other ingredients have risen. While it may be churlish to ask whether they have to pay more for a dead sheep, it is worth noting that their published profits seem to go up as steadily as farmers' incomes go down.

Just what are these other ingredients? The companies are coy about them. Long before the salmonella and BSE scares revealed how dead animals were being recycled, the NFU urged the Ministry of Agriculture to introduce legislation to require the compounders to disclose what they put in their feeds – a reasonable request, given that farmers are responsible for the health of their animals and for the quality of the food produced therefrom. The compounders saw it differently; they had to play the market by buying a variety of ingredients according to price and availability, so the contents of the feed might vary. Their argument won the day. Critics of the ministry claim the compounders' victory as further evidence of the cosy relationship existing between them. The UK Agricultural Supply Trade Association has its offices only a few steps away from the ministry, in Whitehall Court.

So farmers remain in the dark. Is arsenic still put in pigs' rations, as it used to be, as a growth stimulant? Ask the Ministry of Agriculture whether it knows the answer, and you are liable to be told that officials cannot disclose what they call 'commercial confidentialities'; pressed further, they have been known to quote Official Secrets legislation. Then there is copper, which also makes pigs grow faster, but is a carcinogen.

As for offal, we now know that the regulations governing its use are quite inadequate. The original draft regulations were much more stringent, but would have added substantially to the costs of the feed industry. So it set about the task of persuading the ministry to treat it more kindly. Instead of requiring the industry to follow a code, the ministry redrafted the regulations so that the main safeguard was to be an occasional inspection by officials of the plants where offal was processed. These inspections proved ineffective; many plants were found to be infected by salmonella and when inspected again were still infected, the ministry seeming averse to take any firm action against the owners. Only when Edwina Currie came on the scene were more satisfactory controls introduced.

Alongside these three heavyweights – the NFU, the agrochemical industry and the feed compounders – there have been a swarm of other interested parties, all eager to have their share of the hand-outs. In *Farming in the Clouds* I listed sixty-seven trade associations in the food and farming industries which have found it worth their while to maintain offices in central London. Some of them may not behave like the NFU and may never pour the best claret down the throats of the Cabinet. But what draws them, like bluebottles to a cowpat, to the metropolis? Drawn they have been, for many of them once had offices far away in places like Birmingham and Bedford which were geographically closer to their members. The offices are where they are, despite the high rents and rates, because for most of them it is functionally necessary to be near Westminster and Whitehall. So each one is within striking distance of 'where the action is'. It indicates their primary purpose: to influence the government so that it will interfere in such a way as to assist their members.

To give this help without injuring either the taxpayer or the consumer may be possible, but a few moments' reflection ought to make us realize that such help is likely to be trivial or peripheral. When a producers' association asks the government for some form of assistance it is one of three kinds: advice, money or regulation. Advice, in itself, may cost the taxpayer no more than the time of some politician or civil servant over a cup of tea, but how often will it end there? We can be sure that when a producers' association approaches a branch of government it is to ask it to 'do' something. Now, there is one truth about all governments that is certain; they can only 'do' something for us by taking away either our money or our freedom. As often as not, they take both. Whenever the government decides to spend more money in any field of expenditure, by even the smallest amount, without spending less in another field, it must take that money away from all the people in the form of inflation or from some of the people by taxation. Freedom of choice and purchasing power go hand in hand. The more purchasing power is entrusted to the government, the less freedom is left to the consumer to buy what he chooses, and this is particularly true if the consumer is a poor family which has little money left over after buying essentials.

Of course, the scores of producers' associations that beaver away in the environs of government do not see themselves in this light. Most of them would be deeply hurt to be told that they were making inroads on the consumer's freedom of choice. Yet simple logic makes it difficult to draw any other inference from what they are doing.

HOW THE GAME IS PLAYED

Let us explore the methods used to influence the government. Not much harm may be done when the chairman of the producers' association takes a deputation to see an official or a minister to urge him to consider some change of policy. Nor is much achieved when this is the only step taken. Every government department receives so many representations from outside bodies that merely making a point across a table is seldom enough to secure a change of direction. Long before any direct move is made, it is wise to get on good terms with the minister and his top officials; and the engagement for luncheon or dinner has become the accepted means to that end.

An incoming minister receives plenty of invitations. John Silkin tells the story that as soon as he was appointed Minister of Agriculture in the 1970s a letter arrived addressed to 'Dear John'. It was from the president of the NFU, until then a total stranger to him, but the familiar approach was presumably intended to begin a nice, friendly relationship. The first task of the producer associations is to get themselves on good terms with their counterparts in the government departments. Having been a member of the Select Committee on Agriculture for some years I have seen many of them come before us as witnesses. And I have seen the same faces in the Reform Club together with ministry officials or members of the public relations business, a large part of which serves also the business of lobbying. 'There is no such thing as a free lunch,' I say to myself as I pass by their table.

In these proceedings Parliament has not been left out. The lobbyists have tried to influence individual MPs, knowing that they can exert pressure upon a minister to coincide with their own direct approaches. Nor are journalists excluded. The modern reporter in this field does not have to go out of his office to get his stories, and the newspaper proprietors, always conscious of rising costs, are only too glad to allow outside sources to feed in news items. Each newspaper has the opportunity of receiving the same information. The facts themselves are sure to be correct, but like a brief to a barrister, they are not intended to be an objective assessment of the whole matter. They are what the producers' association would wish the reader to digest, and though there may be occasions when the two are the same, it is probable that they will be quite different. Why, after all, should the producers' association want to influence the press in the first place? If its object is to change government policy by getting a minister's decision in favour of its members, the newspaper reader's interest, as a consumer, is almost sure to be prejudiced.

The interest of the consumer does not end with the price he has to pay. A question mark must be put against the way some of the herbicides, pesticides and other poisonous chemicals have been allowed to be sold in the UK, as described in Chapter 2. Elsewhere, the sale of a poison like 2,4,5-T is forbidden by law on the simple ground that the evidence of its danger to people and the environment generally is too great. The market for the sale of hormone-based weed-killers is immense, millions of pounds a year; and if the Ministry of Agriculture were to form the same opinion about their dangers as its counterparts in other countries, the companies that make and sell these extremely toxic chemicals would stand to lose a great deal of money. The amount of research required of these companies is not as extensive as it is in other countries, and a cynic might suggest that the companies will try to persuade the ministry that it is unnecessary for us to adopt the higher standards that prevail elsewhere. Such doubts are hardened when the ministry refuses to reveal the nature of the safety tests that are conducted.

Little of this can be known to the poor consumer. Secretaries in the office who make the engagements, and waiters as they serve the lobster, may have an idea of what it is about. But as consumers themselves, do they appreciate how their own interests are being interfered with?

There is one very important way in which the big producer interests have worked to influence government policy, and worked with notable success. At a very early stage they saw the potential of the Common Agricultural Policy, and the ICI boardroom became the scene of the first fund-raising for the European Movement. It set up a department for the specific purpose of influencing MPs and civil servants. The head of the department, Peter Thring, shared an eccentricity with me – we were members of both the Carlton Club and the Reform Club. Our motives, I hope, were different. He set himself up as an excellent host; he knew a good wine, as the saying goes, and an invitation from him was a promise of generous hospitality. At the Carlton he entertained politicians, and the frequency with which he entertained civil servants at the Reform was well known. It gave the observing cynics plenty to speculate about.

In the 1970s he was particularly active. The late Asher

Winegarten, director-general of the NFU, was also a member of the Reform Club at that time; so, too, was Sir Freddy Kearns, the Permanent Secretary at the Ministry of Agriculture, and later recruited by the NFU to be its consultant. Several others of considerable influence in agricultural policy were also to be found regularly at the Reform. The irony of it! As they stood to drink their gin-and-tonics before lunch, they were but a few feet away from a portrait of C. P. Villiers – the MP for Wolverhampton for sixty years, who long before Cobden and Bright came to the fore was the lonely campaigner against the Corn Laws and proposed a motion in the House every year against agricultural protectionism. When by themselves, they would eat together in a room set aside for members, the very room where the Cobden Club was founded to resist a return to the Corn Laws. Then, after lunch, they would climb the stairs to drink their cups of coffee and glasses of port in the gallery, beneath two portraits that adorn its walls: of Richard Cobden and John Bright.

Also involved in the campaign to get us 'into Europe' were the banks. The clearing banks and the larger merchant banks, which have lent money to agriculture on an increasing scale, also spent large sums on advertising to the British people the advantages of the Common Market, especially the Common Agricultural Policy. Those that lent the most spent the most. One of them was particularly keen to persuade the British people of the benefits of the Common Market, in all its aspects, at the time of the 1975 referendum. That it has invested more money in agriculture than the others may be a mere coincidence. But I have before me some of the material put out by this famous high-street bank; some of the arguments are pitched at an uncommonly high note, and the facts recited could not have stemmed from the thorough research that banks usually insist upon.

TIME TO END THE PARTY

The process of lobbying does not stand still. Within it are forces that propel it on its way to try to get even more out of the system. Far from producers' associations being dissolved, their number steadily increases. Government intervention makes them necessary; protectionism breeds them. Journalists weary of the newspaper world and politicians defeated at the polls have not been backward in filling in the gaps and suggesting to various groups how their interests can be looked after by them. After all, it is quite an agreeable job to have, and there is a lot one can do with the expense account.

Just as soft pornography differs from the hard stuff, so there is hard and soft corruption. No one suggests that politicians and civil servants are compromised by money or generous gifts; the soft corruption takes the form of hospitality, eating and drinking together and the camaraderie that follows. For a business man it is a legitimate part of his job. He may feel that he is justified in treating a politician or civil servant in the same way as a business contact; for in most cases he is furthering the interests of his business. But if his lordship's gamekeeper spends too much time with old Bill down at the King's Arms, what will he do when he catches him poaching the pheasants?

The only possible way to reverse this tendency is for the government to begin the process of disengagement, in plain words to stop interfering with the consumer's freedom of choice. Sadly, this is a tall order, for governments thrive on power. The pursuit of power is the motor that drives nearly every politician and administrative official. To give power back to the consumer would entail giving up what they would prefer to keep.

For all that, there are now unmistakable signs that the process of disengagement may be about to begin. The costs of protectionism, and of the CAP in particular, have now risen so high that everyone, even the policy-makers of the NFU, must recognize that the public will not go on paying the price for ever. The price has always been outrageous, but lately the attempts of the lobbyists to keep it quiet have been less successful. Similarly, the anxiety now expressed by consumer organizations about the quality of our food is something that every livestock farmer concerned about his feedstuffs should share. At last those who speak for the general interest are making themselves heard over the special pleadings of the commercial beneficiaries of the present system. It is this that in the end, and perhaps quite soon, will defeat the efforts of the manipulators. In the face of this rising tide of protest, even the most dedicated believers in the agricultural status quo are having to admit that the party is over.

· 7 ·

FALLACIES IN THE ARGUMENT

Those who support the system of agricultural subsidies and tariffs that has done so much harm have used six main arguments to justify it. One of them, that it would help conserve the countryside, has, as we saw in Chapter 4, proved lamentably wrong. Subsidized destruction, rather than subsidized conservation, has been the rule. The argument that subsidies would help farmers to stay on the land in conditions of reasonable prosperity has proved equally fallacious, as shown in Chapter 5. Here we examine the other four arguments that proved so persuasive: the need for security of supply for the consumer; the need to help feed a starving world; the strategic argument; and the balance-of-payments argument.

DOES THE CONSUMER NEED SECURITY OF SUPPLY?

It is only since the United Kingdom entered the European Community that we have heard the argument about the need to secure our food supplies. No one would have dared raise the idea before we began to cut our trading links with low-cost suppliers in the Commonwealth and elsewhere. Now we are told that it is sensible to pay an extra premium over world prices to be sure of getting the food that we want. Let us therefore not be 'penny foolish'; better to give the farmers a reasonable price for what they produce, although that price may be rather more than we might pay elsewhere, because in return we know that they will not let us down.

This is a plausible argument, especially when it is accompanied by horrendous stories of a population explosion and a lengthening queue of human mouths to feed. The argument does not hold water, however. The elements of the argument are these:

- We have already witnessed shortages of wheat and sugar that have made our supplies insecure.
- A hungry Third World will demand a fairer share of the existing food supply.
- We cannot rely upon other countries to give us preference in the future.
- Our own farmers and those in the EEC can be trusted to give us that preference.

Let us look at each of those elements in turn to see whether any of them are valid.

It is perfectly true that in the 1970s the major suppliers of wheat – the United States, Canada, Argentina and Australia – reduced their production. There is no doubt that as a result a world shortage ensued. The governments of each of those countries, by one means or another, induced their farmers to grow less wheat in the years immediately before 1974. The governments intervened because farmers, if left to themselves, would have continued to grow wheat as before, since for most of them it was their main livelihood. Why then should those governments have felt it necessary to dissuade their own citizens from producing what they wished? No one has dared suggest that their farmers were inefficient or their prices too high. On the contrary, it was because they were too efficient and their prices too low that their governments had to coerce them. Because their wheat was of the kind and quality that the world's markets wanted and because its low price could secure it a sale in the world market, the EEC – with surpluses of wheat produced at high cost – had to resort to a policy of dumping to get rid of what it did not want.

Despite the fury and despair of such countries as Argentina, Australia, Canada and the United States, whose economies should depend largely upon grain exports, the EEC has maintained that it has a right to undercut the price of their wheat on the world market with huge subsidies which it euphemistically calls 'export refunds'. Nor has the EEC admitted any duty, whether under GATT or morally, to limit the scale of its dumping. On a visit to Australia in 1988 I met farmers unable to sell their wheat at £45 a tonne (less than half the price the EEC farmers were receiving) as a direct result of the Community offloading its surpluses in a market that they would otherwise have supplied.

The world food market has always, to some extent, been a place for dumping. It happens where there is an unexpectedly large harvest and a glut worldwide. Millions of food producers in 150 different countries must each make their estimate of what they can sell for a satisfactory return. Their main guide must be the price they received the previous year, but this, of course, is seldom the same for any two years in succession. No one can assess the size of a harvest when the ploughs first take to the field, not even when weeks later the seed is planted.

The total supply of food depends partly upon these millions of estimates. But whatever the food being produced, meat and dairy products as well as arable crops, the ultimate supply will be determined by the behaviour of the climate. A few days of extra sunshine in just one country can make a surprising difference; so also can another inch of rainfall.

The total supply of food will always be unpredictable. In a world where only a minority of the human race are rationed strictly, and the majority are free to buy their food as they can afford it, the demand for food will also be unpredictable. A slight rise in the price of beef on a Thursday or Friday may cause 100,000 families in Britain to switch to pork or lamb for their weekend joint.

There can never be a tidy balance between supply and demand. The food trade nationally knows this, and internationally knows it even better. In such circumstances, it is not surprising that producers, when they have had a crop that exceeds their expectations, have been willing to dispose of some part of it at less than the cost of production. When done across frontiers we may denounce this as dumping; while it can cause difficulties to other producers, some degree of dumping is inevitable in a free market. However, no producer would want to sell at below the cost of production, and he plans his production on the assumption that he will not do so. Thus, as a general rule, dumping, if it takes place at all, is on a modest scale; and it is seldom that any serious or permanent harm is done to producers in other countries. This is the case in a free market, but when governments intervene by goading farmers into producing more than they would otherwise do, they are bound to increase the risk of dumping. This is precisely what the EEC has done with numerous commodities.

In the case of wheat, the European Community has been a notorious dumper. Year after year, it has placed vast quantities on the world market; and, as every ounce of it has been grown at high cost, its sale has been possible only with the aid of export subsidies. The EEC Commission, sensitive to the charge of dumping, does not make available (not even to our own Ministry of Agriculture) the cost of these subsidies. In its published budget, the subsidies of all exported cereals are given in one aggregate figure. We can assume that most are for wheat. In 1980, not an unusual year, £687 million was spent in this way.

Export subsidies paid out on this scale, and paid out year after year, have a most damaging effect on other exporters. Australia, for example, used to have a valuable market for its wheat in Sri Lanka, a market virtually destroyed by the EEC. The worst effect is that no bona-fide exporter can anticipate the quantity of wheat that is to be dumped on the world market by the EEC. Unless he also is to be subsidized by his own government, he faces the danger of both losing some part of his export market and finding he must sell his wheat at a loss. Small wonder if he loses confidence and decides to plant another crop or put some of his acres back to pasture.

A decision to reduce production will not be made by just a few isolated farmers. It never works like that. When confidence is lost, it is lost by the majority. In the 1970s most of the best wheat producers of the world cut their production or were so disheartened that they went out of business altogether. But their land is still there, waiting to grow wheat again at low cost.

Sugar is the other commodity that is mentioned to support the 'security of supply' argument. We are reminded that in 1974 the world price rocketed to over £600 a tonne, and British shoppers had to queue for their rations. A kindly Common Market came to the aid of its new members and sold us sugar at less than half the world price.

I was giving a talk to the Mauritius Chamber of Agriculture when news came through that the world price had reached £200 a tonne. Although the Mauritius economy depends upon sugar, from which some 80 per cent of its export earnings come, the news was greeted by a mixed reaction. All those present knew well enough that the world price for sugar is very volatile, and this is not surprising because it is an artificial creation. About 88 per cent of the sugar exported was sold then under the International Sugar Agreement or the Commonwealth Sugar Agreement; their purpose was to provide stability of prices for sugar growers, most of whom are in developing and poor countries and are for various reasons unable to grow other crops. Hence only some 12 per cent of the sugar exported had its price fixed by day-to-day free market forces. Most of this sugar went to Canada, Japan and a few smaller countries where consumption was low. The smaller the quantity in a free market, the more uncertain and volatile is the price likely to be. The Mauritius growers realized that an excessively high price in one year would prompt an over-optimistic expansion of production for the following year, and the consequent glut would cause havoc in the limited free world market.

This is what happened in 1968. The world price fell as low as £13 a tonne for a short while and was about £20 a tonne for much of the year. The latter price represented roughly half the cost of production. Not every sugar producer was affected, especially among the smaller producers who sold all their crops under the Commonwealth Sugar Agreement. So the collapse of the world market was not the catastrophe one might have expected. But the essential reason why the world market collapsed was because of a coincidence of, first, an unusual growing season and, secondly, the dumping by the EEC of one million tonnes of sugar on to this narrow world market. Canada and Japan bought what they wanted from Europe at bargain prices.

The experience of 1968 was not forgotten. In the UK's negotiations to enter the EEC in 1970–2 it was uppermost in the minds of the Commonwealth producers. They knew the principle of Community preference, that once we were inside we would have to conform to a policy that required us to buy our sugar from within the Common Market in preference to any that was available outside, regardless of whether the latter was naturally cheaper. I visited several of the producing countries at the time to explain the dangers of the CAP to the leaders of the sugar industry. For them, the most important was the end of the Commonwealth Sugar Agreement. The best that Mr Heath, then Prime Minister, was able or willing to do for them was to get Brussels to 'take to heart' the needs of the Commonwealth producers in the developing countries, that is, all of them except Australia.

This assurance was futile as the basis for confidence. And it is to the credit of the following Labour government that in renegotiating the UK's terms of entry it secured permanent access for 1.3 million tonnes of sugar a year from the developing countries of the Commonwealth.

The new agreement, however, was not finally established until 1975. By then the Commonwealth Sugar Agreement was dissolved, and the sugar producers were apprehensive for their future and convinced that Britain was deceiving them. They could not forget their history. Maybe it was long ago, but the inhabitants of the Caribbean islands, Mauritius and Guyana know that their countries were peopled to grow sugar for us, and that their forefathers were torn from their homeland and transported across the ocean, enslaved and humiliated in the process, to satisfy the sweet tooth of the Englishman.

Then came the sugar shortage of 1974 – almost the first there has ever been and one never likely to be repeated. The sugar crop failed in two key countries, and the free world market went into disarray. If the Commonwealth Agreement had continued – as it would have done if we had not joined the EEC – our own supplies would have been secure; for the Commonwealth producers had enough for our needs. But why should they give Britain preference when they had a chance of gaining a place in the world market and opening up for themselves an outlet for their produce to replace the one they had lost in Britain? It was obvious that they had to act as they did.

Cynics have asserted that the sugar producers would have done the same anyway, whether or not we had joined the EEC, but it would have been particularly stupid of them to break the terms of the Commonwealth Sugar Agreement, especially at the very time that the agreement would have been renewed. The agreement survived nearly a quarter of a century; in those years the Commonwealth acted honourably, although there were occasions when producers could have made a short-term gain by acting dishonourably. The agreement gave Britain secure supplies of sugar and gave the producer a secure market. Although the so-called world price was sometimes above and sometimes below the price in the agreement, both parties enjoyed stability.

As with wheat, the example of sugar does not prove that an extensive policy of supporting agriculture is necessary to secure supplies. Indeed, the contrary is true. Some years ago our sugar beet crop was disastrous. It was blighted by a yellow leaf disease, and the disease could have affected every acre of sugar beet in the Common Market. Another year like that and we could have witnessed the spectacle of Europeans scrambling in the world market as the price rocketed upwards.

The second element in the argument about secure supplies is that a hungry Third World will demand fairer shares of the existing world supplies. This really turns on the word 'demand', which has two meanings. There is the everyday one, in the sense that we ask for something in a determined way; and there is the economists' meaning. By muddling up the two, this part of the argument gets muddled too.

A hungry Third World may need more food; but demand, in the economists' sense of the word, implies both need and a capacity to buy. Now, if the Third World can demand in this sense, the supply will be forthcoming. World food production could be doubled without any practicable difficulty (I will come back to this point later), and it is not necessary for anyone to go hungry, let alone to suffer from malnutrition or starve. The earth is there; the skills are there; the seed, the stock and all the tools and machinery could be made available within a few years.

Is there any risk of the other kind of demand? We are given the example of oil and how the members of OPEC have ganged up against the rest of the world. Could the suppliers of certain kinds of food do the same? The answer must be a resounding 'no'. We can list the foodstuffs that could possibly be controlled by a Third World cartel. They are cocoa, coffee, tea, rice, sugar and bananas. But what else? I doubt if any other items can be added to that short list, other than some exotic fruit which we could well do without. This brings home an essential fact about Third World agriculture to which I will return; it is that economic colonialism has, by fair means or foul, expropriated the greater part of the most productive land in the Third World, so that it yields crops mainly to be exported to the developed countries.

There was a time when these developing countries grew a variety of crops to provide for their own needs alone. Of course, there were famines that accompanied droughts, and there were other disasters that caused many people to go hungry or starve (as they do today). Yet the evidence indicates that some of these countries carried larger rural populations than they do now, especially in Africa. Their system of agriculture, although primitive, was able to produce a big enough range of goods to enable each country to be broadly self-sufficient.

Economic colonialism changed all that. Monoculture was introduced. If one country was better fitted to grow cocoa than bananas, then the Western planters so arranged it. Thus Ghana concentrated upon cocoa, Ceylon on tea, Brazil on coffee, Jamaica on sugar, and so on. The decisions were not taken by the farmers themselves, but by European or American-based companies that were established to set up the plantations. Control still rests, for the most part, with such companies. Are they likely to promote a cartel to deprive their fellow-Europeans or fellow-Americans of any of these foods?

One attempt has been made to emulate OPEC. In 1974 the five countries producing most of the bananas decided to set up the Union of Banana Exporting Countries. Their governments decided to impose on every box of bananas an export tax that varied from some 12 pence to 30 pence. The attempt was an almost total failure. The great corporations that effectively control the world market, such as United Brands, refused to pay the tax, threatened to abandon the plantations they owned or resorted to bribery to reduce the tax. The cartel, to all intents and purposes, soon came to an end. Three of the international banana corporations (United Brands, Castle & Cook and Del Monte) used the export tax, even when it was not paid, as an excuse to reduce their purchases, and at the same time increased their prices to the customers, so that their profits on each box of bananas increased from 10 pence to about 30 pence.

The banana countries having failed, it is unrealistic to expect those countries producing coffee, tea or any other foodstuff to succeed. Competition between them is intense, and the governments concerned cannot successfully impose a cartel without the co-operation of the plantation owners. Moreover, they know that the risk of failure is all the greater because they are trading, not in foods that are essential to the needs of the West, but in luxuries to which there is always an alternative.

Now let us look at the third element in the argument – that we cannot rely upon other countries to give us preference in the future. Let us briefly imagine that some disaster overtook the UK, making it impossible to grow any food at all, or that the UK decided that as from a certain date, say three or four years from now, no food at all would be produced on our islands – no milk, no potatoes, no meat, no vegetables, no eggs, no butter or cheese, no fruit of any kind. At the same time it was also announced that our ports would be opened to any ship bringing in food and that all tariffs, levies, quotas and all the other restrictions on the import of food were to be abolished. Would we go hungry?

We can imagine how the news would be received among the farmers and food manufacturers of the world. It would be a sensation. In all those countries like Argentina, Australia, New Zealand, South Africa, Brazil and Canada the exporters would look across to us, as they used to do, and once again study our market. They would conclude that Britain is the most perfect market for the export of food. It has everything they want. In the first place, its people are among the most prosperous in the world. Everyone has a guaranteed income; even the unemployed, the sick and the disabled receive enough money from the state to enable them to buy a reasonable amount of food. Every one of its 55 million people would be purchasers; they would want food and they would be able to pay for it. They are very different from the hundreds of millions in other countries who want food but go hungry because they have no money to pay for it. This fact removes the first anxiety of the prospective exporter of food to us.

Next the exporter looks at the British market and finds that nine-tenths of the consumers live in or near large towns, that distribution to them all from the ports is cheap, speedy and efficient. Again how different from other countries, where the cost of distributing food to the consumer adds a disproportionate amount to the cost of the food itself. Then the food exporters in all those countries would see who would be doing the importing in the UK, and they would rub their hands with glee. More than half the food sold in Britain goes through supermarkets which have central buying agencies. A few days spent in London, in the offices of Tesco and Sainsbury, and the contract is signed. Now, this is not how they sell to other countries, where the retail markets may be in the hands of thousands of independent shopkeepers who may not be tied to any one importer or distributor.

All these are major tangible advantages to the exporters; but the greatest, most helpful and most positive advantage of all would be the knowledge that access to the market was assured. Whoever could supply the needs of the British people at the lowest cost would get the orders – this would be the signal that went out to them. The exporters of Argentina, Australia and the other countries could then accordingly go to the farmers and say to them, 'We have a market which is secure.' It would be the only market in the world – with the exception of Hong Kong – that was truly open, where no government would intervene arbitrarily and without warning exclude imports of food. There would be total security. Security of supply is important to the consumer, but security of demand is vital to producers. No one is going to produce food unless he is reasonably certain that it will be sold at the price that he can afford to sell it at. Where is the farmer who is willing to buy or rent land, purchase or hire his ploughs and tractors, then cultivate his land, sow his seed, nourish his crop and, months later, bring in his harvest, unless he has some security in his mind that his years of labour and his working capital will have their reward?

If the British people were to say to the food producers of the world, 'Our ports are open; provided you can grow your food more cheaply than our farmers, you will be assured of a market in the UK', we can be sure that they would respond, rather than lose such a market. It would be their sheer self-interest to do so. Then the UK could be sure that its people would have preference over all others. Greater security of supply than this is impossible to conceive.

Finally, there is the fourth element in the argument, namely that our own farmers and those in the EEC can be trusted to give us preference over other outlets. This is undoubtedly true if food prices are higher within the EEC than outside. As this is normally the case, and is likely to remain the position in the future, it is clear that our farmers will dispose of their produce on the home market. They have no other choice. But if a market outside the EEC offers them a higher price, we cannot be sure that their charitable sentiment will outweigh their own interest.

While export controls can always be introduced to make sure that their food stays here, the real weakness of this element of the argument is that it fails to recognize that farmers themselves do not make the ultimate decision as to how much food is grown. At least once in a generation both the UK and Western Europe suffer from a prolonged drought that may reduce cereal yields by 20 per cent or more. Some years ago, as noted already, sugar beet was affected by a disease that made much of the crop useless. The scourge of foot-and-mouth or BSE could devastate our home supplies of lamb or beef. These are the occasions when we are forced to turn to the world market; and the narrower it becomes, with other countries pursuing a policy of self-sufficiency, the higher the price we must pay for such imports.

Agriculture is, in fact, 'unplannable'. No group of high-powered officials can ordain how much food will be grown at home, no matter how large the battery of computers to assist them, nor how skilful they may be in marshalling their research, nor even how great their authority may be in ordering farmers what to do. Whatever their forecast, it will always be more than what is ideally desired, or less.

It might just be possible to base an autarkic, mercantilist policy upon a calculation of how many gas stoves, refrigerators or deep-freezes will be made and sold in any one year. To make a further calculation about the quantities of all the different kinds of food that will be put inside them, however, is far beyond the realm of possibility. The uncertainties for the consumer can be minimized only when he has access to supplies from every corner of the world.

FEEDING THE HUNGRY

There is no doubt that many millions of the human race do not have enough to eat, and a tragically large number die from malnutrition. Certain pressure groups, financed by international food companies, have persuaded many of us that this evil can be overcome only by the richer countries becoming self-sufficient. The argument is plausible enough, yet it is the very opposite of the truth.

The human race is not like one large family eating its meal together, where if one eats more than his fair share, others must have less. Were that the case, the argument would be incontrovertible. The real scarcity, however, is not of food but of people capable of buying the food that is available and could be made available. In a word, it is poverty that is the cause of hunger. This point has been made over and over again by the United Nations Food and Agriculture Organization, especially by Dr A. H. Boerma, its former director-general. Much of this poverty is the direct result of the selfish policies of the developed countries, as I show in Chapter 9, in the section on the Third World poor. Here we need to look at the basic question, do the resources exist that would allow the countries of the world, including the poor countries, to feed themselves?

Both the FAO and another United Nations agency, the World Health Organization, have published what they consider to be the nutritional requirements of the human race. Our age, sex, height and occupation and the climate we enjoy are obvious factors that vary our needs, and these have all been assessed in the tables they have prepared. They have also invented 'reference man'. He is aged 25, weighs 65 kilograms and spends eight hours in bed, eight at work and eight in non-occupational activities. While the amount of energy he exerts depends on numerous factors, assuming that his work and leisure engage him in moderate activity and the climate he lives in is neither excessively hot nor cold, such a man should have 3,000 calories a day. The world produces food at that rate for every man, woman and child in grain alone – that is, wheat, rice, maize, barley and oats.

One pound of grain provides not less than 1,500 calories, and in 1989 the world's grain harvest amounted to 1,870 million tonnes. Thus an equal distribution of these basic foodstuffs would ensure that the world's present population of 5,300 million would all have enough to eat. It must be admitted that most of us in the developed countries would recoil from such a dreary diet, but this takes no account of any of the other kinds of food that would also be available if we were all given equal rations, especially the enormous quantities of fish, fruits and vegetables that could also be produced. An equal distribution of all foodstuffs now available would provide nutrition in excess of what the world needs.

It will be noticed that I have not referred to eggs, meat,

milk, butter and cheese. Modern methods of producing these require the use of concentrated feeds for the livestock that produce them. No less than one-third of the world's grain goes into the mouths not of humans but of livestock to feed the relatively rich. Since the war it has become profitable for farmers not only in the UK but throughout Europe and the United States to feed intensively kept farm animals grain rather than the kinds of feed they were given for centuries, and to keep them in expensive buildings instead of yards and fields. These methods are only profitable because capital from other parts of these nations' economies has been diverted to agriculture by means of taxation. If governments remained neutral in this respect, the profitability of such farming methods would evaporate. Among the beneficiaries of this change would be many of the millions who now go hungry and whose suffering is a disgrace to humanity.

The lobbyists and log-rollers in Washington, London and Brussels who have done so much to persuade governments to support this policy insist that these intensive methods are essential. Further, they argue, the policy should be extended to the Third World, to meet the needs of some 6,000 million human mouths by the end of this century.

The truth is that no problem need arise, because, as matters now stand, less than one-half of the world's arable land is cultivated. The potential for increasing food production is still enormous – a finding confirmed in several studies carried out by the FAO and other agencies. One of the most detailed surveys was *The World Food Problem: A Report of the President's Science Advisory Committee* published in 1967 by the US Government Printing Office. This report showed that only about 44 per cent of the land potentially capable of growing arable crops was being cultivated. All the evidence shows that, despite more than two decades having passed, the percentage is still approximately the same, and the report's main conclusion is still valid.

According to the *Production Year Book* of the FAO, this planet of ours has a land surface of 33,750 million acres. More than 23,000 million of them are mountains, deserts or places where no vegetation can prosper except at inordinate cost. Another 5,000 million acres are forest which, if we are

Table 5 Land availability and use (million acres)

	Australia and NZ	North America	South America	Europe	Africa	USSR	Asia
Total area	2,030	5,210	4,330	1,180	7,460	5,520	6,760
Area available for arable crops	380	1,150	1,680	430	1,810	880	1,550
Area cultivated	40	590	190	380	390	560	1,280
Cultivated area as percentage of potential arable land	11	51	11	88	22	64	83

Data from: *Action for Development* (Voluntary Committee on Overseas Aid and Development, May 1975).

sensible, we will let remain. Not quite all the remainder is suitable for arable cropping; but making every reasonable allowance for setting aside the poorer-quality land (though it is the kind of land we have seen fit to grow wheat upon in Britain) there remains an area that is still vast. Christopher Robins, in a paper for War on Want in 1975, prepared a table from data obtained from the Voluntary Committee on Overseas Aid and Development – see Table 5 (above). I have compared the salient figures with those in the FAO *Production Year Book*, and though there have been some changes, they confirm the essential point made by Mr Robins, that the human race has all the land it needs to cultivate.

Europe, the table shows, makes considerable use of its arable land, and by now this use probably exceeds 88 per cent. Of course, this refers to Europe in the proper sense (twenty-five countries, not just the twelve in the EEC) and it gives us quite a good benchmark to judge what is happening in the other continents. Asia's 83 per cent is due largely to the remarkable achievement of China. There, despite its hundreds of millions, visitors confirm that no one seems to go hungry. The principles of farming followed are an example to other countries whose natural disadvantages are trifling compared with China's. A huge area of the country cannot be cultivated at all – in fact, most of it is unploughable – so to feed its massive population China has done almost the opposite of what others have been doing. The land itself is not nationalized; most of it belongs to the local communities, and each district or village owns its own land, with elected representatives managing the village estate. What does not belong to the local community is vested in individuals who are thus able to cultivate their own smallholdings. This means that every peasant (an honoured term in China) has a close and personal interest in making the land prosper.

Once, millions of Chinese might die in a single year from floods devastating huge areas or from a drought that might last a whole season through. These may be now a matter of history; rivers have been dammed by the work of hundreds of thousands, fetching and carrying stones and earth, and now an even flow of water never seems to fail them. The villages do not buy fertilizers or expensive machinery; they rely on low-cost methods at every stage of their year's work. Livestock are fed on food that costs nothing except the labour of bringing it to them, and much of it is in the form of human left-overs. Cereals, such as rice and wheat, are grown for human consumption; and these are fertilized by the livestock's manure, compost and anything else that can improve the soil, including human excreta. Herbicides, pesticides and fungicides appear to have no place; the hoe and the hook serve instead – they are cheap and find work for the many hands available. Besides, by adhering to rotations, as we used to do before the agrochemical industry entered the field, the Chinese have little need for weed and pest control.

To applaud Chinese methods of husbandry is not to imply that they should be imported into the West; but they deserve applause because they succeed, suiting the needs, resources and temperament of the Chinese people. That 317 million arable acres can be enough to feed 1,100 million people is, at least, an indication of what can be done. In terms of cost, Chinese farming is low-input farming; it is also very efficient indeed, if efficiency is about doing a job in a competent and cost-effective manner.

Less successful is the USSR, where according to the table

only 64 per cent of the arable land is cultivated – eloquent testimony to the ineptitude of decades of central control. Even Russia, however, is able to make better use of its land than Africa and South America, two continents where terrible hunger is to be found.

In Africa as a whole, only 22 per cent of arable land is cultivated, and the situation in its hungriest countries is even worse. At the World Food Conference in 1974, held under the auspices of the FAO, the Sudanese Minister of Agriculture stated that only one-tenth of his country's arable land was being farmed; the proportion remains about the same today, despite the hunger of many thousands living in Sudan. Throughout most of the African continent a similar story could be told. Nigeria and Tanzania are making determined attempts to raise their production of cereals and have a great deal of excellent land for the purpose. Zaïre, however, has perhaps the greatest potential, with an incalculable acreage capable of producing food, yet a population with one of the worst dietary standards. Even an approximate estimate of the percentage of untilled land in Zaïre is difficult, such is the state of that country and its people. It is likely to be over 90 per cent, and most Zaïrans fail to have one proper meal in the course of the day.

South America possesses 16 per cent of the world's arable land; it possesses also millions of people who, though they may not starve to death as many do in other parts of the world, suffer acutely from malnutrition. They eat the wrong kind of food, to some extent because too much of their farming is orientated towards cash crops for export, and an excess of bananas, coffee or sugar makes for a doubtful diet. Still more importantly, the South Americans cultivate only 11 per cent of their arable land. In Colombia more than half of the good farmland lies idle, and in Chile, Uruguay, Argentina and Brazil millions of cultivable acres are no longer farmed.

The world's population is, of course, increasing. But let us ask ourselves why this should be so. Susan George and others have done much to establish the link between poverty and large families. A succession of children (preferably sons) are believed to provide security in sickness and old age in a society where state benefits and social security are unknown. The poorer you are in a poor country, the more children you want to bring into the world. In the other direction, one cannot establish any necessary connection between a high density of population and hunger, as numerous countries such as Belgium, the Netherlands and the UK can show. Zaïre is the opposite extreme.

In all, the FAO *Production Year Book* tells us, we have 3,500 milion acres of the world being cultivated; and this represents about seven-tenths of an acre per head of the population. Without much difficulty and without doing any ecological damage, we could make it an acre and a quarter. In the UK there are some 21 million arable acres, yielding half the food eaten by 55 million people. True, the comparison is not altogether fair, as it excludes our pasture used for sheep and cattle; on the other hand, we can afford to be very extravagant in how we produce our food – most of our cereals, for example, going to feed our livestock. An acre and a quarter should be enough for the grossest feeder wherever he may live in the world.

Two further points can be made to rebut the argument that the plight of the starving millions requires us to curb imports of food into the UK. The first is that different methods of husbandry could transform the world's consumption of food. One-third of all the grain produced goes, as noted, into meat, eggs and dairy products. Little is so used in China.

The other point that the protagonists of extreme protection overlook is that the fertility of our land, and thus the quantities it will yield, is neither static nor permanent. Fertility will improve immeasurably through the right methods of use and cultivation. Two centuries or so ago most of Europe consisted of poor-quality land; now it is much improved. The land in Japan was generally inferior to that of India; today the reverse is the case, and Japan's yields, having been less than India's, are now five times greater. Good farming can work miracles.

The conclusion seems irresistible. There is no reason to be filled with neo-Malthusian gloom about the world's population outpacing the capacity of the land to supply its needs.

Experts are agreed that virtually every country in the world, apart from such obvious exceptions as Hong Kong, is physically capable of being self-sufficient in food; and this includes the UK. Some countries could feed many more than their own populations.

THE STRATEGIC ARGUMENT

After the Second World War a favourite argument for supporting agriculture was the strategic need for the UK to grow a substantial proportion of its own food lest another war occurred. This was used to underpin the Agriculture Act of 1947 and it still lingers on – although it tends to be mentioned rather hastily, as if it no longer stood up to scrutiny.

During the war the fifty million people on our island fortress ate very much better than either our enemies or those they subjugated in Europe. It should have been the opposite; continental Europe being almost self-sufficient before the war and France always an exporter, the problem of feeding those millions should have been much easier. The bravery of the Merchant Navy is one part of the answer. Another is that we began the war with a massive merchant fleet that existed because of the trade we carried on with so many countries across the seas. Our policy of free trade gave us that fleet; because of it, the UK was able to survive, despite the appalling number of ships sunk by enemy action.

While it is true that food supplies can be cut off by blackmailing producers as well as by an enemy navy, it would be churlish to see our particular suppliers as being prone to blackmail. The producers of Australia, New Zealand, Canada and the United States were steadfastly loyal to us during both world wars, and they would fill the main gap if we reverted to a liberal policy of importing food.

Those who insinuate that blackmail is a danger fail to see that, even if successful, it would achieve little for the offenders. The blackmail, presumably, would take the form of demanding an inordinately high price for the continued export to us of the food we needed. Our succumbing to the threat would have the effect of putting into the hands of the blackmailers a larger quantity of our currency, all of which would remain in the UK where it would have to be spent.

The strategic argument for protection really rests on the assumption that a future war will not be a sudden nuclear holocaust, but a conflict that might be extended over a year or more. It is argued that in such circumstances a strong agriculture capable of providing most of our country's needs should be part of our plans for national defence.

Again it is useful to draw on our memory of what happened in 1939. In that year we in Britain produced only about a quarter of the food we ate, and only a small part of our cereals. Most of our farmland was under grass, and in the war years that followed, millions of acres of that pasture – the equivalent of several counties – were ploughed up for the first time for generations. The resulting yields were quite remarkable. Very little in the way of artificial fertilizer was applied, and there was not much farmyard manure to go round. The quality of seeds was mediocre, and the skills of the farmers and farm workers, who were more accustomed to livestock than to arable farming, were not as good as they are today. None the less, those millions of acres produced some marvellous crops. The reason was that grass stores up fertility, and for all the years that land was under grass it had stored up in the soil a great bank of fertility.

Much of the land reverted to pasture immediately after the war, but in recent years the high prices that have been paid for cereals have caused it to return to the plough. The green bank of fertility has gone. Come another war, it would not be possible to repeat the great achievement of 1939–45. In fact, in the event of another war, much of the expansion of British agriculture could not be sustained, and over a wide area there would be a cut-back in agricultural production. The reason for this is that, to a dangerous degree, our present level of production has been made possible by increasing inputs that are imported from abroad and cannot be obtained from our own natural resources.

In 1939 the cart-horse was still the main source of power on many of our farms. Now it is exclusively the tractor, and unlike earlier and lighter models, the modern tractor, like the modern combine, uses an inordinate amount of fuel.

Imported fertilizers have doubled the stocking rate for many a dairy herd and enabled herds of beef cattle and flocks of sheep to graze land which would otherwise be incapable of supporting such numbers. Modern feedstuffs include protein additives of soya bean or fishmeal, both of which come from across the sea. A major decision would have to be made if the UK were plunged into another war. Would it be right to endanger our already diminished merchant fleet, and to put in peril the lives of our seamen, to bring to this country the necessary oil, fertilizers and protein, so that British farmers could go on producing the kind of food they do now, and in the way that they do? Or should our farmers adapt their methods of production to the need to save British ships and British lives?

Our modern and efficient farmers – efficient in the sense that the word is used about agriculture today – are not equipped to carry on in a siege economy. Anyone doubting this should visit a large dairy farm where a herd of more than 100 cows may flourish on perhaps as many acres. Remove imports of oil, fertilizers and protein, and the farm would be lucky to keep half that herd.

So the strategic argument is not a valid one. Indeed, it is really a counter-argument. It can be stood on its head and shown to be a reason why we should return to the conditions before the war which enabled us to eat so much better than our enemies.

THE BALANCE-OF-PAYMENTS MYTH

Another reason advanced for giving support to agriculture is the balance of payments. Agriculture, we are told, could save Britain another £1,000 million on the balance of payments; and we are further assured by the NFU and others that 'agriculture is the UK's biggest import saver'. The premise of the argument is that imports are 'bad' and exports 'good'. This is a fable that has blighted our economic thinking ever since the end of the war. Succesive governments have exhorted business men to export, have set up agencies to underwrite the losses, converted half the Diplomatic Service into supernumerary salesmen and even gone so far as to give loans to foreigners at derisory rates of interest to persuade them to buy our exports. While exporters are given knighthoods, importers are made to feel distinctly inferior and perhaps a little lacking in patriotism when they are told by their bank managers that *their* borrowing must be reduced.

The other countries that themselves have an adverse trade balance with us are the ones that used to supply us with food. Because of the deteriorating terms of trade, some of them have put up serious obstacles to our exports. Many of our business men have found it so difficult to export to them that they have given up the effort. Their consumers have lost the opportunity to choose a British-made article, and the British industrialist has lost a market that was once freely accessible. The converse is equally true. The British people no longer eat beef, butter and cheese from Australia and cannot eat as much lamb, butter and cheese from New Zealand as formerly. This is because Australian producers have entirely lost the outlet they used to have in the UK, and New Zealand producers have lost most of theirs.

The balance of payments, which is something of a nation's virility symbol, is made up of two accounts, the current and the capital. The current concerns the exports and imports, both visible and invisible. Into this account go all the payments for visible and tangible items that are imported or exported, such as cars, television sets and other manufactured goods, together with food; also the 'invisibles' which are payments for services such as banking, insurance and shipping. The total value of the UK's visible and invisible exports, amounting to some £20,000 million in a year, is never likely to equal precisely the total value of visible and invisible imports. It is matched by a counteracting surplus or deficit in the capital account. When the UK has a balance of payments deficit in the current account, it has a surplus in the capital account – and each sum is exactly the same because the two accounts must balance.

Pound notes are intrinsically useless pieces of paper. Their value exists as a means of exchange in the UK; once out of this country, they can still, sometimes with difficulty, be exchanged, but they remain valueless unless they can be returned here. Thus pound notes do not in practice leave these shores. If an exporter to the UK is paid in pound notes, they stay here and are spent by him in this country. However, virtually all imports are paid for in the currency of the exporter's own country; and in the world of today the necessary currency is bought in the foreign exchange market.

It is this institution, hectic but fascinating, that makes trade multilateral and not bilateral as it used to be. It no longer matters (even if it ever did) for one country to have an adverse 'balance' with another. Great concern is expressed at the way we import more from Japan than Japan imports from us, and the Japanese are criticized for not taking steps to restrict their exports or to increase imports from us. In fact, Japan imports from Britain almost as much as it exports to us. None the less the Japanese have been warned that failure to change their policy will invite retaliation. A moral obligation is invoked, as if some code of international ethics existed which prevailed over the simple proposition that a willing seller and a willing buyer should be allowed to do business together.

People who think like this – and they are in high places – do not seem to understand how the foreign exchange market operates. The Japanese television set is sold for pound notes to a British customer. The retailer, wholesaler and importer trade in pound notes, as of course they must when the transaction takes place in this country. The Japanese exporter, however, needs to be paid in yen, so the British importer arranges with his bank the purchase of sufficient yen to pay for the imported television sets. The bank's representative buys the yen in the London foreign exchange market from a dealer who may have bought as a result of a transaction that has taken place thousands of miles away in a different currency. The currencies themselves never have any cause to leave their country of origin. Sterling, dollars, francs, yen, pesetas, marks and dozens of other currencies are being bought and sold every day in the foreign exchange market. The more a country trades with others, the more its currency is in demand. Obviously, if a country exports, visibly and invisibly, more than it imports, the demand for its currency will exceed supply, and this will cause its value to go up in the foreign exchange market. Whether the increase in value will be reflected in a higher rate of exchange must depend upon the currency's freedom to float.

When there is a fixed rate of exchange a government has to enter the foreign exchange market by borrowing in other currencies if it is a net importer or lending its own currency if a net exporter. But a government that allows its currency to float freely imposes a system of import control that is the most natural and effective form of protection. Indeed, it is a perfect one. When the country imports more than it exports, its currrency is automatically devalued; and the more the currency falls in value, the dearer its imports become, thus making its own products more competitive in the domestic market. At the same time they become more competitive in the world market, since less of the country's currency must be purchased in the foreign exchange market in order to buy them. The converse is, of course, the case when a country's exports exceed its imports. The impersonal forces at work in the foreign exchanges make sure that the cost of importing its goods goes up.

Canada can supply the UK with as much wheat as we would wish to have. That we would pay in Canadian dollars does not make it necessary for us to acquire the same amount of dollars by exporting to Canada goods that the Canadians might buy from us. If Canada could send us wheat cheaper than any other country, it would be to our advantage to buy it, regardless of whether Canada imported anything from us.

The simple analogy is to be found in our everyday lives. To buy a joint of beef from the butcher, we do not inquire whether he will engage our services or purchase whatever we may make in the course of our occupation. We buy his joint of beef because it is the cheapest or because his shop is the most convenient or because a neighbour recommended his meat. Trade across frontiers is carried on in precisely the same way. Just as we may buy all our meat from the butcher of our choice, regardless of whether he buys anything from us, so it matters not how much or how little another particular country buys from us. What does matter is that we should be able to buy our needs in the cheapest market.

That is just what we cannot do when our trade policies are bedevilled by the balance-of-payments argument.

Any country that unilaterally declares a free trade policy and brings down all tariffs and other barriers to imports, irrespective of whether other countries reciprocate, takes an immense stride forward towards its own prosperity. Wealth in the real sense – that is, goods, not cash in the modern form of intrinsically worthless pieces of paper – will pour in, and the people of that country will be set free to buy whatever they prefer. The country that permits its people more of this freedom than any other is Hong Kong. A country of scarcely any natural resources, densely and dangerously overpopulated, producing only a fraction of its own food, Hong Kong nevertheless succeeds in affording its people a level of prosperity that is the envy of the East.

To assert that free traders are against any import controls and that they are willing to see their country's industries unprotected is a mistake. They believe that just one kind of protection is necessary: an exchange rate that is allowed to float up and down without any interference by the government or central bank. The floating exchange rate is a mechanism that regulates the flow of imports and exports in the cheapest way possible and to a degree that each individual industry deserves.

Paper money cannot be eaten; it cannot be worn or provide shelter or energy. It has but one use: to be a means of buying something in the land where it belongs. Every pound sterling 'lost' in the so-called balance of payments is a pound spent, sooner or later, in this country. It will go towards paying for one of our exports or for some capital investment here. It must be spent in Britain. The greater our deficit on the current or trading account in our balance of payments, the greater must the surplus be in the capital entering the country.

A sensible government need never worry about the balance of payments, still less bother the people with the topic. It allows its currency to float cleanly – that is, without interfering by spending taxpayers' money in the foreign exchange market. Thus is provided a self-regulating mechanism that automatically corrects the volume of the country's exports and imports. The harder the population work, the more efficient and inventive they are, the greater the volume of imports the mechanism will permit. And imports, let it be emphasized, consist of wealth entering the country to raise people's standard of living. The converse follows; the less industrious and efficient the population are, the more the same mechanism will require them to export – to lose wealth. Those who argue that we must not import food from abroad because of the balance of payments fail to see this difference between wealth in the true sense and paper money.

These, then, are the standard arguments that have been used in the UK to justify government interference in agriculture, in pursuit of greater output at almost any cost. They are all fallacious. The further argument, that our farmers need protection and that, though so many of them have been forced off the land under the present system, without it their case would have been even worse, was examined and dis-proved in Chapter 5.

· 8 ·

WHAT IT ALL COSTS

The cost to the United Kingdom of its present policy of agricultural protection is so huge that most people, confronted by the figures, simply refuse to believe them. For many years, the NFU and the Ministry of Agriculture have tried to persuade us that we are better off – and certainly better fed – than we would have been under free trade. The true facts are very different.

A government can favour one sector of the economy only by taking wealth away from other sectors. For the consumer, this means that he must be induced to buy things he would not have bought of his own free will at their true cost of production. For the economy as a whole, it means distortion: the bleeding of resources away from activities that could have used them more profitably. We are all made worse off, and the results are cumulative. The longer the distortions persist, the more other industries are held back.

THE PRICE OF A LAME DUCK

As a farmer, and one who strongly sympathizes with farmers, I hate to admit this, but the straight fact is that British agriculture, once a symbol of rugged independence, is now far more of a charge on the state than any of the great loss-making industries of the recent past, such as the shipyards, docks and car factories. Agriculture is the biggest lame duck of all.

There is sometimes a case for subsidizing domestic industries, but it is a social not an economic one. Money can, and should, be spent on preserving rural Britain, but this should not be confused with profitable farming. Whatever our aims are, we should pursue them honestly with a full knowledge of the facts; so the first thing is to see what the facts are.

One obvious measure of the support received by agriculture is the proportion of farmers' incomes provided by subsidies of one kind or another. We saw in Chapter 5 that by no means all the money poured into agriculture by the government ends up in the farmers' pockets, and that as time goes by the process is becoming more inefficient in that way. Even so, the amount that does get through to them is staggering.

Table 6 (p. 179) shows how dependent upon subsidies British farmers have been since we adopted the Common Agricultural Policy. The first column shows total farming income as measured by the Ministry of Agriculture; the second sets out the total of the various subsidies and other forms of support given to British farmers; and the third column represents the support as a percentage of farming income.

It is important to note that the figures in the middle column of Table 6 do not consist of the principal kind of support given to farmers in the form of import levies and duties. The net figure is given in the table because the refunds from the EEC are paid for out of the revenue it receives from these import levies and duties.

Table 6 therefore tells only part of the truth. The true cost of supporting agriculture in the UK is considerably more than the table indicates. When butter is sold to the Soviet Union for 3 pence a pound, the export subsidy does not of course go directly to the farmer. Yet the cost of getting rid of the surpluses to countries outside the EEC has run into many thousands of millions of pounds. Consumers not only lose the benefit of buying butter, wheat, wine, citrus fruits and numerous other items at lower prices, but are required to pay prices made artificially higher by levies and duties. A substantial part of the VAT receipts that are passed over to Brussels also go to pay for the operation of the CAP.

When, in the early 1980s, I first published figures showing

Table 6   Agricultural support in the UK since 1973–4

	Farmers' net income (£ million)	Cost of agriculture support (£ million)	Support as a percentage of income
1973–4	1,283	392	30.5
1974–5	1,263	488	38.6
1975–6	1,676	306	18.3
1976–7	1,751	378	21.6
1977–8	1,301	460	35.4
1978–9	1,263	538	42.6
1979–80	1,145	677	59.1
1980–1	1,162	1,012	87.1
1981–2	1,368	972	71.0
1982–3	1,817	1,432	78.8
1983–4	1,508	1,728	114.6
1984–5	2,033	1,714	84.3
1985–6	1,160	2,215	190.9
1986–7	1,557	1,449	93.1
1987–8	1,623	1,630	100.4
1988–9	1,240	1,380	111.3
1989–90	1,441	1,255	87.1

Data from: *Annual Review of Agriculture* and *Agriculture in the UK*.

how agricultural support had worked during the first ten years of Britain's participation in the Common Agricultural Policy, the table was denounced as 'fiction' (by the NFU), 'a libel upon farmers' (by the Country Landowners' Association) and 'farmer-bashing' (by the editor of *Farmers' Weekly*). The figures showed British farmers – for so long hailed as the epitome of efficiency – as having 166 per cent of their income coming from the taxpayer in 1980–1; that is, taxpayers were paying out to farmers, in one form of subsidy or another, 66 per cent more than farmers' incomes. Treasury officials could not believe that they had been taken for such a ride for so long, but eventually the awful truth was accepted.

The same trend has continued throughout the 1980s. The Organization for Economic Co-operation and Development, with its access to impeccable sources and to statistics beyond suspicion, calculates that British people paid £7,500 million more for their food in 1988 than would have been the case had they been allowed to buy it outside the Common Market. To this form of protection we must add £1,255 million, which is the figure given in *Agriculture in the UK 1989* for the amount received by British farmers from the taxpayer either directly from Whitehall or via Brussels. This gives a combined total of £8,755 million – which, no senior wrangler is required to tell us, represents a greater percentage of farmers' incomes – £1,225 in 1988 – than it did at the start of the 1980s. The percentage 166 per cent has become 700 per cent. For every £1 the farmer and his wife have by way of income, then, the taxpayer, directly (through subsidies) or indirectly (through higher shop prices), provides £7.

The UK Treasury now estimates that the true cost of supporting agriculture is £16 a week for the average family. The same figure was given by the Prime Minister in July 1990 at the Houston summit on world trade. For the British people this is some £250 million a week or, in round figures, £12,500 million a year. It is more than we spend on teachers, doctors or the police.

The OECD has recently produced a table to show how much money some of the food-producing countries give to their farmers over and above the market price for their produce – see Table 7 (p. 181). Readers may have some difficulty in believing these figures. They portray agriculture in the European Community as a lame duck so hideously crippled that its neck ought to be wrung as speedily as the deed can be done. Neither New Zealand nor Australia subsidize their farmers to any significant degree. In Australia, having rid themselves of price support, the National Farmers' Federation have declard their objective to oppose the principle of subsidies. New Zealand farmers, now totally unsupported, show no inclination to return to the old system. In their case, the New Zealand government swept away the support system virtually overnight. The price of land was halved; dairy farmers now find themselves some 40 per cent better off than they were; and beef and sheep farmers are 20 per cent better off. Those who borrowed excessively or were not all that good at farming (often the same) have gone to

Table 7   Total transfers associated with agricultural policies (US $ billion)

	Transfers from taxpayers (1)				Transfers from consumers (2)				Budget revenues (3)				Total transfers (1)+(2)-(3)			
	1986	1987	1988	1989	1986	1987	1988	1989	1986	1987	1988	1989	1986	1987	1988	1989
Australia	0.4	0.3	0.2	0.3	0.5	0.4	0.4	0.4	0.0	0.0	0.0	0.0	0.9	0.7	0.6	0.6
Austria	0.4	0.5	0.6	1.1	2.2	3.0	2.7	2.2	0.0	0.0	0.0	0.0	2.6	3.5	3.2	3.3
Canada	4.4	5.7	5.7	4.2	3.6	3.6	3.6	3.1	0.1	0.1	0.1	0.1	7.9	9.2	8.6	7.2
EEC	31.7	38.2	45.8	44.1	71.9	78.3	63.7	54.1	0.7	0.7	0.7	0.7	102.9	115.9	108.8	97.5
Finland	1.3	1.6	1.8	1.7	3.5	4.0	4.4	4.3	0.1	0.4	0.2	0.1	4.8	5.3	6.0	6.0
Japan	13.9	18.4	18.7	15.6	48.8	55.3	60.8	52.5	8.6	10.4	13.7	10.2	54.1	63.3	65.9	57.8
New Zealand	0.9	0.1	0.1	0.0	0.1	0.1	0.1	0.1	0.0	0.0	0.0	0.0	0.9	0.1	0.2	0.1
Norway	1.5	1.8	1.8	1.8	1.4	1.8	1.8	1.6	0.2	0.2	0.3	0.2	2.7	3.3	3.4	3.3
Sweden	0.5	0.5	0.5	0.4	3.2	3.5	3.3	2.9	0.1	0.3	0.2	0.1	3.5	3.8	3.6	3.2
Switzerland	1.1	1.4	1.5	1.3	3.8	4.9	5.2	4.3	0.6	0.8	0.9	0.6	4.3	5.5	5.8	4.9
United States	59.4	50.3	49.1	46.3	29.6	30.4	26.0	21.6	0.9	0.7	0.8	0.7	88.1	80.0	74.3	67.2
Total	115.5	118.7	125.2	116.9	168.5	185.3	172.0	146.9	11.2	13.6	16.8	12.7	272.8	290.4	280.4	251.1

Source: OECD, *Agricultural Policies, Markets and Trade* (Paris, 1990).

the wall. The great majority who have survived the trauma of change are entitled to claim that, if one is competent at one's job and able to satisfy the customer, support is dispensable. Of course, there is one proviso; countries such as Australia and New Zealand depend greatly upon fair terms of trade in the export market. When the EEC subsidizes its sale of cheese to Japan, for example, with the intention of underpricing the lowest-cost producer of cheese in the world – which is New Zealand – it is scarcely possible for New Zealand's dairy farmers to compete.

The year 1984 was the high point of the EEC subsidy system. Various controls on production began then, and 1984 also marked the end of Peter Walker's influence on agriculture in the UK; no minister before or since has been so addicted to the belief that the giving away of public money has a benign effect upon agriculture, regardless it seems of how the money is spent. In that watershed year of 1984 I compiled two tables: the first showing total price support for agriculture in the UK in the post-war period – Table 8 (p. 183) – and the second showing the consequent rise in land values – Table 9 (p. 185).

Table 8 sets out how much money the British taxpayer gave to agriculture from the fiscal year 1955–6 to that of 1982–3 for the purpose of supporting prices. The left-hand column of figures states the cost of price support in terms current for the fiscal year in question. These figures are meaningless in conditions of inflation, so the right-hand column sets out the cost to the taxpayer as measured in 1984 terms (the year I compiled the table). These figures, it must be emphasized, do not reveal the full cost of supporting agriculture. They leave out the thousands of millions of pounds of other money given to agriculture in the way of subsidies, production grants, advisory services and tax allowances. They relate purely to price support.

Stated in 1984 terms, the cost from 1955 to 1983 comes to a total of £50,697 million. Before 1955 the cost of food subsidies given to the consumer was subsumed in the cost of price support to the farmer. To disentangle the two with precision is not feasible, but it is reasonable to assume that the cost of price support for the previous years was broadly

Table 8   UK expenditure on price support for agriculture, 1955–83

	Cost in current prices (£ million)	Cost in terms of 1984 prices (£ million)
1955–6	206	1,696
1956–7	239	1,863
1957–8	284	2,124
1958–9	241	1,750
1959–60	257	1,846
1960–1	263	1,852
1961–2	343	2,336
1962–3	310	2,048
1963–4	295	1,903
1964–5	264	1,631
1965–6	238	1,405
1966–7	229	1,296
1967–8	261	1,436
1968–9	265	1,390
1969–70	268	1,335
1970–1	256	1,179
1971–2	411	1,731
1972–3	395	1,542
1973–4	289	1,051
1974–5	398	1,214
1975–6	703	1,706
1976–7	739	1,584
1977–8	1,061	1,999
1978–9	1,329	2,268
1979–80	1,500	2,191
1980–1	1,928	2,372
1981–2	2,500	2,799
1982–3	3,000	3,150

in line with what it was for 1955–6. The cost in current terms for that year was £206 million and in 1984 terms £1,696 million. To assume £1,500 million for each of those years must be fair. To find the cost to the taxpayer from 1947, when price support began, to 1983 we therefore add £12,000 million to our previous total, to make £62,697 million.

Divided among 220,000 post-war farmers, £62,697 million would provide £285,000 for each of them. But as we saw in Chapter 5, many farmers have not received this kind of support; indeed, they have had to pay for it. So for those who have been the benficiaries, the average must be raised still higher. (Of course, there were once more than twice as many farmers as there are today – a fact which shows the failure of price support – but in counting the cost of the system it is only sensible to divide it among those who survived with its help.)

In 1946, the last year before the system of price support began, total farm incomes were £220 million. Since then the pound has fallen to less than one-fifteenth of its earlier value; so farm incomes should now be over £3,300 million to maintain their value. *Agriculture in the UK 1990* stated that they were £1,441 million. The basis of the calculation has changed somewhat over the intervening years, but making every possible allowance for this there remains a considerable fall. British farm incomes are now half of what they were before we began spending thousands of millions of pounds to support them. If those farmers who have survived are better off, it is only because half of them have *not* survived.

THE MISUSE OF LAND

So where has our money gone? One explanation is that it has been lost in the sheer state of inefficiency of modern agriculture. Farmers are goaded into producing at high cost a great deal of food which cannot be sold at an economic price because the customer has not enough money to pay for it. Obviously there is some truth in this, for the pattern of food consumption has changed remarkably; yet this cannot be the complete explanation when the price support is now in the form of import levies which are passed on to the consumer to pay. We must look elsewhere.

As farmers have not had their incomes raised, this vast sum of money must have gone in some other direction. One clue came to me when I discussed with my constituents their difficulties. The tenant farmer with less than 60 acres – of whom there used to be many fifteen or twenty years ago –

Table 9   UK agricultural land values, 1939 and 1984

	Acres	1939 value per acre × 15	1984 value per acre	Excess value per acre
Grade I	1,263,628	£750	£3,500	£2,750
Grade II	6,588,921	£600	£3,000	£2,400
Grade III	22,068,374	£405	£1,800	£1,395
Grade IV	8,890,531	£150	£1,200	£1,050
Grade V	6,318,144	£ 75	£ 900	£ 825

seems to be in a markedly different position to an owner-occupier with the same size and type of farm. Agricultural rents have been rising steeply, and the very rich land in my constituency can fetch over £100 an acre a year. The owner-occupier, once he has paid off his mortgage, finds himself placed quite differently, his asset steadily increasing in value. The gap between the two grows wider each year. Could it be that this money given by the taxpayer has gone into inflating land values?

In 1984 I compiled a table to show how the value of agricultural land rose in the first ten years after we adopted the Common Agricultural Policy, over and above the rate of inflation – Table 9. To obtain an accurate picture, I divided the land into its five official grades, then with advice from agricultural valuers who practised before the war I put down the average value of each grade in 1939. Assuming that the pound had fallen to one-fifteenth of its pre-war value then (1984), I multiplied that estimate by 15, so the second column states what the value of our agricultural land would have been by 1984 if it had risen according to the rate of inflation since 1939. (I took 1939, rather than 1946, as the base year since there were obvious distortions of the price mechanism during the war). Next, with the aid of valuers then practising, I calculated the actual value in 1984. The last column in the table shows the 'excess value per acre': the difference between the value of our farmland in 1984 and the 1939 value when brought up to 1984 terms.

Now let us calculate the excess value of each grade reached

by 1984 by multiplying the excess value of each acre by the number of acres per grade. The following is the result:

Grade I	£ 3,474.98 million
Grade II	£15,813.41 million
Grade III	£30,785.38 million
Grade IV	£ 9,335.06 million
Grade V	£ 5,212.46 million

Adding up those five together we reach a total of £64,621 million, virtually the same as the amount of money given away in subsidies and price support by 1984 (see Table 8). Well, now, is that a coincidence? People with money to invest will look for places to put it where the return is highest. If a government is foolish enough to spend taxpayers' money to raise the return on one kind of asset rather than another, it is natural for investors to take advantage of the folly by investing in that kind of asset, and as they compete to get hold of it, inevitably its price is pushed up.

The price of farmland went up in a similar way under the Corn Laws. The more the government raised the duty on imported wheat, the more farm rents rose to wipe out the advantages of the higher price of corn. What happened then and is being repeated today suggests an economic law: when the state artificially raises the value of a product, the benefit to the producer's income is nullified by an increase in the value of the asset that yields the product. It follows that a farmer who is a tenant receives no benefit from protectionism in the short term; a farmer who owns his own land, however, will benefit from his asset's appreciation in value.

What has happened since 1984? The price of farmland continued to increase for a further few years until total 'excess value' reached about £70,000 million. Production having thus been artificially stimulated by the EEC Council of Ministers, bringing the Community to a state of technical bankruptcy, steps had to be taken to reduce output. The price of land then went into decline.

THE MISUSE OF CAPITAL

As well as raising the price of land, to the benefit of landowners and the detriment of farmers, the drive to invest in land has been part of a general distortion of the UK economy – the diversion of capital away from efficient business into a loss-making agriculture. This is a serious matter, since we in Britain badly need all the capital we can raise to modernize our outdated industries and build up our infrastruture. To waste capital in unproductive ways is to impoverish ourselves without making anyone else richer. It reduces our ability to care for the needy and to protect our environment.

By any test the diversion of capital to agriculture by the government is enormous, even if there is difficulty in assessing how great is the enormity. And there can be no doubt that the diversion of capital must be from other branches of our trade or industry or services, which would have been able to hold on to their capital but for interference by the government.

Although ministry figures show that the total of grants and subsidies received by British farmers since 1956 comes to thousands of millions of pounds, this is not the full cost to the taxpayer of supporting agriculture. We must also take into account the expenditure incurred by the Ministry of Agriculture in administering the subsidies. In terms of expenditure and staff, the ministry has been one of our largest government departments in the post-war era. It has steadily increased the amount of public money it has spent. In 1938, at a time when the UK had twice as many farms as today, when 950,000 people were employed on the land and when agriculture, especially in the livestock sector, was expanding rapidly and profitably, gross expenditure by the Ministry of Agriculture and Fisheries was a mere £3,985,654 – £8 per farmer! In 1991 terms this gross expenditure would be £120 million.

Looking at the 1990–1 estimates for the Ministry of Agriculture we see that Parliament has approved the sum of £874 million for its expenditure after deducting receipts from Brussels. Taking out items not attributable to agriculture, such as help for forestry and fisheries, this is a sixfold increase over 1938 in real terms. Yet this does not include the main support which agriculture receives from the operation of import duties and import levies under the Common Agricultural Policy. Nor does it take into account numerous other kinds of financial assistance given to agriculture. As the number of farms decreases and their size increases, they seem to need an ever greater degree of support. This is contrary to what we have been led to believe about the necessity of making farms 'viable' with public money.

In looking through the government estimates, one finds many benefits going to agriculture, other than in cash, which none the less cost money to provide. They all have one common denominator: money spent to induce farmers and growers, in one way or another, to increase their production. They can be described as short-term benefits with long-term disadvantages. Perhaps the most important is the Agricultural Development Advisory Service (ADAS). Although the farmer now makes a contribution towards the benefit he receives, ADAS's services will still cost the taxpayer £138 million for 1990–1. Members of its staff are, in effect, the business and technical consultants to any farmer who wants advice; and there are about 4,700 of them. It is noteworthy that there are only a very few consultants in private practice, despite agriculture being an industry whose methods are constantly changing and one in which the expertise demanded of most farmers increases year by year. Why pay a £500 fee when you can get the services of a consultant heavily subsidized by the taxpayer – as well as being supported by a massive team of research workers? ADAS is, in fact, a nationalized service: the nationalization of the agricultural consultant's profession.

Agricultural research paid for by the ministry is another large item. It now costs about £120 million a year. Every facet of conventional agriculture comes within this ambit, and some notable advances have been made in animal health, plant breeding and other fields. The results are made available to the farmer through ADAS and the farming press. No other industry in the country is supported by so much free research (free to the customer, that is).

Much of the research is undertaken at British universities, so some of the cost is borne by another set of estimates, those of the Department of Education and Science. It is quite impossible to disentangle from the education estimates just how much goes indirectly into supporting agriculture, but sixteen of our universities own or rent farms for purposes other than investment. These farms add up to more than 13,000 acres and must be worth not less than £30 million.

There are also other government-funded bodies such as the Agricultural Training Board. But far more important are the tax advantages that have gradually been made available to farmers. Such advantages do not fall to all of them, but to certain categories – none more so than those who own their land or farm on a large scale.

Until recently none of this money was spent upon organic farming. Still vivid in my mind is a visit I paid with a most distinguished dean of an agricultural faculty to the Minister of Agriculture. We tried to convince him that a modest grant of £20,000, even £10,000, would enable the university farm to embark upon a particular form of research into the organic growing of wheat. He was not to be persuaded, nor were the officials sitting beside him (whose faces were a study in cynicism). They were unmoved by our plea that the demand for organically produced food was likely to increase and that, if our farmers failed to satisfy the markets, imports would fill the gap. Our forecast, which we considered rather obvious, has been proved correct, with some 70 per cent of organic food sold in the UK being produced in other countries.

Even now the taxpayers' money for agricultural research is almost entirely spent upon devising methods of increasing output. Higher output in conventional farming as a general rule requires the use of more inputs. This in turn means higher sales for the products of the chemical and other companies that supply the farmer. His costs go up but not the price he receives for what he is selling; as the agricultural research enables him to raise his production, however, he may manage to stay on the treadmill described in Chapter 5 by selling more for less. It is arguable that it is not the farmer who benefits from this research but rather the companies that manufacture and sell the inputs whose increased use is the result of much of it.

It is also arguable that a great deal of the research is rather futile. At the Babraham animal research establishment near Cambridge, goats have their udders removed from where goats have had them for thousands of years and stitched on to their necks to see whether they will produce more milk that way. I also saw there a solitary pig placed in a simulated lorry and then thrown around by the shaking of the artificial structure; this was to find out how pigs were affected by being transported from the farm to the slaughterhouse. The researchers were unable to tell me how much it had cost to build the pretend lorry, and a glimmer of dismay passed over their faces when I pointed out that no farmer in his right mind would send away a single pig in such a large lorry but would pack in many together so that they would not be hurled from side to side. Indeed, pigs suffer easily from stress, more so than any other animal on the farm, and the simplest way to measure this is to weigh them before and after a journey. To do this in a real lorry undertaking a real journey on real roads would have cost the taxpayer a fraction of the money. Also at Babraham they decided to find out how many times a pair of rabbits could copulate in the course of the day.

A kind of Parkinson's law can be applied to the amount of public money allocated for research. Never mind how much it is, there will always be scientists with a limitless number of ideas on how it can be spent. At another publicly funded establishment at Compton, Berkshire, it is said that more than £4 million was spent upon erecting a single building where grotesque experiments are carried out on pigs. When the House of Commons Select Committee on Agriculture paid a visit to the establishment, committee members were prevented from seeing the experiments. Tighter security is maintained there against anti-vivisection demonstrations. At Babraham, on the other hand, they show less fear of public concern and on two occasions welcomed the select committee to see everything. Members were able to report that, although they doubted the value of some of the experiments, the animals were well looked after – which led some of the parliamentarians to wonder what extraordinary experiments were being done at Compton.

These experiments are not only paid for by the Ministry of Agriculture but commissioned by them. The ministry's understanding of what is meant by welfare is rather strange. In defending its attitude to the welfare of farm animals, the minister of state in the House of Lords told the peers that the ministry was spending £500,000 a year on research into pigs' welfare. This amazing figure not unnaturally satisfied their lordships. Subsequent correspondence between the minister and myself about how this £500,000 was spent conveyed a different story. Most of the money was going on research into how to keep pigs in ultra-intensive conditions without them dying of various diseases – and it was difficult to see how any of it was being spent on research into their welfare in any ordinary sense of the word. Any farm animal deserves to be treated humanely; intensive factory farming makes this impossible; yet most of the public's money allocated to research relating to livestock is spent trying to make intensive forms of husbandry more profitable.

Then there is the delicate subject of business rate relief. Farmland itself has never been rated in the UK, unlike in the Republic of Ireland where domestic housing is exempt but land is charged. Legislation has been passed to give all farmers relief from rates on buildings, and this includes the so-called factory farms. The dividing line lacks any logic. If a poultry producer slaughters his stock on the premises, the building maintained for the purpose is exempt, but if his stock is taken down the road to a poultry slaughterhouse, it is not. This exemption from rates is worth an annual £800 million to farmers on the modest assumption that the rateable value of farm buildings is 5 per cent of their capital worth.

There is also a tax privilege that goes back more than fifty years. Farmers are entitled to repayment of the excise duty on fuel oil. This is 0.77 pence per litre on oil other than kerosene and 0.22 pence per litre on kerosene. Although the Treasury loses only £3 million a year as a result, this is still some indication of the vast quantities of oil that are used up by agriculture.

We now come to the most grievous and damaging item.

This is £7,500 million a year, the cost of 'price support' calculated by the OECD. This is the sum total of the extra cost for food that the consumers in our country must pay: the difference between the prices they pay and the prices they would pay if they were able to buy on the world market.

It is frequently said that, were the UK to re-enter the world market for its food, the extra demand would force up prices, and so there can be no guarantee that we would be able to buy what we needed at existing world prices. An increased demand for a limited supply of any kind of food will cause its price to rise; but as we saw in Chapter 7, the resources exist in the world to increase food production. Once it became known that 1 per cent of the world's population (the UK's 56 million inhabitants) had been set free to buy from the remaining 99 per cent, it is inconceivable that the statistically small increase in demand could not be met by the millions of farmers in other parts of the world who have the capacity to expand production and would be only too glad to improve their incomes. We can thus assume that we could buy the food we need at ordinary world prices. The British consumer would be able to spend that extra amount of money saved on his other needs, and the consequent gain to our depressed manufacturing industries could be considerable. The import duties and levies imposed upon so much of what we eat are a form of hidden taxation, and it is taxation to the extent of £7,500 million.

The total annual sum paid out to agriculture in the UK is, however, £10,000 million. This represents £40,000 a year for the average farmer. As this money is diverted each year to agriculture away from where it would otherwise be spent – in effect, from other industries and services – it may be instructive to compare this figure with the capital of some of our largest companies. It is over two and a half times more than the total capital of our four main clearing banks (£3,546 million), five times more than the capital of ICI (£1,936 million), eight times that of Unilever (£1,133 million) and forty times that of Courtaulds (£246 million). To suggest that forty new companies the size of Courtaulds could be established every year, were a different policy pursued, cannot be entirely unreasonable.

The total burden, while falling directly upon individual taxpayers and consumers, is one which also has to be borne by the rest of British industry. The effect must be devastating, not just because of the enormous amount of taxation paid by industry as a direct result of these demands upon the Exchequer, but also indirectly because of the higher wages made necessary by both costlier food and a higher level of taxation imposed upon employees. Every penny collected by the Chancellor of the Exchequer comes ultimately from industry in some form or another. The more the Chancellor collects, the less is available for allocation by industrial and business managers in such areas as research and development, the building of new factories, increases in wages or dividends or some other step needed to meet the demands of the public.

Ten thousand million pounds a year divided by the number of ultimate taxpayers in industry remains a great deal of money. But for the policy of supporting agriculture, other industries would have had a very large proportion of this money to spend upon their own development and expansion. We cannot calculate the extent to which their efficiency has been impaired, but even the most prosperous must have been affected. Of the less prosperous, a large number have gone out of business, and for at least some of them high taxation may have made the crucial difference.

There is another important way in which our subsidized agriculture has drawn capital away from other sectors of the economy. Anyone associated with farming knows how readily bank managers have offered to lend their money on the security of a farmer's title deeds. The total amount lent to agriculture is now some £7,000 million. No one would suggest that none of this money should have been lent; none the less, it is proper to ask whether agriculture has borrowed more than it would have done had there not been the present high level of protection.

The answer lies in the mouths of the bankers themselves. In the last few years, since the crisis in the CAP began to impose limits on agricultural expansion, banks have been less free in their loans to farmers; but for decades before that there was not a bank chairman, chief general manager, local director or even branch manager on record saying anything bearish about agriculture. Better to lend against land than against a shop, a factory or indeed any other business enterprise, especially a small or medium-sized one. The very large companies – the kind that give the banks so much business that they can insist on the lowest rate to borrow money, the so-called blue-chip rate – have little difficulty in borrowing as much as they want. There may be 100 such companies. But what of the rest? The future wealth and prosperity of the UK are at least as dependent upon these in the aggregate as they are on the existing top 100.

Let us assume, for the purpose of the argument, that agriculture had borrowed only a quarter of what it has succeeded in getting from the banks today. This would mean that the bank managers of the UK would have further funds to the extent of £5,250 million available for all the other small and medium-sized businesses – many thousands of pounds for each of them. A reduction to one-quarter may be an underestimate of what is possible, however. In 1970 agriculture borrowed only £546 million and in 1939 a mere £63 million. These figures must go a long way to confirm that the higher the degree of protection and support given to agriculture, the greater the prospect of it being able to borrow the capital it wants. This is another serious example of the way capital has been diverted from the efficient to the inefficient.

Two further comments may be added. The first is that, on the principle 'to him that has, it shall be given', the large farmers have received the lion's share of this fresh capital. The banks realize that the small farmer is forever being squeezed out; as the number of holdings of fewer than 100 acres grows less each year, the risk of lending to the small farmer increases. Naturally the banks will prefer the large farmer to the small one, and this makes it still more difficult for the latter to compete.

The other comment is that this huge sum of borrowed money does not include loans to the industries that service agriculture. Shell, BP, ICI, Rank Hovis McDougall and Boots are among the large companies that have undoubtedly reached their present size because they have shared in the advantages of agricultural protection. Their borrowings from the banks compare with the amounts that have gone direct to agriculture. The total amount of capital invested in these companies that supply and service agriculture runs into thousands of millions of pounds; and, of course, only a part of it would be needed if Britain pursued a different agricultural policy.

It is not possible to assess precisely how much extra capital has been absorbed by these companies, but it cannot possibly be less than £2,000 million in total. The capital employed in the industries that supply fertilizers, compound feeds and agricultural machinery is many times more than this, and they are only three (albeit probably the three largest) industries that have expanded along with agriculture.

Industries that supply or service agriculture are themselves a source of capital for farmers. The competition between compound feed companies is so great that it has been quite normal for them to provide most of the initial capital for someone beginning a pig or poultry enterprise, and they may allow him credit for up to a year. Machinery distributors may reach a similar agreement with a newcomer to arable farming. As the loans come from the capital employed by the company, and are therefore part of the above estimate of £2,000 million, they should not be added as a separate item of capital diverted.

Loans advanced by the Agricultural Mortgage Corporation should undoubtedly be included in the calculations. The AMC is a quasi-official body that exists to provide working capital to the owner-occupier farmer. On 31 March 1947 farmers had loans outstanding of £8.2 million; but on 1 August 1990 the outstanding loans had reached £750 million. If farmland had risen in price at the same rate as inflation, these loans would have been considerably less. Taking into account the excess value of land as assessed above, it would be right to estimate the excess value of capital lent by the AMC as somewhere in the realm of £475 million; such a sum is a further diversion of capital from other industries.

The insurance companies are another source of fresh capital. Like the banks they have been only too pleased to pour their money into agriculture. The same applies; every extra pound invested by the insurance companies in agriculture, because it is protected and supported, is a pound diverted away from other trades and industries which would otherwise have received that injection of capital.

Until the UK entered the EEC, British insurance companies owned only a modest area of agricultural land, about 83,000 acres in all. This was the result of selective purchases made over the years, mainly for their pension schemes. As soon as they realized what the effect of the Common Agricultural Policy would be, the companies' attitude completely changed. Caution was swept aside. In the first year of the CAP their farmland purchases doubled; the second year they trebled; and by the end of the 1970s they had acquired nearly 300,000 acres. Most of this land, not surprisingly, was arable. Within a decade the insurance companies' investment in agricultural property had leaped to £600 million. Because the land was already there, this money did nothing to create more wealth. Yet, had it not been tempted by the CAP, it would necessarily have been invested elsewhere; at least a large part of it would have gone to other industries where there was a likelihood of new wealth being created. Now that the EEC has had to curb the growing of surplus cereals, the insurance companies are losing their interest in arable land.

British agriculture has become, not just capital intensive, but the most capital intensive of all our industries. This is the judgement – or is it the confession? – of the Country Landowners' Association. As long ago as January 1978 the CLA submitted a memorandum to the Treasury disclosing that for every person employed in agriculture there was a capital investment of £38,000. This, the CLA said, compared with £16,000 for the chemical industry, which the less well informed may have assumed to be the most capital intensive of all. The memorandum went on to say that annual investment in agriculture equalled £804 per person employed in the industry, 30 per cent higher than the figure for UK industry as a whole. The CLA gave the game away. In case the picture had since changed, I looked up in *Agriculture in the UK 1989* to see what the estimated gross capital formation was for that year.

The figure was no less than £1,036 million. Divided by the number engaged in agriculture, 573,000, simple arithmetic tells us that investment is now £1,808 per person per year.

What, then, is the grand total amount of capital that has gone to agriculture as a result of a policy of protecting and shielding it from overseas competition, and has therefore been taken away from others who would have made more efficient use of it? This sort of reckoning is always difficult, and some readers may think that simply adding together all the figures so far listed would involve an element of double accounting (though others may find omissions). Neverthe-less, by any reckoning the grand total must come to many thousands of millions of pounds. If the reader divides what-ever total it may be by the British population (a mere 56 million), one is still left with a fortune – and a large one to most people. If this money had been wisely invested, it would by now have multiplied to the point that all of us would be noticeably better off.

THE MISUSE OF NATURAL RESOURCES

Finally, in this catalogue of distortions, let us look at two major resources which government support of agriculture has caused to be diverted on a massive scale: oil and fertilizer. In both cases the diversion has been artificial and would never have taken place to the extent it has but for the policy of support.

Sir Kenneth Blaxter of the Rowett Research Institute, in one of the most refreshing papers ever delivered to the Annual Oxford Farming Conference, illustrated in 1978 how oil has been swallowed up by British agriculture. Before we had tractors, he said, our farmers produced 41 per cent of the food we ate. Now, with the aid of tractors, they produce 46 per cent of our food. The population during these years has increased from 38 million to 56 million, so yield has risen by almost two-thirds (65 per cent). But – here is the rub – it has needed a sixteen-fold increase in power consumption to achieve it. Moreover, he calculated that producing, process-ing and distributing our food use up 26 per cent of the nation's commercial energy.

The UK's annual commercial energy consumption is 209.3 million tonnes of oil or oil equivalent; 26 per cent of this is 54.4 million tonnes, or rather more than one tonne to the acre. Obviously, the figure also includes fuel used up by the processors and distributors, but it is none the less quite a startling quantity. Until North Sea oil came on stream in the mid-1970s this oil had to be imported and was an item in our balance of payments current account. The NFU and the oil companies, which have campaigned so successfully for an expansion of British agriculture on the ground that it would 'save money' on the balance of payments, would never concede that nearly all such 'saving' was eliminated by the contrary dependence on imported oil. Their argument was not validated once the UK became, in effect, self-sufficient in oil; every extra barrel of oil going to agriculture has meant one less barrel going for export.

Until a few years ago the British farmer was given every inducement to mechanize and to buy larger and more powerful tractors and combine harvesters, particularly through his privilege of being able to set off the complete cost of any new machinery against income tax in the year of purchase. This was a most valuable tax concession; the larger and more prosperous the farmer, the greater was its value to him. Many of the farmers who ploughed up their pasture to take advantage of high CAP prices had incomes of over £50,000 a year. By investing in new and more powerful tractors and combine harvesters they were able, quite legitimately, to avoid much of the income tax they would otherwise have paid. However, this heavier machinery uses twice the amount of fuel that the older machines needed.

In mechanizing our farms we have replaced manpower with oil. The transfer has been made because it was profitable to do so, but the profitability has been contrived and artificial. If the price mechanism had been allowed to operate without intervention by the government, a more efficient use of both manpower and oil would have ensued. A man with his hoe who grows his own food is among the world's most efficient producers of energy; and the farmer who uses his own muscle finds it cheap, reliable and wasteless. While a tractor will obviously enable him to produce a great deal more than he would with his hand tools, the optimum of efficiency is not likely to be attained by the taxpayer's money being used to induce him to become more mechanized than he would otherwise. And if the taxpayer's money does not have this effect, there seems little point in giving it to him.

Perhaps it may not matter very much if we exhaust our oil resources sooner than we need because of their unnecessary diversion to agriculture. Other forms of energy may be devised in the next century; and tractors and combines may be replaced by machines which work off forms of energy that are yet unknown. But although the energy in the universe might, for our own purposes, be limitless, other kinds may cost more to bring into use, and once we have found them we must be ready to pay the extra price.

On the other hand, fertilizers (more strictly speaking, artificial fertilizers) are unquestionably finite. Their reserves are exhaustible. What is more, the ones we now use are in danger of becoming exhausted sooner than we may realize. Many of us would like the Third World to adopt more sustainable methods of agriculture; but most farmers in the developing countries are already on the chemical treadmill, and there is little prospect of their being able to get off it for many years yet. The consequence to the Third World, where millions of acres more must be cultivated to prevent as many millions of the human race from starving, is desperately serious. These acres need fertilizers, and we are depriving them of what they need. It may seem sensible to improve our own marginal land so that it can grow arable crops: but this can be done only by applying fertilizers much more heavily than they would need to be applied on the better-quality land that could be brought into cultivation in the Third World. This is a perfect example of the misapplication of resources.

World fertilizer prices have increased faster than the rate of inflation. Farmers in the developed countries have been able to afford to pay for fertilizers at these high prices, and so manufacturers have charged accordingly. This is borne out by the figures. Every year the Fertilizer Manufacturers' Association publishes a report about the sales of its member companies. These reports show a steady 5 per cent increase in the annual consumption of nitrogen fertilizers in the UK during the 1970s and early 1980s, although purchases have since levelled off.

One of the reasons why our farmers have continued to buy the fertilizers is that for many years they were cushioned from the true world price by a government subsidy. Such subsidies have not been available for farmers in the developing countries, and so they have had to reduce their purchases. Food production has declined in some of these countries, and more people have gone hungry, even starved, as a result. Is it morally right to use taxpayers' money to divert fertilizers away from developing countries?

Some major international companies have been responsible for this policy, ICI, British Petroleum and Shell among them. Their stake in a policy of agricultural support is enormous, and they and the others in the fertilizer business have been considerable beneficiaries. Not for nothing do they spend their millions upon advertising for ever larger sales to farmers.

Hundreds of millions of our fellow humans in the Third World have too little to eat. How many of them would have a fair share of the world's supply of fertilizers if this policy were not pursued we are not to know. But we can be sure that the greater the number who go hungry because of this policy, the greater the shame upon those who persist in arguing in favour of it.

FALSIFYING THE SIGNALS

Farmers must work the system given to them. Unless they happen to be millionaire dilettantes, they have no choice in the matter. No one should blame the tens of thousands of British farmers who cultivate their land and rear their stock in the way the policy-makers bid them to do. In so far as he is still a business man and not a public servant, anyone engaged in agriculture must respond to the signals of the market-place. What has gone wrong is that the politicians have taken over the signalling system and reduced it to a state of chaotic disorder. Wrong signals have been sent out – only the customer who wants to eat some food can send out an accurate message about the particular kind of food he happens to want.

The Minister of Agriculture in London and the EEC Commissioner of Agriculture in Brussels are both very clever and conscientious men. Yet neither they nor any of the thousands of officials who advise them are qualified to manage something so delicate and complicated as the food market. Not even in the most *dirigiste* economy can this be done. A totalitarian minister can control the manufacture and sale of mechanical things, like refrigerators and deep freezes, but the growing and marketing of food depend upon elements beyond human control. It is astonishing that such a simple truth is not understood and the consequences of it acted upon.

I suspect, however, that the truth is understood. Unfortunately, it is rather enjoyable taking over the powers of the signalling system. All ministers enjoy power; some enjoy it too much, and these are the ones who cause the most trouble. It is easy for them to tell themselves that they are correcting the mistakes and injustices of the market-place. In reality, as we have shown, the market would have made fewer mistakes and been far less unjust than the interventionism of the last forty-five years. It is not only British consumers, taxpayers and farmers who have suffered. A heavy price has been paid by millions of people throughout the world, many of them among those least able to bear it. They are the victims of our policies. Chapter 9 studies their plight.

· 9 ·

THE VICTIMS

THE CONSUMER

A generation ago people scarcely ever spoke of 'the consumer'. Now consumer councils have been set up, a Consumers' Association formed, newspaper columns are written about consumer affairs, radio and television programmes advise consumers, local authorities have departments of consumer protection and, to top it all, the United Kingdom has a Minister for Consumer Protection. Unfortunately the consumer affairs industry has grown up behind – and a long way behind – the growth of protection for producers. The more we draft rules to help consumers, the more consumers' interests are under other forms of attack by the government of the day. In a plain word, this is humbug.

The most effective protection the consumer can have is the freedom to choose. If he wants to buy a banana he must be free to do so, not be told by some law-maker or civil servant that it would be in the national interest for him to buy an orange. This is not being fanciful, for we are induced to eat some kinds of food rather than others for that very reason. The bananas we eat in the UK are from either Jamaica or the Windward Islands, and only when their crops fail are we allowed to buy bananas from Ecuador and elsewhere.

Freedom to choose implies freedom to buy in one place rather than another and from one place rather than another.

So far as most of us are concerned, it is the freedom to go to a supermarket, a market stall, an ordinary shop or any other place where the goods are honestly traded. It is, of course, a very obvious kind of freedom, and we take it for granted. But we overlook how limited it can be in its effect. It becomes almost worthless if every shop and supermarket has the same kind of food on offer and sells it at the same price. The freedom to 'shop around' has value only when the retailers themselves can also shop around and give the customer a variety of choice. If all the bananas in all the retail outlets in the country come from the West Indies, and they all sell at much the same price, the customer's freedom does not add up to anything worth having.

'Protection' is such a cosy, comforting word. The motive of the protector must be good; no doubt he is a kindly, well-meaning sort. How difficult it is to criticize someone who wants to protect and who assures us that British farmers must be protected. Indeed, they must; but how and from whom?

The protection they are now given is the wrong kind, for two reasons. First, it fails in its objective, as Chapter 5 showed; secondly, the protection is against what the British people want. This should be a self-evident truth, for if the British people did not want to buy North American wheat or New Zealand butter there would be no point in setting up an array of fiscal fences, quota restrictions and levies to stop them doing so.

These simple truths get washed away in the flood of fine words about free trade heard at Mansion House dinners. No one stands up to say he is positively against free trade. More humbug! Protectionism is favoured by industries that think they will benefit from it, and it is now rampant throughout the world. The officials of the General Agreement on Tariffs and Trade, based in Geneva, have identified forty-four categories of non-tariff barriers.

The interests that ask for protectionism – whether the NFU leadership or anyone else – and the powers that give it, in Westminster or Whitehall, never acknowledge the loss of freedom. Over the years there has been so much special pleading that it seems to have blinded them to what should be obvious. Nor is it self-evident to most of us. In this respect, people living in Eastern Europe have had an advantage; they were sharply aware of the limits put on their freedom and in 1989 they rebelled against them. The control over the British people is not so blatant, but it is there none the less, invisibly. We are allowed to pretend that our freedom is unfettered as if intangible fetters were no fetters at all.

The chief method used to divert our decision is fiscal. The food we would prefer to eat is taxed. We are not aware how much we are taxed in this way, because we do not pay the tax directly to any agency of the government; it is passed on to us by the retailer, who has himself had the tax passed on to him by the wholesaler or importer. The more we would like to eat a food which the government does not want us to eat, the more heavily it is taxed, to the point where we are pushed into buying some other kind of food which the government does want us to buy. On some kinds of food the tax is so high that no one finds it worthwhile eating them any more, so that no retailer or wholesaler any longer trades in them. A considerable range of goods come into this category. Tinned salmon from Canada used regularly to appear on the table of hundreds of thousands of British families twenty years ago, and it was so cheap that even poor families were able to enjoy it. Now there is an import duty on it. There are still plenty of salmon to be caught in Canada, and the tax is not imposed for any reason of conservation. The trouble with Canadian tinned salmon was that it was too cheap and too popular with the British people. They preferred it to the food produced in the Common Market.

Canada also used to send us great quantities of cheese and apples. The tax on Canadian cheddar is now 55 pence per pound (weight), and that effectively doubles its price in the shops. Some people, it may be remembered, particularly liked it. Every high-quality grocer supplied it, and many thousands of us bought it regularly, simply because we liked the taste.

The same can be said for many other kinds of food that used to be imported into our country. These days comparable foods are much more expensive, and many people eat cheaper 'junk' food instead. The instrument of taxation is used to keep better-value food out of our shops; and in most cases it is to protect not our own producers but others in the Common Market.

Even the foods that are not entirely excluded from our market are almost all taxed to some degree. The exceptions are those foods that we do not want to eat in any quantity, usually those chosen by the ethnic minorities, such as yams. The exceptions serve to emphasize that the more of a kind of imported food we want to eat, the more it is likely to be taxed.

So the fiscal weapon is used against the British people. Other weapons are also used. Quotas, prohibitions and the whole gamut of grants and subsidies are there to serve the same purpose. Of course, the government (I use the term in its wider sense, of embracing all the institutions of the state) needs to curb our freedom in a lot of ways; but when it comes to controlling what we want to eat (need it be said, after breathing, the most essential of our activities), the need to exercise that control should be proved. In plain words, we should eat what we like, unless it can be clearly shown that we ought not to do so. The burden of proof lies upon the government.

When prices rise, we not only have to buy rather less than we would otherwise have done; our pattern of consumption changes, and we tend to eat food of a lower quality. Table 10 (p. 206), compiled from the *National Food Survey*, illustrates what has happened to the British consumer since the import taxes began.

In less than two decades our eating habits have undergone a major change. Being more conscious of our health, we are buying fewer of the items listed in the table, but common sense suggests that a tax of about £1 per pound (weight) on beef, for example, is also part of the reason why we are eating almost 21 per cent less of it. The truth of the matter is known in every household; we are eating differently, and not just because we wish to do so. Except for during wartime, the diet of the British people has never altered as quickly as it has these last twenty years.

Even if we choose (and can afford) to eat the same

Table 10   Average weekly consumption of main foods in the UK (in ounces unless stated otherwise), 1971 and 1988

	1971	1988	Percentage change
Milk	4.46 pints	2.54 pints	43.0
Beef	7.96	6.30	20.8
Mutton and lamb	5.41	2.77	48.8
Bacon and ham	5.12	1.13	77.9
Butter	5.53	1.99	64.0
Sugar	15.80	6.94	56.1
Eggs	4.66	2.58	44.6

categories of food, the food itself is not the same. The treadmill of high-input/high-output farming fostered by subsidies and protection presents us with meat and other products that may contain additives, hormones, pesticides and other harmful substances (see Chapters 2 and 3). As intensively produced food has taken over the bulk of the market, it has forced low-input products on to the margin and, by making them more difficult to market, has forced up their price. It is to be hoped that the arrival of the 'green consumer' will counter this trend, at least to some extent, but at present our money is being used by the government to keep it going.

There is now general agreement on the financial cost to the consumer and taxpayer of our agricultural policy. The broad figures were set out in Chapter 8. They leave no escape from the conclusion that the average family of four is paying out £16 every week that does not need to be paid, and in return is getting a more restricted choice of food.

When I first asserted in *Agriculture: The Triumph and the Shame* that the system cost the consumer £3,000 million a year (about £5 a week for a family of four) on top of the cost to the taxpayer (about £2,000 million), there were mutterings of disbelief in high places. In the debate that followed, a consensus emerged, and the figure of £3,000 million was accepted. The Institute of Fiscal Studies agreed, and so did the Treasury. Christopher Johnson, group economic adviser to Lloyds Bank, prepared a detailed independent assessment which was published by the Centre for Agricultural Strategy and the Centre for European Agricultural Studies, and his conclusion was the same.

Even Peter Walker, in one of the last statements he made as Minister of Agriculture, agreed! Writing in the *British Farmer and Stockbreeder* in January 1983, he admitted that a system of deficiency payments would cost £3,000 million a year, which of course is really the same as saying that this is the difference between world prices and our own. Robert Jackson in his booklet *From Boom to Bust?* (1983) chided me for a 'pervasive lack of contact with reality' and went on to concede that £3,000 million was probably the right estimate. Yet on the very same page he said that the gross product of British agriculture was worth £5,420 million. The awful significance of the extra burden upon the consumer being more than half agriculture's gross product passed him by; and when the Exchequer's costs and the actual net cost of food at the farm gate are added, the total cost becomes greater than the value of agriculture's gross product! The inference to be drawn, even from Mr Walker and Mr Jackson, amazing though it may seem, is that agriculture had reached such a high-cost level that we would have been better off if our farmers produced no food at all. There was certainly a 'lack of contact with reality' somewhere!

The taxing of food strikes at everyone, no matter how low their income may be. The poorest in the land can escape the net no more than the millionaire. The difference is, of course, that while the millionaire might not feel the pinch, the poorest men and women find themselves carrying a particularly heavy burden. A family of four living on income support will probably have a disposable income of less than £80 a week. For them £16 is an important sum, and the bitter irony is that the farm worker who is supposed to benefit may be no better off. In my own constituency there are several thousand farm workers on low pay, and there is seldom much difference in income for many of them whether they work or not. A farm worker with four children is often better off financially when he loses his job. We have introduced a system of 'protecting' farm workers, but its real effect is to tax them 5 to 10 per cent of their income.

THE UNEMPLOYED

Unemployment in the UK peaked in September 1986 and has fallen considerably since then. Nevertheless it remains a serious problem – painfully and grindingly so for the long-term unemployed – and at its height was worse in Britain than in other comparable countries.

In northern England, Scotland, parts of Wales and Northern Ireland a serious percentage are still registered unemployed. Many thousands of others, particularly married women, would seek a job if there were hope of getting one; and a further 200,000 or so others would be added to the unemployed but for the various job-creation and early retirement schemes. Economically speaking, the true total of unemployed must still be more than 2 million. Even the registered number is as many as it was before the war (and those were the days when the Civil Service and local government had not mopped up between them a further 2 million men and women).

Ever since the UK's entry into the EEC, our rate of unemployment has generally been worse than that of other Community countries. In the search for an explanation, one favourite is the familar bogy of monetarism. Yet the government's decision to keep the increase in the money supply broadly in line with the growth of our gross domestic product is similar to what West Germany has been doing for many years, and the blaming of monetary policy for our unemployment is difficult to reconcile with the German experience. Nor does it account for the south-east of England being largely unscathed.

That the rest of the UK has suffered so much more goes some way to confirm one particular danger of our membership of the EEC in its present form. A number of distinguished economists have maintained throughout all the debates on the subject, from the very beginning, that being outside the hub and nave of the Common Market – the growth point in the middle – these areas would suffer a recession and large-scale unemployment as our own national economy became merged into that of the rest of the Community. No industrialist is likely to set up a new enterprise or expand an existing one on the periphery of the market. This is the first of the reasons why unemployment is so much worse in the UK than in other EEC countries, and it certainly commends itself to common sense.

This is sometimes spoken of as the 'golden hub' or 'golden triangle' argument, the triangle being the area of which Paris, Hamburg and Milan are the apexes, where the Community's main industrial growth is to be found. This triangle compares with the middle parts of England in the nineteenth century when a common market of the four countries of the British Isles came into being, and the Industrial Revolution was followed by the growth of the railway system, the two together giving us an integrated economy. Hundreds of thousands of Irish, Welsh and Scots moved into the middle parts of England, the golden hub of the UK, to share in the prosperity. They left behind depressed areas. The periphery was no place for an industrialist to go.

Similar thoughts, it seems, have prompted the leaders of many of our largest companies in deciding to invest their capital in the golden hub of today's Common Market. Very many millions of pounds are involved, and by setting up new plants and factories over there, they have created jobs for many tens of thousands of French, Germans and others.

A notable example is ICI. ICI has established plants in this golden area to produce plastics, paints and pharmaceuticals, and has recruited 11,000 workers. The company's investment runs into hundreds of millions of pounds, and now no less than half its sales to Western Europe are produced over there. Interestingly no company has done more than ICI to raise money for the campaign to persuade the British people to support membership of the Common Market. Fundraising for the European Movement began – as I described in Chapter 6 – in ICI's boardroom; and when the 1975 referendum came, the company released a prominent member of its staff to help run the campaign with the slogan 'Out of Europe, Out of Work'. At the very time that ICI made the largest contribution to the campaign to persuade the British people that they would lose their jobs unless they voted 'Yes', it is now known that the firm was planning to invest many millions of pounds to export jobs from the UK to France, West Germany and Italy.

Rowntree Mackintosh gave a more modest contribution to the campaign to scare the British people about unemployment, only £10,000, and its directors forthwith put up a factory in Hamburg to supply our market as well as the Continent with sweets. The European Movement is shy about giving any information about the source of its funds, even to its members, but enough is now known to confirm what a cynic might assume. The list of British industrial companies that have given it money is much the same as the list of those that have chosen to invest and expand in the golden hub of the Common Market, instead of in the UK.

The decision by all these companies to manufacture in the golden hub is one of the reasons why our trade with the rest of the Common Market in manufactured goods has changed with such dramatic speed. The drama is tragedy for the many thousands who have lost their jobs. Table 11 (p. 211) tells the sorry story of Britain's worsening balance of trade in manufactures with its EEC partners.

Fortunately, our trade with countries outside the EEC is much better and shows a surplus, but our total trade in manufactured goods is now worse than it has been for centuries. Indeed, it is an extraordinary fact that for the first time since the reign of Henry VIII we import more manufactured goods than we export. Another dismal fact is that our manufacturing output is now 10 per cent less than it was in 1973, the year we joined the Common Market, and this represents a fall comparable to that between 1929 and 1933. Again, it is useful to compare this fall in output with an increase for France and West Germany. French manufacturing output is up 12 per cent compared with 1975 (France has no records before that), and West Germany's is up 13 per cent.

Several comments can be made about the figures in the table. For a long period of time we succeeded in exporting more manufactured goods to the EEC countries than they exported to us. Then the position changed, and the change came at the very time we entered the Common Market. The longer we remain inside, the worse the balance of trade in

Table 11   UK trade balance in manufactures with EEC countries (£ million)

	1979	1980	1981	1982	1983	1984	1985	1986	1987	1988	1989
France	−727	−439	−595	−535	−1,082	−1,154	−1,222	−1,510	−1,151	−1,152	−976
Belgium–Lux.	−403	−168	−380	−525	−499	−558	−518	−357	−528	−608	−695
Netherlands	84	184	−191	−466	−803	−844	−747	−1,128	−1,117	−1,914	−2,157
West Germany	−2,523	−2,001	−2,152	−3,314	−4,926	−5,069	−5,833	−6,713	−7,465	−8,676	−9,631
Italy	−796	−368	−498	−826	−1,175	−1,302	−1,387	−1,590	−1,553	−1,787	−2,087
Irish Republic	954	793	690	547	471	495	548	584	484	491	698
Denmark	147	114	−5	−1	−71	−81	−21	−1	−58	−140	−197
Greece	184	140	137	137	172	163	167	149	152	173	222
Portugal	14	79	49	39	−74	−236	−238	−217	−98	−49	−77
Spain	−78	−79	−71	−80	−84	−257	−294	−54	251	257	442

Source: UK overseas trade statistics.

manufactured goods appears to be. A deficit of thousands of millions of pounds a year must represent a large number of jobs. Economists are generally agreed that it is not less than a million.

This decline in the UK's manufacturing industry was for many years attributed to a workforce obsessed with restrictive practices, lengthy tea breaks and other heinous matters. It may be a reason why the Ford Motor Company and the former British Leyland – now Rover – have both put up a new plant on the Continent; but the other companies, such as ICI, that have invested so heavily in Europe have on the whole had good industrial relations in Britain. Besides, our manufacturing industries have a strike record generally no worse than that prevailing in France, West Germany or Italy. In the last ten years there has been a sharp fall in the number of strikes, and they are now a small fraction of the number that used to take place. In fact, working days lost by various forms of industrial action in the private sector are almost insignificant, and absenteeism is also much reduced; so it seems contrary to the evidence to suggest that the British people are worse employees than those fortunate enough to be in the golden hub.

The explanation that we have 'priced ourselves out of the market' cannot be totally true, because we sell our manufactured goods to countries outside the Common Market as successfully now as we did in 1970. But the deficit with the other EEC countries has been gradually mounting up and now exceeds the surplus gained elsewhere. No one could dispute the estimate given by a Labour MP in the House of Commons in the early 1980s that the other Common Market countries 'send us ten cars for every one we send them, and for every £8 worth of manufactured goods we import from them we only export £5 worth in return'. Since then the position has worsened further. It is true that British manufactured goods tend to be more expensive in the Common Market than those they compete against. Too little has been said about why this should be so. Among the reasons are two that are not sufficiently discussed: the cumulative effect that agricultural protectionism has had upon other industries since 1946; and the way the Common Agricultural Policy has militated against our interests since 1973.

Because the chain of cause and effect is not so evident, these reasons for the UK's bad performance in Europe are much less discussed than some more obvious ones. For example, a lot of attention has rightly been given to the way we have used our North Sea oil, extracting it as fast as we could and pushing it on to the international market. This has raised the value of sterling and so put up the prices of our exports in terms of foreign currencies.

Then there is the fact that, compared with those in other EEC countries, our industries are less modern, less streamlined and less well equipped. Since the Second World War we have not spent enough capital on up-to-date plant and machinery; we have not pursued productivity or innovation sufficiently. One reason for this has not received much attention and has its roots in recent history. Although the CAP came into being only after the Treaty of Rome was signed in 1957, its protectionist principles were already in force in each of the member states; indeed, they had been, with varying degrees of severity, for generations.

In 1940 the late Professor C. W. Guillebaud published an interesting study of *Hitler's New Economic Order in Europe* in which he attributed to Dr Walter Funk, the Minister of National Economy in Nazi Germany, the idea of a system of stable agricultural prices, 'insulated from the wide fluctuations of the world market and divorced from the general level of prices at which food can be raised overseas'. Professor Guillebaud went on to say that France would benefit no less than Germany from such an agricultural policy. Dr Paul Einzig, one of the most prolific of all economic writers, spent much of his subsequent career attacking Professor Guillebaud's views and, after the war, when the Treaty of Rome was signed, showed that there was not a scintilla of difference between the principles of the CAP as set out in Article 39 of the Treaty of Rome and Hitler's 'New Economic Order'. This distinguished European (Dr Einzig was born in Transylvania and educated in Budapest and Paris) described the Common Market as the 'New Economic Order' without Hitler. The Treaty of Rome did little more than formalize the high level of protectionism that each of the original Six – Belgium, France, Italy, Luxembourg, the Netherlands and West Germany – had experienced for many years previously.

The Six were therefore accustomed to high food prices, and industrial employers in these countries had to pay higher wages in the post-war years than those in the UK to compensate. As a broad generalization, one-quarter of employees' incomes went on food in the Six, compared with one-fifth for the British employee. His labour costs being lower, it was less necessary for the British industrialist to concern himself with labour productivity; so, unlike his continental counterpart, he was not under pressure to invest a high proportion of his capital in new plant and machinery. Once we became bound by the CAP and food prices began to rise, our employees, anxious to maintain their standards of living, demanded and received considerable wage increases, necessarily greater than those of the original Six over the same period.

British companies were now in a dilemma. They were compelled to pay wages comparable to those of their competitors. But while the latter had the advantage of having obtained a higher rate of labour productivity by modernizing their factories in the past, ours had failed to do so because it had not been necessary for them. The sudden artificial rise in food prices therefore had the effect of pricing us out of the market.

If the EEC had been founded upon the principles of a free trade area instead of a customs union, this difficulty would never have arisen. The difference between the two is significant for the British, as a people who have traded in the markets of the world. In a free trade area, each country brings down its barriers against other member states but pursues whatever trade policy it likes with other countries outside the area. A customs union requires its member states not only to bring down the internal barriers but also to put up the same barriers as the rest of the union against every other country in the world. Membership of a free trade area would have allowed us to go on buying our food from the low-cost suppliers of the world and so continue with comparatively low wages while keeping the same standard of living.

To quantify the number of jobs lost directly as a result of the sudden rise in labour costs that occurred is obviously not possible. Yet it must be equally clear that it has been a major factor in the UK's loss of a large share of its domestic market, as well as making it extremely difficult to sell British manufactured goods in the rest of the Common Market. At least, every industrialist seems to blame his high labour costs for the failure to export; if these costs were 10 per cent less, most industrialists say their disadvantages would be overcome. Reducing the nation's food bill by £16 a week for the average family, as we could outside the CAP, would not go as far as that, but it might remove one-third of the disadvantage.

A more serious matter is the way our own agricultural protectionism has diverted capital away from manufacturing industries to agriculture. It is a process that began the day the system of price support came into effect. In fact, a policy of price support would be pointless unless it gave resources to farming by taking them away from other industries where they would naturally have gone. The cost of the price support was calculated in Chapter 8. It comes, in 1990 terms, to an accumulated total of more than £80,000 million. It is a sum of money so staggering that it is difficult to comprehend; one way to grasp it is to compare it with the capital of our largest manufacturing companies – as was done in Chapter 8. Another comparison is with total government spending; it represents 40 per cent of all current expenditure.

This diversion of public money not into farming but into landowning has been to the prejudice of our manufacturing industries in two ways, and both are important in considering the problem of unemployment. In the first place, the means by which this money has been transferred is, of course, through taxes, and every company has had to pay over a proportion of its profits. Money lost in this way cannot be invested in new plant or modernization. Worse still, the research and development that are a vital part of any modern enterprise tend to be the first casualty. If only 10 per cent of the £80,000 million that the government has extracted from the general body of taxpayers since price support began came directly from manufacturing industries, it would still be the capital of tens of thousands of companies, and the cumulative effect over the years could be very serious.

The second reason why this diversion of public money to agriculture was bound to hit industry was also mentioned in Chapter 8. It triggered off a huge diversion of funds from banks and other private investors at a time when businesses badly needed those funds for modernization, and often just for survival. The thousands of businesses whose applications for a bank advance were rejected were in the aggregate the employers of probably hundreds of thousands, perhaps millions, of people. Many of the applications were for only £10,000 or less; if bank lending to agriculture had remained at more modest levels, perhaps 250,000 businesses could have had the help they sought. We enter the realm of speculation in trying to gauge what number of them would have survived if they had got the loan they asked for, or how many would have expanded. What is reasonably certain is that this massive transfer of wealth away from industry has been a substantial cause of the UK's unemployment problems.

If we take all these factors together, it is reasonable to believe that, at the peak of our unemployment in 1986, not less than 2 million people in the UK had lost their jobs because of the country's agricultural policy. Many are still out of work, and it is a bitter irony that more than half our farm workers have been forced out of their jobs by the very measures that were supposed to help them.

WAR BETWEEN ALLIES

When the government of a country allows its people to trade freely with others who live beyond its frontiers, it makes it possible for links to be forged. There cannot be trade without communication; and the very moment we begin to talk to people in another country, the barriers that have kept us apart must start to come down. As trade increases, the links get stronger. There are exchanges of visits and meetings together. Then follows the discussion of markets, of what suits the consumer in one country and not the other, and all the problems of commercial dealings. As the talks go on, each party comes to understand more about the other's country and its way of doing things. The narrow question of how much is to be paid for the goods is left behind, as many matters about the two countries are discussed and understood.

While the people of the two countries talk together and the talks lead to satisfactory trade between them, which in turn brings to both a higher degree of prosperity, sheer self-interest must reduce the prospect of the two countries' wanting to fight a war against each other. So when a government lets its people trade unrestrictedly with the people of another country, it is making a declaration of peace.

Is the converse equally true? Let us see what must follow when a government takes away from its people the freedom of trade that they have hitherto enjoyed. It says to its people: 'Until now you have traded freely with those who live in Ruritania, but you will do so no longer. We shall put a tax upon the food you import from Ruritania and also place a limit on the amount you will be allowed to buy from the Ruritanians who supply you.' Put in such words, this may sound a trifle whimsical, yet substitute the United States for Ruritania and it is what scores of British firms, whose business was founded upon imports from the USA, have been told. Wheat, maize, beef, butter, cheese, dried fruit, tinned and even fresh fruit used to be imported without any restriction at all. Free trade in food used to be complete and absolute. The Wheat Act of 1932 made a slight difference to the amount that came in; the policy of deficiency payments indirectly reduced supplies, and so also did a few other measures introduced by the UK government. But until we decided to go over to a system of import levies and import duties, preparatory to entering the EEC, a policy of free trade in food generally prevailed between the United States and ourselves.

It is beyond doubt that the farmers of North America are able to grow wheat and maize more cheaply than we can in the UK. It is not that they are, in any technical sense, more efficient than our own farmers; it is simply that nature has given them advantages denied to us. Both Canada and the USA have many millions of acres of soil that are excellent for growing wheat and maize, and a climate that is as perfect for the purpose as one could wish for. Just as our mild and wet climate can afford us good grassland, so their cold winters followed by their hot summers are better for cereals. Their cold winter puts a curb upon the diseases afflicting crops, while we have to spray our land with herbicides and other toxic chemicals on a scale that increases every year, as do the costs and dangers. The hot summers on the other side of the Atlantic enable the harvest to be garnered without it being dried, while we use corn driers, each one now costing many thousands of pounds. True, farmers can write off the entire financial cost of it against their income tax in one year; but the economic cost remains, and it is insidiously paid for by the British public as taxpayers and consumers. There are other advantages of climate conferred upon North American grain growers; and maybe the most important is that the sun never fails to shine down upon the ripening corn at the time it is most needed. Oh lucky Americans! What would our arable men give for such solar comfort.

Despite all this, 82 million acres of the United States were set aside – as the euphemism goes – in 1983. This is an area the size of Texas and about twice the total area of our own farmland. It is an area capable of growing arable crops at low cost. All of it was taken out of cultivation to lie fallow for at least a year.

In return for the farmer agreeing not to cultivate his land, the US Department of Agriculture brought his previous year's crop of wheat and maize and gave it back to him so that he could sell it the following year and in the meantime offer it as security for money he needed to borrow. All this, and some other forms of aid, cost the US taxpayer about $67,000 million. It is about two-thirds the true cost of supporting the famers in the EEC. If the world were a more sensible place, there would be no need to give the American farmer a single dime; as a low-cost producer, he would be certain of a place in the world market. The world not being a sensible place, at least as far as agriculture is concerned, the American farmer has become a charge upon the US taxpayer. His income is steadily decreasing, and his indebtedness to the bank is rising to a level that puts at risk a large part of the US banking system.

US farm incomes have plummeted. Since Britain adopted the CAP and ceased to be one of the US farmers' main customers, their incomes have fallen to less than half of what they were in real terms. According to the 1989 *Fact Book of US Agriculture*, published by the US government, the average farmer's annual income is $15,000; and 18 per cent of the rural population now lives in a state of poverty, compared with 12 per cent in the cities, a gap wider than it has been for many years. Resentment is widespread and it has naturally made US farmers ask several questions. Why has this happened? Who is responsible? How much longer must they experience this decline into poverty? They cannot sensibly accuse themselves. They remain the same kind of farmers they have been for decades: the lowest-cost producers of wheat and maize. And their low costs should still enable them to overcome fair competition from any quarter of the globe.

Resentment extends beyond the farmstead. Tens of thousands of businesses that service and supply the US farmer are no less affected. Manufacturers of and dealers in machinery and fertilizers are obvious examples. Agriculture is the only industry over a vast area of the United States; it is the mainspring of the economy of over half the states. So when the purchasing power of the farmer falls by over a third, the effect upon business and professional people throughout most of the United States is serious. They too ask who is responsible.

Nobody has become more anxious than the bank manager. Total indebtedness on the part of the farmers has reached $188,000 million. As there are 2,200,000 farmers, this represents an average debt of $85,000. This indebtedness is dangerously out of proportion to US farm incomes. If farmers cannot pay the interest charges and their debts continue to grow, the consequences facing those banks in the USA that depend upon the fortunes of agriculture are deeply serious. In fact, no bank, not even the most powerful, is isolated from the impending crisis. Unless some change of fortune comes, US bankers say, it is no longer fanciful to speak of a crash comparable to that of 1929.

The annual *Fact Book of US Agriculture* shows how important agriculture is to the US economy. About a third of US farmers' crops are exported, and this makes the USA the world's largest food exporter, dependent upon food more than any other kind of export for its trade abroad. So any decrease in food exports will cause the value of the dollar to fall. Wheat and maize are most important factors in this. Ten years ago (in 1981) US wheat exports were 1,771 bushels, which was two-thirds of production; since then exports have been cut by more than one-third almost entirely as a result of EEC dumping. The effect upon farm-gate prices has been extremely serious, with US wheat growers' receipts falling from $3.69 to $2.42 a bushel. The 1990 harvest in the EEC has yielded yet another surplus, this time of 35 million tonnes. Surpluses must either be destroyed (as fruit and vegetable surpluses usually are), be stored in intervention (at great expense, to deteriorate and cease to be fit for human consumption) or be dumped on the world market at even greater expense.

There was a time when the UK used to be one of the principal markets for US wheat and maize. That, of course, was before 1973, when the system of import levies and duties was put fully into effect. In 1972 we imported 788,004 tonnes of wheat and 1,645,173 tonnes of maize from the United States. In 1983 it was 18,444 tonnes of wheat and 709,021 tonnes of maize. Since US wheat costs about two-thirds of the price in the Common Market, the fall in our purchases is some measure of how much our most basic of foods is being taxed.

Once Britain entered the EEC, the USA's share of the world food market went into decline. To some extent this has been arrested by US food exporters finding new outlets for grain in the Third World. Public Law 480 (Food for Peace) enables the US federal government to promote these exports with taxpayers' money, and thousands of millions of dollars are available for the programme. But what is the effect upon the Third World? It is scarcely an inducement for poor agrarian countries to grow more of their own food. The danger is recognized in Washington; it is seen as a short-term device to prevent the collapse of the rural US economy. Whether it continues depends largely on what is decided in Brussels.

During the 1980s the US trade deficit reached staggering heights of many thousands of millions of dollars a year. If today the dollar still appears 'strong' against other currencies, this is due to a cause which cannot benefit the US economy – the inordinately high interest rates that have enticed considerable amounts of money from Europe and elsewhere. These high rates have stifled the American business man desiring to expand, and so long as he is faced with them he cannot play his full part in the economy. The prosperity of all industries is set back.

The US Department of Labor is also anxious. Twenty-three million Americans work in some phase of food production; and more Americans are engaged in the actual growing of food in the fields than the combined number in the steel, automobile and transport industries. No less than 5 million Americans are employed in providing feeds, fertilizers and other supplies to agriculture. Altogether one American in five working in the private sector works in or for agriculture. The United States cannot prosper, and its people cannot enjoy full employment, unless it is the principal exporter of food to the markets of the world. Were its agriculture to be allowed to face fair competition, the USA would be in a position to lead a much-needed worldwide economic recovery. But talk of this is futile while the EEC denies fair competition to the largest and most naturally efficient agriculture that any nation in the world is able to enjoy.

Wheat and maize, it might be added, are not the only items in a future food war. Dairy produce is the second most important sector for US farmers. The total amount received by all US farmers for dairy produce is some $18,000 million – a figure that has remained constant for years despite inflation. Unless a substantial proportion of it is exported, the second largest part of the country's agriculture is put in jeopardy. US dairy exports, however, have been cut by half.

This inability to sell farm produce abroad is undoubtedly the main reason for the US trade deficit.

Retaliation can take a very simple form. The United States could do what the EEC does and subsidize its exports, in this way regaining the market it has lost. It will feel totally justified. In 1976 the EEC's share of world food exports was 8 per cent, almost the whole of it gained by undercutting competitors with the aid of subsidies from the guarantee fund of the CAP. By 1982 the share had more than doubled to 17 per cent, making the EEC the world's largest food exporter after the United States, a position it retains. Every inch of this progress has been made by using more taxpayers' money to increase the subsidies, and most of the inches gained by the EEC have been inches lost by the USA. In most years more than half the money the EEC spends is used to try to take away the trade – and the livelihood – of farmers who live in other countries. Australia, New Zealand, Canada and a host of poorer countries in the Third World have been too weak to retaliate by matching subsidy with subsidy, at least not on the massive scale of the EEC. So they have lost their markets, and are the poorer for it. The EEC is also the poorer for what it has done; it has no more money available for the fight unless the member states agree to ask their taxpayers to pay still more money. Its budget ceiling has been reached. The USA is in a more favourable position. Were the President to ask Congress for more money to save the nation's farmers, there is little doubt what the answer would be. Uncle Sam can fight back, and he can win. Defeat for the EEC would be certain.

Let us look next at Latin America for another example of what happens when historic ties are cut by protectionism. The amount of trade that took place between Argentina and the UK used to be immense. It was British business men, engineers and other experts who gave the Argentine economy the size and shape it enjoyed. For nearly a century we purchased beef in quantities that increased year by year, and the more we purchased, the more dependent the Argentinians became upon us. Although they imported many of their needs from us, a large part of their beef was paid for by increased investment in railways, property, banking and other sectors that enhanced their country's wealth. We also imported wheat and several other commodities from Argentina, so that altogether the UK was its best customer. Argentinian prosperity depended on the British people.

Then came our entry into the Common Market. Within two years our imports from Argentina were cut in half, from £106 million worth in 1973 to £53 million in 1975. They continued to decline and within a few years were of trifling importance. The effect upon Argentina was appalling. Unemployment rose; bankruptcies became common; government revenue declined; and every part of the country's agriculture, its main source of wealth, was blighted. Cattle ranching covers about half of the total land area of Argentina; one-third of its exports used to be meat, and agriculture contributed 90 per cent of its export income. The EEC tariff of 70 pence on each pound of Argentina's meat was a punishing blow. It was an aggressive and hurtful act, from which Argentina's economy has not recovered.

For all those years that we traded so amicably with Argentina, a thousand or more settlers from the British Isles lived on the Falkland Islands. The UK and Argentina prospered together, and the economic alliance kept the two countries clear of open conflict. Today, despite the resumption of diplomatic contact, the Falklands dispute remains unresolved. The Argentinian claim has not been abandoned, and the cost to us of coping with the threat it poses is going to run into hundreds of millions of pounds, the equivalent of many, many years of beef supplies. As long as the British consumer is denied the supply of cheap beef from Argentina, which means as long as we subscribe to the CAP, and as long as the British taxpayer has to pay these massive sums of money to ward off the Argentinians, we are entitled to ask one or two questions. Would Argentina, while so dependent upon its export trade with us for its prosperity, have deliberately cut off that trade? What could the Argentinians have gained by acquiring those bleak islands when they could have lost so much? Common sense seems to suggest that the British people would have remained blissfully unaware of the Falklands if we had not severed the economic alliance with Argentina in 1973.

The other question is, what would happen over the Falklands were we to open our ports to Argentinian food again? That impoverished, bankrupt country would have a chance of recovery; its farmers and meat processors would be glad enough to respond, and no Argentinian government would be so short-sighted as to stand in the way. An economic alliance would begin again, hesitatingly at first perhaps, but as it grew, so would the threat to the Falklands recede. British taxpayers would be able to spend their money, and British servicemen their time, in other ways.

What of Australia, New Zealand and Canada? Going over to Canada for the first time, in 1983, I met an elderly Canadian, brought up on an English farm, who had, like so many other younger sons, had to leave his home as a young man to farm abroad, 'to go to the colonies'. By the time war came in 1939, he was just established on land that had taken some years to bring into economic cultivation. The Canadian government then decreed that, as part of the war effort, the farmers would sell their wheat to the UK – 'to the people back home' – at 30 cents a bushel below the world price. They did not demur; they did it gladly, and their sons went off to fight as well. By the time the war was over, the discount had caused the Canadian wheat growers to forfeit no less than $600 million. Given that a dollar was worth a great deal more in 1945, it represented quite a fortune to every farmer.

Within two years, our system of deficiency payments began the process of displacing Canada's exports to us and, at the same time, putting a gentle squeeze upon the price we paid them. Once deficiency payments gave way to import levies on wheat, the gentle squeeze became more like strangulation. As our own high-cost production of cereals increased, so the Canadians' exports to us diminished. They looked elsewhere for their sales, and they were not always successful. Within three years the Canadian government had to tell its farmers to grow less wheat and to punish them if they disobeyed.

I passed on to the Canadian Minister of Agriculture what we in the UK were being repeatedly told, but which I suspected to be a falsehood, namely that Canada had found other markets for its wheat and was no longer interested in ours. His denial was plain and blunt; a moment later he said how sad he was that Canada and Britain had moved so far apart that statements such as this could be made. The fact is, we are being forced apart by a policy that has deliberately cut off trade between us. As a result we no longer meet and talk together as we used to do, and misunderstandings arise, even mistrust.

The amount of low-cost food entering Britain from Canada used to be considerable. How different it is today. The decrease in imports has made both our countries the poorer. We are also both the poorer as a result of our huge surpluses having to be exported. Canada, like the United States, Argentina and Australia, has been forced out of its export market by the EEC's dumping policy.

In cutting our trade links with Canada we have made certain that our own manufacturing industries will be the casualties. In my visit to Canada in 1983 I cannot remember seeing a single motor vehicle manufactured in England. I did, however, see scores of Renaults, Citroëns, Volkswagens, Fiats and others from the Continent. I was told that ten years earlier our cars would have been seen in far greater numbers than those, in every city and village. The reason was that they entered Canada free of duty, under the Commonwealth Preference System, while vehicles from outside the United States or the Commonwealth had a tariff of 17 per cent imposed upon them. Such a tariff was enough to exclude, almost entirely, any car made in the EEC as it then existed.

Not only cars, but all British manufactures, previously exported to Canada under preferential terms, have been affected adversely. When we deliberately put up barriers against Canada, we made it inevitable that we ourselves would get hurt. Only a small part of the export trade we lost in that way has been diverted to the Common Market; most of it has been lost altogether, and as a direct result many thousands of jobs in the UK have also been lost.

The case of Australia is in some ways even worse. When Malcolm Fraser, then Prime Minister of Australia, spoke in the City of London a few years ago, he told his audience that one-third of Australian dairy farmers had gone out of business as a direct result of the UK's entry into the Common Market. He was trying to rebut the argument, made so often, that Australia had gained markets elsewhere and was now indifferent to ours. The fact is that our own domestic market is, without question, the most coveted of all for food exporters, for reasons that were pointed out in Chapter 7. Every Australian concerned with the exporting of food would say, even now, that the UK would have first preference in his trade abroad – that is, if we allowed him to choose.

It is not quite so easy to see the effect on our exports to Australia, but any visitor will soon see and hear about the demise of our trade in manufactured goods. The British car, once ubiquitous, is now a rarity. Not even the staff of our own High Commission in Canberra seem particularly anxious to purchase our cars. Walking by its car park some years ago, I stopped to count how many of the thirty or so vehicles were of British origin; apart from what looked like the High Commissioner's Daimler, there was just one very elderly Morris. Most of the others were continental – Renaults, Volkswagens and suchlike. Curiosity prompted me to go on later to the French Embassy. All the cars there were French!

To gain alternative markets to replace ours, the Australians have had to fight very hard. As often as not they have been defeated, and it has been the EEC that has usually defeated them. The main weapon used by the Community has been, of course, the export subsidy. The vast sums made available under the CAP have enabled it to undercut the prices of the Australians, while the revenue received by the Australian government could never have been large enough to allow it to retaliate. Agriculture is the first industry of Australia, as it is of the United States and Canada, and the country's farmers are expected to support the government financially. Australia's other industries are neither rich nor numerous enough to carry the deadweight of a highly subsidized agriculture.

Australia has tried to diversify. Cotton, for example, can be grown in place of wheat in parts of New South Wales, and this is being done. But diversification out of the crops which a country can grow most economically in conditions of fair competition seldom succeeds, because usually the crop is already being grown in some other part of the world to meet the existing demand. It has been the experience of Australian farmers that diversification is not generally a practical policy. So hundreds of thousands of acres capable of growing wheat at low cost now lie idle. Some have gone over to grass, but the lack of rainfall has prevented this from being a success.

One side of the agricultural depression in Australia can be illustrated anecdotally. On the occasion of my visit to the country in the 1980s, I went up to Queensland to see at first hand the problems of the cane sugar growers. By every conceivable yardstick, the whole industry, from the farms via the sugar factories to the sugar terminals, is highly efficient. What upset me most of all was to see the standard of living of these farmers, who had felt for so long a strong bond with what many of them still called 'home', though they may not have been born here nor even visited our shores. Linoleum on all the floors seemed universal, cheap wooden furniture, little if any modern equipment in the kitchen and outside an elderly and dilapidated car. What I saw took me back to the 1930s; it was just how our farmers lived then. Farm workers in my constituency are among the low paid, and the minimum weekly rate of pay of £140 usually prevails, but even their houses are more comfortable and up to date than those I saw in Queensland. I doubt if there is a single farmhouse in England, encircled by its two hundred acres, looking as poor as those I saw in Queensland; and if there is, it is the fault of its owner.

The quality of life in Queensland is the fault of the EEC in dumping on to the world market between one-quarter and one-fifth of its total supply of sugar at a price that may be half its cost of production. No matter how efficient they are in Queensland, that kind of competition cannot be endured.

New Zealand, too, has seen its agriculture go through a crisis. Like Australia's, New Zealand's trade deficit has grown worse, and tens of thousands of its farmers have become the poorer by what we have done. The fault is certainly not nature's. Grass grows some ten or eleven months in the year in New Zealand, compared with six months in Britain; vast flocks of sheep and great herds of cattle can eat all they need at low cost. They can, as a matter of hard fact, be fed more cheaply in New Zealand than anywhere else in the world. When the 1,309 ton *Dunedin* sailed into the Port of London in 1882 with the first refrigerated shipment of meat and butter exported from New Zealand, it was the beginning of an enormous advantage to us in the UK. From then on we were to have preference over all others for the supply of all the butter, cheese and lamb that we might want, and every bit of it at the cheapest price in the world.

Some 80 per cent of New Zealand's exports were of food before we put up the barriers, and they are much the same today. New Zealand is still, as nature ordained it to be, a pastoral country, so it has had to search elsewhere for a market. Like the United States, Canada and Australia, New Zealand has had to compete against the dumped surpluses of the EEC, and although successful in some places, its food exports can no longer provide the degree of prosperity enjoyed by its people until we entered the EEC. Fighting a trade war has cost New Zealand a great deal of money. Not only are its farmers individually the poorer in consequence, but as the country's prosperity is so heavily dependent upon agriculture, her whole economy has suffered grievously.

So our policy of overproducing and dumping food has hurt and alienated our friends throughout the world. If an American or Australian farmer finds his standard of living reduced, however, at least he is not forced into starvation. Shamefully for us, it is not an exaggeration to say that the effect on some Third World countries of our dumping of cereals, sugar and other foodstuffs has meant starvation for many of their farmers. These are the people we must consider next – the poorest and the most defenceless victims.

THE THIRD WORLD POOR

For many years we have been told of the millions of our fellow humans who go without food and who die prematurely simply because they do not have enough to eat. In 1980 the World Bank estimated that 'the diets of 730 million people . . . did not contain enough calories for an active working life', the annual report *World Resources 1988–89* tells us. This is a quantitative measure of undernutrition and fails to record many millions more suffering from malnutrition through lack of vitamins and other ingredients of an adequate diet. A 1988 update of the World Bank study put the number of Third World people with deficient diets at 950 million. Any agricultural policy we pursue that causes more people to go hungry in the world is indefensible. Yet that is exactly what is happening; the Common Agricultural Policy plays a major part in causing millions of people to go very hungry, and as each year passes it affects even more.

Because this is undoubtedly the gravest charge to make against our agricultural policy, and as it reflects against those responsible for pursuing it, the facts to support it must be examined very carefully. So we need to answer the following questions:

- Are there resources available to enable these hundreds of millions to eat enough food?
- If the resources are available, what are the reasons for them not getting that food?
- What, if anything, have we ourselves done wrong? And how can we put it right?

The first question was largely answered in Chapter 7. The fundamental resource is land, especially arable land, and this exists in plenty. It may be argued that some of the poorer countries are in need of land reform, for in parts of South America especially international companies hold on to vast areas that they fail to cultivate. But where land reform has been carried out it has seldom been a solution in itself; besides, the amount of land that could be released in this way can come to only a small fraction of what is now uncultivated.

So to speak of any shortage of the most important resource of all for the production of food is to take us far into the realm of the fanciful. Labour and capital are the other factors of production. Labour is manifestly there: people by the millions, and the millions can grow the food for further millions. As to capital, very little is needed, because it would be foolish indeed to introduce capital to displace labour, as First World farmers have found it profitable to do. The simplest ploughs, the most elementary reaping methods and all other kinds of low or intermediate technology are what is needed. To send our 78 horsepower tractors and massive combines (the sort of thing some people have suggested in the past) would be self-defeating. Seed suitable for the soil, climate and terrain is less easy to supply, but the Taiwanese are in a position to help many countries, even those dissimilar to their own, and so also are several other Third World countries which have overcome their own difficulties. Lack of irrigation is a problem in most developing countries, and here capital is required. It is generally agreed that there need be no shortage of water, even in some of the driest regions of Africa; but extracting it, either by making wells or by drawing it from rivers on a modest scale, requires money. So does the planting of trees – perhaps the most necessary strategy in the fight against drought. External funds may be needed in most of the countries concerned, but comparatively speaking the sums would be small.

Two other resources must not be overlooked: fertilizers and pesticides. While it may be undesirable to encourage the Third World to become dependent upon chemical inputs, it would be idle to deny that both of these are already in widespread use and have succeeded, at least in the short term, in raising Third World food production. Each year Western Europe consumes about twenty-one times as much fertilizer as the whole of Africa, yet its area of cultivation is less, as Table 5 on p. 165 shows. Western European farmers can afford to buy it; Africans cannot. The price of fertilizer has risen considerably in the last two decades, from less than £20 a tonne in 1971 to eight or nine times as much in 1990,

but European farmers can still afford the price because the
more it rises the more their farm-gate prices also tend to
rise. The price that farmers in the EEC receive for their
wheat, their milk or nearly every other kind of food they
produce is fixed for them by the EEC, and in fixing the
price the EEC takes into account their costs. In short, the
higher price of the fertilizer is passed on to the customer
who buys the food.

The Third World cannot do business like that. Its customers, most of them too poor to buy enough food anyway,
are in no position to pay higher prices every time farmers
want them. The fertilizers, of course, are manufactured in
the main by a few giant international companies; they are
controlled in the West, and their first market is Western
agriculture because it is for them a certain and profitable
outlet.

A high-input/high-output system requires the use of ever
more fertilizers, but as with most other inputs, the law of
diminishing returns applies. In the UK the average amount
of fertilizer applied to an acre in 1961–2 was 31 units; by
1981–2 the average had increased to 93 units. This threefold
increase in fertilizer applications failed to increase yields
proportionately. The figures available for fertilizer use apply
to all agricultural land, and no separate estimate is obtainable
for individual crops. But I think most arable farmers would
agree that the increase in the use of fertilizers on their wheat
has been at least as great as the national average, and I suspect
they would concede that it has been substantially more. The
average wheat yield in 1961–2 was 1.40 tonnes an acre; in
1981–2 it was 2.55 tonnes. This means that the increase in
the use of fertilizer during the intervening period was in the
ratio of 3 to 1, while the increase in yields was only 1.82 to
1. The downward trend is pellucidly plain, and every agricultural scientist sees it continuing. Scientists also recognize
that much of the increase in wheat yields is due to better
varieties of seed; were it not for this improvement, the ratio
would show an even worse downward trend.

The only good news about the use of fertilizer in the UK
is that it is now on a plateau and in some areas it has gone
down. In the Third World the use of fertilizer is also

diminishing, but there the reason is higher cost. Instead of being able to use more fertilizers to grow more food, higher prices force farmers in poor countries to use less and thus to grow less food. Yet one tonne of fertilizer applied on previously unfertilized land there could yield an extra ten tonnes of grain. A tonne of fertilizer is likely to produce about five times more food in the Third World than applied on land in our own country.

In the language of the economist, this is a gross misallocation of resources. If there were a genuine free market, the resource would go where it would yield the greatest return. That does not happen because the price support for our farmers – and for farmers in other developed countries – makes it impossible for resources to be allocated in the most sensible manner. When certain politicians and farming leaders in the UK call for still higher output, they are in a position to have the farm–gate prices increased to make good the higher costs of the inputs. Neither individual farmers nor governments in the poor countries can compete.

This is not the end of the matter. These artificial fertilizers are exhaustible. Great reserves may still exist, but they get less all the time.

Some years ago I went to see a great area, several square miles in size, in Senegal, in West Africa, where phosphate is extracted. Enormous trucks take several tonnes at a time to the docks about eighty miles away, and there it is despatched to farmers who can afford to buy it, ours included. In that same country there are tens of thousands of people who are fortunate if they get a single meal in a day; families suffer from the diseases of malnutrition, and many people die as a result.

Experts repeatedly sound the alarm about the way we are using up these fertilizers. Again and again, they repeat that there will not be enough by the end of the present century. Perhaps one quotation will be enough; it is from *By Bread Alone* (1975) by Lester R. Brown and Erik P. Eckholm:

> Farmers in much of the world are confronted not only
> with higher fertilizer cost as the cost of energy rises, but
> also with lessening returns on fertilizer use. The amount

of grain produced with each additional ton of fertilizer used is beginning to diminish at the global level, largely because of the high levels of use in such areas as North America, Western Europe and Japan. Each additional million tons of fertilizer applied by the world's farmers now adds less food than was added by the preceding million tons. The total level of chemical fertilizers required at the century's end may be more than four times the 800 million tons being used today.

No country in the world is more to blame than the UK. Even the rest of the EEC does not use fertilizers on the scale we do; the Dutch are as extravagant as we are per farmer, but the total quantity they use is very much less. The United States, Canada, Australia and other major grain-growing countries have plenty of land to spare, and their land is much cheaper, so they are not under the same pressure to maximize yields.

As to pesticides, their importance to the Third World is greater than it is to us in the West. Ecologists can present a very persuasive case against their use, and in an ideal world it would be possible for the African and the South American to farm as the Chinese do. But a century or more of colonial influence has had its effect, and a great deal of both those continents is now dependent upon monoculture. If land can be made to grow coffee, tea, cocoa, sugar, bananas, copra or anything else more economically than some other land, then it has been. In one sense, it is eminently sensible that agriculture should be arranged like this; but it would be unfair to infer that this is the result of a free market system. The latter implies free trade and the removal of all barriers that separate a willing buyer from a willing seller. Such a robust principle did not fit in with the paternalistic thinking of the colonial rulers. France, Belgium, the Netherlands, Spain and Portugal, as well as the UK, all had bilateral arrangements with their colonial possessions that militated against the most elementary principles of free trade. A Frenchman trying to buy sugar in Barbados or an Englishman trying to buy maize in Mozambique would soon have been sent packing. Barbadian sugar was planted, grown and harvested for Britain or some other part of the Empire and for no one else. All the old imperial powers behaved in the same way. In return, each of the empires took its colonial chicks under its wing and protected them from the ravages of a rival power. Cash cropping has been the consequence.

A great part of an erstwhile colony, once made over to a single kind of crop, cannot easily now diversify into other forms of agriculture. Pundits from Brussels or London descend, from time to time, on these countries and tell them they should plant this or that instead, but the pundits usually arrive in total ignorance of how each kind of monoculture has developed subsidiary industries. Mills, factories, processing plants, research stations and a whole transport network, including perhaps a railway company to take the cash crop to the mills and then on to the docks: all these have grown up in most of the former colonies to handle the coffee, sugar and other cash crops, and they may employ more people than the plantations themselves. Since all these monocultures are prone to disease and pests that can decimate a crop, they cannot continue without pesticides.

The other special feature of the Third World is that most of it is tropical. The insects, mites, ticks, nematodes, fungi, bacteria, weeds, rodents, molluscs, crustaceans and viruses that can blight the life of a farmer tend to be more virulent, persistent and otherwise troublesome than those we encounter in our kinder, temperate climate. It has been said that food lost on the stalk through pests and disease in poor countries can be one-third of what is harvested, and 40 per cent of what is harvested can be lost in storage.

The price of all pesticides has rocketed upwards, however, and even in real terms they are now many times more expensive than they were ten years ago. As with fertilizers, the cost of pesticides is taken into account when farmers in the Common Market have their prices fixed for them. The agrochemical industry can charge accordingly. Also, as with fertilizers, our high-input/high-output ratio requires increasing use. This higher demand has the inevitable result of causing prices to rise still further, to the detriment of others in the world. It follows that we do not pay the true cost of our high-input/high-output system. We pass some part of it on to the poorest people in the world.

So let us now answer that first question in a sentence. All the resources are there on our planet to enable everyone to eat the food they should have, but so long as we pursue a high-output policy, financed by a price-support system, there is little chance of fertilizers being used to the best advantage; and fertilizers and pesticides will be made artificially more expensive and beyond the means of those who need them most. In this respect the policy-makers of Britain are as responsible as anyone else in the world. These men have been influenced by our agrochemical industry and have listened to its special pleading too much. Why were our policy-makers induced to give British farmers a subsidy of taxpayers' money to buy phosphate fertilizers in 1951? Why was that subsidy later extended to other fertilizers? When a definitive history of agriculture in the UK for the post-war years is written, perhaps its author will lay bare the truth.

Now let us turn to the second question, namely, if the resources are available, why do these hundreds of millions of hungry people not get the food they should have? Granted that fertilizers and pesticides are important and we are being selfish in their use, this still does not explain why those millions of acres of good arable land are not cultivated. The answer is really a matter of common sense, once one thinks a little about it. The business of growing food can be long and laborious, and from the time one begins the process to the time one gets paid for all the work, a year is likely to go by. There are millions of farmers in the world, from multi-millionaires to peasants in abject poverty, but they have one thing at least in common. None of them are minded to begin growing food for other people unless they are reasonably sure that they will get paid for it.

All those hundreds of millions cannot, in fact, pay for the food they want. Their need for food is one thing; their capacity to exchange some money for it is another. If there are about 950 million people suffering and dying from undernutrition or malnutrition, there are about the same number simply too poor to buy the food they need. The prime and fundamental cause of this mass hunger is poverty.

How then can this poverty be overcome? Doling out money from the exchequers of the wealthier nations is a possibility, but it does nothing to put matters permanently right. Sending them our surplus food is an alternative canvassed by the leaders of the NFU and the UK chemical industry, but this has several drawbacks. Much of our surplus food is of a kind that would be totally unsuitable, nor could its future supply be assured; but above all it would be ludicrous for us, as high-cost producers, to send food to people who cannot afford to pay for it, when the same type of food could be exported to them by low-cost producers in Australia, the United States and elsewhere. If the richer nations of the world are going to organize a scheme of food aid, it ought to be from those low-cost producers, rather than ourselves.

Another remedy is what the Third World has repeatedly sought in words that have become a cliché: trade not aid. Unfortunately, the meaning of that repeated request fails to be understood. Having had the good fortune to visit fifteen of the countries concerned, including two of the poorest of them, I have had spelt out for me in plain terms what they would like; it is that we should allow them to sell to us what they can produce. What they can sell is the produce of their soil. There is little else they can offer us or anyone else, except for the lucky countries that have mineral deposits. The EEC, through the Lomé Convention, may say that the Third World can export its manufactured goods into the Common Market, as if hundreds of thousands of its people were making cars, washing-machines or computers. So long as they remain developing countries, however, any second-ary or manufacturing industry will be primitive or non-existent. Of course, there are some factories in some parts of the Third World, but generally they are small, there to supply a local need and quite incapable of embarking upon any serious export trade. A number of poor countries have textile mills, but the EEC has imposed severe restrictions upon the entry of Third World textiles into its markets. Quotas have been introduced by the Multifibre Arrange-ment, so that fewer textiles are allowed in from the countries affected than previously. This has meant that their workers must now either produce more for lower wages, to allow other markets to be found, or produce less and thus accept a still lower standard of living.

Despite all the pretence to the contrary, the Lomé Convention included, a vast number of trade barriers exist to prevent the Third World exporting freely to us. At the same time, worsening terms of trade – made even more severe by the constant inflation in the West – have quadrupled or quintupled the price of Western exports to poor countries, many of these exports being essential for any improvement in their standard of living.

Let one example illustrate what has happened since the UK joined the Community. In 1972 a Jamaican could grow 21 tonnes of sugar and sell them for the price of a new 78 hp tractor imported from Britain. By 1982 he would have had to work twice as hard to grow 50 tonnes to buy the same kind of machine. But in 1990 it was necessary to produce over eight times more sugar than in 1972 for the tractor – instead of 21 tonnes, 170 tonnes! Not only the Jamaican, but almost every food producer in the developing countries (and they produce little else but food), has been caught in a scissors movement. On one side, they have to pay ever higher prices for what they buy from us; on the other, when allowance is made for inflation, they get reduced prices for what they are allowed to sell to us. The gap will continue to widen as long as the West continues its inflationary course, while at the same time placing numerous obstacles in the way of imports from the Third World. If we choose to make them poorer, we cannot be surprised to hear that they have less money to buy the food that they and their families should eat.

The countries where there is mass hunger tend to be those where, for the great majority of people, there is no other kind of work except farming. If they were able to export food, jobs would then be available for them to grow food and so earn money; and with the money they earned they could pay for their own food. Until that opportunity comes, it seems they can never get off the launching-pad, let alone launch themselves to a height where abject squalor is left behind. Getting rid of food in order to eat may appear, at first sight, too much of a paradox. So let us look at it through their eyes; and let us take one of the countries I visited.

There is a part of Senegal that is a microcosm of the Third World. It is along the banks of the River Senegal that divides Mauritania (one of the poorest of all the poor countries) from Senegal itself. This great river has, over the centuries, brought down from the hinterland rich alluvial silt, so today there are hundreds of thousands of acres of superb land; in the UK we would classify it as Grade I and value it at over £3,000 an acre. It goes uncultivated, apart from some 10,000 acres where a plantation has been established to grow sugar and tomatoes which are sent to Dakar, the capital, for local consumption, though the Senegalese hope to secure an export outlet. The land is much richer than what lies beside the Nile, where a million acres may afford three crops a year, where the sun shines every day and the waters of the Nile irrigate by night. Senegal could do as well as Egypt. Its river may be smaller, but it brings down more than enough water for the needs of the soil, and as in Egypt the sun shines unfailingly. Yet not only is the land uncultivated, but there are many thousands suffering from acute hunger on that very land. I saw small children with their bellies distended and their legs emaciated, and beside them were mothers who looked as if they were in their fifties but who were perhaps thirty years younger.

If anyone set about the task of cultivating that land in Senegal and actually growing food, what would happen to it? He would eat his share; and he could try to sell the rest, but he would look in vain for anyone who could pay for it. All around he would see people without enough money, perhaps with no money at all, and none of them would give him a livelihood for the work he had done.

The area I visited would probably be very suitable for growing maize. It is just the crop that should be grown in the tropics and it is almost as good a basis for a poor person's meal as can be devised. Perhaps rice could also be grown there. But neither can be imported into the UK unless an import levy is paid. Under the EEC regulations import levies are chargeable on agricultural produce from outside

Table 12   EEC import levies on rice, ACP countries and others, 1983

Description	ACP levy (£/tonne)	Other Third World countries (£/tonne)
Paddy rice round grain	121	249
Paddy rice long grain	123	253
Husked rice round grain	153	311
Husked rice long grain	155	316
Semi-milled rice, round grain	189	398
Semi-milled rice, long grain	230	479
Wholly milled rice, round grain	202	424
Wholly milled rice, long grain	246	513
Broken rice	73	152

the Common Market; the Lomé Convention gives a privilege to about fifty former colonies of the European powers known as the ACP group (Africa, Caribbean and Pacific) by which their produce my enter on payment of a reduced levy. For years, supporters of the EEC claimed that the Lomé Convention enabled these former colonies to have free access to our market. As is now increasingly recognized, the truth has been rather different. Table 12 (above) appeared in Hansard in answer to my parliamentary written question in 1990.

Rice, like maize, can be grown in many countries in the Third World, and the more it is milled or processed there the more work is found for those who live there. A *nil* rate of levy would be a considerable benefit to them, but the table shows that the more the rice is processed the higher the rate of levy. In fact, the levy is exactly doubled for milled rice. Third World countries outside the ACP group – and several of them are the poorest of all – pay the full levy; and if they choose wholly to mill their rice in competition with the Italians, the levy is fixed at over £200 a tonne. The levy apart, the prospect of being able to export not only maize and rice but many other kinds of food either to the UK or to any other part of the Common Market dims as the years go by and our quest for self-sufficiency narrows the market for any exporter.

As we know, the EEC's degree of self-sufficiency exceeds 100 per cent in numerous commodities. Beef, wheat, barley, butter, cheese, rice, malt, wheat flour, whole milk powder, skimmed milk powder, condensed milk, pig meat, poultry meat, sugar and wine are all in surplus. Export subsidies have to be paid out to secure a place in the world market for this food and drink we do not want, and these export subsidies fill the Third World with dismay, as they do the United States, Canada, Australia, New Zealand and other countries that depend upon food exports for their trade abroad. For them to compete against us in a food war in which both sides try to undercut the other by lowering their export prices to below the cost of production is out of the question. The result is that the Third World's share of food exports to the world market is declining. Figures taken from the UN *Monthly Bulletin of Statistics* show the percentage of the world trade in food achieved by the Third World falling from 37.1 per cent in 1960 to 27.7 per cent in 1981, a remorselessly downward trend. A fall of some 10 per cent of the share of trade, when it is one's principal and perhaps only source of foreign exchange, verges upon the catastrophic.

Now for the third question: what have we done wrong and how can we put it right? This can be easily answered; the UK should unilaterally declare a free trade policy. Two results would follow immediately for the Third World. First, it would regain the chance to supply our consumers with food (while our consumers regained their freedom to buy that food). Secondly, we would no longer be a party to the EEC's policy of dumping surplus food on the world market in competition with other countries that cannot afford to use their taxpayers' money in that way. As Britain is one of the two chief paymasters of the Common Agricultural Policy, such a decision would effectively bring to an end the guarantee section of its fund that pays for that dumping.

The decision would hurt a few people, but the financial loss to some individuals and a few companies would have to be set against gains that could not be counted in money. True, opening up our own market to the outside world would go only a fraction of the distance towards providing hundreds of millions with an income; but even a few million people given what they should have – and what they will never get if attitudes do not change – would be a giant step forward for them and an example for others to follow.

Having shaped the economies of some twenty or thirty countries so that they grew cash crops to our advantage, it may be said that we still owe an obligation to them to buy those crops at fair and reasonable prices. This is one argument for commodity agreements. Such long-term agreements can also be justified on purely commercial grounds, as in the case of the old Commonwealth Sugar Agreement which had to be brought to an end when we entered the Common Market. Sugar, indeed, highlights the plight of the poorest victims.

Of all the Third World victims, the cane sugar growers deserve a special mention. We in the UK have played a unique part in their declining fortunes, and it was because of our special obligation to the cane sugar growers that, when entering the EEC, we negotiated an agreement to permit their sugar to continue to come into the country, despite the rules of the CAP which would otherwise have excluded it.

What is this special obligation? The main countries concerned – Jamaica, Barbados, Guyana, Trinidad, Fiji, Mauritius and some others to a lesser degree – were peopled by our forefathers. Although slavery came to an end many generations ago, indentured Indians were still being taken to Guyana, Mauritius and Fiji as recently as 1917, in the lifetime of people living today. The system was not so very different from slavery. The Indians were coaxed by dubious promises to sign an indenture and, once transported to their destination, were kept in bond-yards for the hours when they were not marshalled into the sugar factories or out on to the cane fields. Put bluntly, they were imprisoned to stop them escaping.

For this we received the cheapest sugar in the world. It is not a portion of history that we should forget, because even to this day the British people are able to benefit from having had that cheap food. It has made us richer than we would otherwise have been. Cheap sugar enabled us to spend more money on other items and so raise our standard of living and develop other industries. The wealth thus gained has still not been lost; and all of us, to a larger or lesser degree, are to this day better off as a result of hundreds of thousands of men and women gathering in a harvest of sugar cane for generations of British people to eat. It would be hard to deny that we have a moral obligation to protect their descendants from the vicissitudes of a volatile world market for sugar, made even more so by ourselves.

Thus this special obligation became a feature of the UK's negotiations in joining the Common Market. The outcome was an agreement whereby the Commonwealth sugar producers, Australia excepted, would be allowed to export to us 1.2 million tonnes a year at prices comparable to those of Common Market growers. They were joined by Surinam, Zaïre and Malagasy to form the ACP group, though the additional three countries sell only about 30,000 tonnes under the agreement. This 1.2 million tonnes represents about half their production; the other half has to be sold in the world market at world prices. At the time it seemed to the Commonwealth a reasonable arrangement, and only the Jamaican Minister of Agriculture, John Gyles, had the foresight to see the danger ahead – that the European beet growers, armed with modern technology, would have ever increasing yields and ever larger surpluses of sugar to get rid of.

The root of the trouble is that sugar, whether cane or beet, is quite an easy crop to grow, and it can be grown in extremely difficult conditions when nothing else seems to provide a reliable crop. The forebears of today's sugar producers were shipped to those places, and there is little else they can do to earn a livelihood in them except grow sugar. Barbados may not be typical, but its experience is worth recording. It is a coral island, and the soil can be cultivated to a depth of little more than a foot. The Barbadians have been told to diversify into other forms of agriculture, and no less than fifty-five other crops have been tried. They have all failed, with the partial exception of tomatoes and a few other vegetables, which have been only a moderate success. One of my visits to Barbados coincided with Hurricane Allen, when two merchant ships were swept on to the beaches, and trees and houses were uprooted, to be hurled extraordinary distances. Yet the sugar cane survived. Though combed down by the tempestuous wind, it recovered its normal stance to yield only a quarter less than would have been usual. On the other hand, the banana trees and most of the tomatoes and other crops were laid waste.

Perhaps we should confess that we ought never to have peopled places like Barbados for the purpose of growing food; but we cannot turn back the clock now, and those who live in Barbados must take the consequences. They have gone some way in developing a tourist trade, which brings with it many drawbacks when taken beyond a certain stage, as Jamaica and the Bahamas have learned. Some engineering and other industries have been set up but on too small a scale to make exporting worthwhile or to employ as many men and women as the sugar industry.

The problems of Fiji and Mauritius are similar to those of Barbados. Trinidad has found oil, but Jamaica and Guyana, though they have bauxite to extract, are also dependent upon sugar for their people to have a livelihood worth the name. As it is, Jamaica's unemployment rate is one of the worst in the world, about 30 per cent, and its acute poverty (with no unemployment benefit or social security) has brought the country unhealthily close to a Cuban brand of communism. To prevent even more people losing their jobs, the Jamaican Parliament, some years ago, made it illegal for the sugar farmers to mechanize. The decision placed them in a dilemma; mechanization would have lowered their costs and allowed them to compete more easily on the world market, and so part of their export trade was lost. The other cane-growing countries have also put curbs upon mechanization of varying kinds, with the same object of preventing an increase in unemployment. In any case, they can hardly afford the cost of mechanization.

Guyana, Fiji and Swaziland are the three countries that, with Queensland in Australia, can produce sugar more cheaply than anywhere else. One might suppose, therefore, that they would have first place in the world market. They don't. Like the other low-cost producers they have gone through a crisis, through being forced to compete with the world's highest-cost producers, those in the EEC, whose sugar is dumped on the world market with the aid of enormous subsidies.

Because sugar is, compared with most other crops, easy to grow, too much of it is being produced at a time when total consumption is standing still and in some countries, including the UK, declining. Throughout the EEC, consumption is about 9 million tonnes a year, but production is 13 million tonnes. To this surplus must be added the 1.2 million tonnes of Commonwealth sugar. Most of the total surplus has had to be sold on the world market; but 80 per cent of the sugar traded is sold in accordance with long-term contracts at agreed prices, which means that a residual world market requires about only 5 million tonnes of sugar. The sudden addition of another 5 millions tonnes obviously has a catastrophic effect upon prices. At one point in 1982 the world price went down to £83 a tonne, and for weeks on end it remained at less than £100. No farmer, no matter how personally efficient or how favourably blessed with soil or climate, can grow sugar at that price. The lowest of the low-cost producers in the world need a price of £140 a tonne to break even.

Guyana is in the league of low-cost producers. Its rich land on the South Atlantic coast has been for generations a superb area for sugar. When the world price fell to below £100 a tonne, I had the opportunity of seeing at first hand the effect this had upon a country whose main source of foreign exchange was its sugar exports. Unless Guyana can sell sugar, the country comes to a standstill – literally. There is no oil, no petrol; there are no spare parts for cars or tractors, and obviously no new vehicles. It is difficult to imagine what happens to a country when, to carry on at all, it is forced to sell its exports at nearly half the cost of production. The consequences also happen very quickly. My wife and I stayed at the foremost hotel in the capital, owned by Trusthouse Forte, whose manager had been the assistant manager of a famous hotel in London only six weeks previously. High standards would normally have prevailed, and the menu for breakfast would have been pretty good. In fact, we had black coffee; the poor manager could get nothing else: no bread to make toast, no flour in the capital, except on the black market. It didn't matter really to us – it was probably rather good for us – but out on the plantations it was a different story. To maintain yields, considerable quantities of fertilizer are required, so the government gave priority to them being imported; but it could not also give priority to new tractors and other machinery, nor to spare parts. So on one plantation we visited four tractors were in use instead of fourteen, and the men who should have been working hard were standing about in idleness. The costs of the following year's crop would go up, the land might not be so well tilled, and the harvest would suffer.

Perhaps the most vivid impression of all came when we visited a modern hospital, serving a district where many thousands lived. There were only four patients in the men's ward, and there was one in the women's. Yet there were hundreds of men and women waiting for operations or some other treatment in that hospital. The surgeons were there, and so were the nurses, the pharmacists and all the other staff; the operating theatres were open and waiting. Everything was available except just one element: drugs. These had to be imported from abroad, principally from the UK, and there was no foreign exchange available. Whether people died as a result I do not know for certain; one of the surgeons was convinced that they would.

An attempt has been made by the Common Market to stem the rising tide of sugar surpluses flooding over the world market, and the new regime had been introduced before our visit to Guyana. The theory of it is that EEC producers will pay for the cost of their dumping. True, this has caused a reduction from the amount of sugar produced in previous years, but there is still an annual surplus of several milion tonnes. The EEC Commission recognizes that the price given to sugar growers in the Common Market is set so high that they can afford to pay a levy for the surplus to be dumped abroad. Worse still, the new policy assumes that a quantity of sugar equivalent to whatever may be imported from the ACP countries will be re-exported, and the subsidy for its sale in the world market will be paid for by the EEC itself. This policy provides the funds needed to dump between 3 million and 4 million tonnes of sugar. It nullifies the good that the agreement to import the 1.2 million tonnes may give the poorest among the sugar growers. It means that the sugar they grow and sell to us is used to undercut the price of the rest of their sugar.

In round figures, the Commonwealth countries have 2.5 million tonnes of sugar to export. They receive a reasonable price for half of it from British importers; so far, so good. But the remaining half must still be sold and at a price that is, to all intents and purposes, fixed by the quantity of surplus sugar that the EEC chooses to sell. When it resells the Commonwealth producers' sugar, plus its own surplus, the effect is to undermine the chance of cane sugar growers being able to sell at a price over the cost of production.

The longer the EEC behaves in this way, the poorer the people of Guyana, Fiji, Barbados, Jamaica and other Third World producers will become. And the longer we continue to block imports of all kinds of food from the poor countries which produce it, the longer we will prevent them from earning for themselves the only income they are equipped to earn. The direct financial costs of surpluses fall on the people of Europe. The indirect costs, which are far more serious, fall on many people throughout the world, and they fall most heavily on the poorest. There is not a citizen in Europe who, at that thought, ought not to feel a sense of bitter shame.

· 10 ·

FARMING WITH A FUTURE

'Agriculture is a biological system.' Dr Mark Whalon looked me firmly in the eye as he said it. He is one of a team at the Michigan State University exploring how agriculture can be pursued biologically. A visitor is struck at once by the enthusiasm pervading their department. Agriculture becoming ever more dependent upon the drugs of the chemical industry is the danger they see, and if there is not a change of direction now, we may go too far to avert some terrible consequences. The purpose of biological farming, in short, is to get away from the economic and chemical treadmill.

The economic treadmill was described in outline in Chapter 5. Let us take a look here at what it means in practice, and as typical examples let us take first pig farming and then poultry.

THE BIAS AGAINST HUMANE AND HEALTHY FARMING

One effect of the United Kingdom's support policy is to make traditional animal husbandry uneconomic and to foster intensive 'factory farming'. It has been possible to set up a modern intensive unit of, say, 300 sows, with the progeny going to either pork or bacon, very largely with tax allowances. Anyone wanting to start a herd of the same size kept extensively – on free range – has not been entitled to the same assistance.

A factory farm will need only a few acres of land. These, it is true, will have to be purchased out of the owner's capital, but they are unlikely to cost more than £10,000, which represents a very small percentage of the total needed. A much larger amount, at least £100,000, will go on the buildings, and it has been possible to write off all of that against income tax over a period of years. Then fittings and equipment must be purchased, and these are also likely to cost more than £100,000. They include the narrow and inhumane sow stalls described earlier in this book. Sows used to live six or seven years, giving birth to litters large enough each time to make it worth the while of their owners to keep them for that length of time. Now sows seldom last three years; smaller, weaker litters will otherwise be born as a result of these conditions. The cost of sow stalls, farrowing pens, the automatic feeding devices and all the other factory-style equipment has also been allowed against tax.

The advantage to a large-scale farmer with an income of £100,000 or more a year is obvious enough; the advantage to one of the many farming companies that have been formed in the last two decades is still more so. It is the essential reason why this type of animal husbandry has been taken over by the companies. They have paid less tax as each year they have expanded, and plainly their expansion has been at the expense of the small farmer. A farm (if it can be so called) where 1,000 sows are kept in row after row of sow stalls has become not uncommon.

The fourth item in order of purchase would be the pigs themselves and the feedstuffs. Again, tax privileges are available when one comes to expand the size of the herd. Admittedly, the taxpayer is not called upon to pay for the feed, but any farming company or individual farmer large enough can secure favourable terms with one of the major companies, such as Unilever and Rank Hovis McDougall, so that the cost of the first supply of feed is not paid for until the returns come in. Needless to say, the small farmer is seldom able to receive credit so favourably.

Now let us see what happens when someone wants to keep pigs extensively, that is, in fields rather than factories. The 300 sows will be out in the open, and about 100 acres will be needed – more or less, depending on how well the land is drained. This is twenty times as much land as needed for an intensive unit, so the first item of expenditure will be, let us say, £200,000. This price is far higher than it should be, because of the distortions produced by protection and subsidies, but the farmer who pays it receives no tax allowances. Sow huts, fencing and other pieces of equipment will cost a fraction of what his intensive competitor will have paid out, perhaps less than £5,000, and this will have brought relief from tax. It will be seen straight away that, in the matter of tax allowances, the factory farmer has been able to set most of his capital expenditure against tax, while the other farmer has virtually no such advantage.

Despite the great discrepancy of treatment, an appreciable number of arable farmers in the UK, especially when they have well-drained downland, with underlying chalk to provide the drainage, are finding it profitable – but only just – to establish outdoor herds. Such herds are to be found in Berkshire, Oxfordshire, Wiltshire and Hampshire, especially on the higher land, usually acting as a break-crop. A sow may eat a tonne of concentrated feed in the course of a year, so the dung of 100 sows concentrated on some thirty acres for a few months at a time enriches the soil. By suppressing the growth of weeds in that period the pigs also become natural herbicides. Anyone taking possession of a derelict smallholding years ago used to know the value of a few sows being turned out into the worst of the fields. The gain to the soil and natural advantages of such a break-crop have enabled these outdoor herds to make a come-back. Anyone inspecting them would have to admit that, winter or summer, the sows look considerably more contented and healthier than their sisters in the sow stalls. If it is good farming, as experienced observers believe it to be, should it be penalized?

A modern pig unit of 1,000 sows in stalls and many thousands of pigs being fattened by ultra-intensive methods, employing only two or three men, all on a few acres of concrete, resembles a factory in more ways than one. Transformed by the long arm of technology, it has become something quite different to the pig farm of twenty-five years ago when one man looked after thirty sows and made a fair living. In one room there may be a computer, adjusting feed levels daily for every sow, or performing some other function; in another room perhaps a close-circuit television set, recording how the sows are farrowing; and in yet another there will be shelf upon shelf resembling a doctor's pharmacy. In their white coats, the employees look like – and they are – technicians. The sows are numbered and not named, and two or three essential statistics determine the life span, unlike the mixture of different criteria some years ago. All this is done in the name of efficiency, but it is also done with the aid of a tax system that does not choose to give comparable help to the farmer who tries to compete using other methods; and if this aid were taken away it is extremely doubtful whether such a modern pig unit could survive. At least, no one in his right mind would invest £300,000 of his own capital in such a venture, nor would any bank manager lend that money to him. Public money, directly or indirectly, has become available, and a branch of technology has stepped in to take advantage of what is offered.

Once the import levies were imposed upon feedstuffs, the need for further technological advances was made imperative. The British pig farmer was now being put out by a high tax on his largest item of expenditure; and no matter how efficient he might be, he simply could not survive unless in every other item of expenditure he made drastic economies. In fact, they could not be made unless he enjoyed economies of scale. Hence the steady decline in the number of pig breeders after 1970. In 1971 there were, according to Ministry of Agriculture figures, 62,900. By 1976 the number had declined to 35,300; in 1983 it was down still further to 20,600, and by 1989 a mere 13,100. Thus, in less than twenty years more than three-quarters of them have gone out of business, their efficiency notwithstanding.

A critic of what is being done is in danger of being dismissed as a latter-day Luddite, a fuddy-duddy reactionary who stands in the way of farming progress. Such a riposte misses the target, however. Should a new technology be encouraged when it promotes the inhumane and unhealthy treatment of animals? And can such technology as we have introduced to our farms really be described as efficient? Is

Concorde efficient? It is one of the supreme marvels of technology but still has to be paid for by somebody. If the passenger cannot afford the fare, it seems rather hard that the rest of us, who stay at home, must pay the balance. Getting some little pig ready for the slaughterhouse two or three weeks more quickly is efficient in much the same way as Concorde is. It seems marvellous, but not when we have worked out the true cost.

The economics of pig farming have afflicted my life for many years, and I am glad that those of the poultry world have passed me by. The essence is the same, but its effect is still worse. Looking after animals of any kind is a labour-intensive operation. To look after farm animals humanely – to get them to yield profitably, yet retain their health – demands patience, diligence and understanding. Many people possess these qualities, but they have been so penalized for practising their skills that few can now be found on British farms. The humble hen demands such qualities, as do the dairy cow and the farrowing sow. Put tens of thousands of them together in one unit, and no stockman on earth can practise the skills of good husbandry by himself. Modern technology has stepped in, however, and now one man can look after them profitably.

The computer has invented hybrid hens that look alike, eat and drink alike and generally behave alike. This has been its purpose, and it has been very largely successful. But what is the value of such success? It has created conditions for animals which many of us find distasteful, as well as producing a marked deterioration in the quality of our food and the character of our countryside. The hybrid hens are not, however, identical. I own a small farm which is let and where the tenants keep about a dozen hens to supply themselves and a few other people with eggs, housed in an old-fashioned movable chicken house in an open compound of a few square yards. Each batch has come from a modern poultry farm, and theoretically they should behave alike. Yet it is noticeable that soon after they are released in the compound the hens develop distinct characters, and their needs for food and water begin to vary significantly. They look considerably healthier than those in the battery cages, and under these free-range conditions it is profitable to keep them to a much older age.

Once we went over to a system of import levies on wheat and maize, the day of the smaller producer came to an end. He was still efficient in the sense that he could earn a livelihood without a policy of price support, but not when the largest item in his expenditure was grossly taxed. Statistics show how poultry farming has changed out of all recognition.

According to the *Annual Revew*, in 1967 there were 179,000 holdings with up to 1,000 laying fowl. This was a high percentage of the total number of agricultural holdings, which was 338,000 in that year. Of course, many of the birds were kept for household needs, but five years later the number fell to 106,000. The inference must be that a large number of producers were driven out because their flock ceased to be profitable. This is confirmed by the sharp increase in the number of large flocks in the same period. In 1967 only 39.9 per cent of all laying fowl were in flocks of over 5,000. By 1973 the percentage had risen to 67.4 per cent. Then the *Annual Reviews* had to increase the largest unit to 20,000 birds. In 1976, 50 per cent of laying fowl were in flocks of 20,000 or more; by 1983 the figure had risen to 64 per cent, and by 1989 to 72 per cent. The broiler figures are even more startling. In 1989 most broilers were in flocks of 100,000 or more, with 39 million birds on only 200 'farms'.

These trends have divorced British poultry production from farming in the ordinary sense of the word. Through their subsidiaries, two great corporations – the Hillsdown Group and Unigate – took over from the farmer's wife with her modest flock. This useful supplement to the income of nearly every small farmer has been removed by the tax system. A multi-million-pound commercial concern can set up huge factory farms, each one keeping tens of thousands of birds, and the cost of every item of the factory can be written off against tax.

The new approach has now extended to turkeys. Tens of thousands of farms used to fatten about thirty or forty turkeys every year for the Christmas market. They provided an extra job on the farm after the harvest was in; and, being housed in a barn or two or three stables, they were easily attended to when the shorter days of November and December came. In a word, they fitted very neatly into the farming year, and they gave the farmer another source of income that seldom failed him. For the work and risk involved, the return was well worth his while. This convenient sideline has gone. Two large companies have put up a series of 'turkey farms', and several of them are now in my constituency. They consist of perhaps four or five acres, all concreted, and six or more huge turkey-houses, each taking up nearly half an acre, into which go tens of thousands of baby turkeys. The land itself is bought for 'agricultural use' and costs perhaps £15,000. All the rest of it – the concreting, the erection of the buildings, the putting in of all the plant and fittings – can be set against tax by these companies. The effective net cost to them of a 'farm' costing £250,000 may be comparatively small.

The economies of scale achieved have to be acknowledged, and they have given the public the chance to buy both eggs and poultry meat at prices, in real terms, lower than those that prevailed years ago. But how much lower would they be if the most expensive input were not taxed? If, as most producers claim, feed costs are about 70 per cent of the total cost of production for most eggs and broilers, and the main part of the feed is taxed at over £100 a tonne, it must follow that getting rid of the tax would have two consequences. First, the price of eggs and poultry meat would fall substantially, and the public would be able to buy more of both of them. Secondly, the pressure upon the poultry producers to adopt the more aggressive and intensive methods of husbandry would diminish. Lower costs would have a relaxing effect upon the producer; and the consumer would be the beneficiary – as well as millions of birds.

An additional bias is introduced into the system by the way research is funded. Aside from the money spent by the big agricultural supply industries, far more public money has gone into developing intensive methods that into more humane alternatives. A visit to the animal research establishment at Babraham is enough to convince anyone that this research has no limit (see Chapter 8).

Yet, despite all the obstacles put in their path, there are still farmers who are ready to pioneer better, less intensive methods, and their numbers are growing. The farming establishment thinks them cranky. NFU leaders dismiss them as inefficient. ADAS officials shake their heads and call them hopeless. The agribusiness salesmen pass them by as loonies, for obvious reasons. But when the leaders of agriculture smirk at farmers who make a profit without taxpayers' money, while they give their respect to those who cannot make a livelihood out of their farm unless given ever more government help as each year goes by, other people may suspect that their sense of values has gone awry. In no other branch of the nation's economy is there a similar attitude of mind.

SUSTAINABILITY

There are various types of low-input agriculture, going by different names. Some speak of biological agriculture, others of organic farming, biodynamic agriculture or ecological husbandry. There are differences between the four, but the differences are far less important than their common aims. Standards have been laid down for organic farming, but there is no single definition; biological agriculture, on the other hand, has been given an accepted definition by Dr R. D. Hodges, editor of *Biological Agriculture and Horticulture*, the official journal of the International Institute of Biological Husbandry:

> Biological agriculture can be defined as a system that attempts to provide a balanced environment, in which the maintenance of soil fertility and the control of pests and disease are achieved by the enhancement of natural processes and cycles, with only mode rate inputs of energy and resources, while maintaining an optimum productivity. The introduction into a biological system of chemicals such as fertilizers tends to short-circuit these natural processes and thus a proper interpretation of this definition should not allow the use of soluble fertilizers or synthetic pesticides into the system.

Official wisdom has been to discount any need for a change, and has also supported the claim of the chemical industry that without the use of its methods, especially pesticides and fertilizers, there would not be enough food for the world's population. In tropical countries it is undoubtedly difficult to keep cereals and other foodstuffs in store without them being devastated by various pests, and often in the past a whole harvested crop of a community has been lost in this way. So much of the Third World being in the tropics, the advance of monoculture has certainly added to the risk of potential damage done by pests. Thus – having seen all the problems arising from high-input methods – it is fair to ask, can biological farming sustain the world and yield enough for several billion humans?

The question posed by the chemical industry and its supporters is wrong, however. The world is not going biological for a long while yet. The majority of farmers in the West have neither the experience nor the knowledge to do so, and only a minority have the temperament. What is important is that official policy changes direction now and encourages the handful of farmers who are leading the way towards a practical alternative, despite government indifference.

In one respect, it will mean going back to what countless farmers have done in the past. Chemical agriculture as we know it today is a phenomenon of the post-war period, and to revive skills of half a century ago should not be excessively difficult. In the main, however, biological farming is not a return to what our forebears may have done. It is forward-looking or it is nothing; it is about how we can sustain agriculture on a secure footing with both the methods that have been proved reliable in the past and a host of others which are still being experimented upon.

One way to illustrate the divide between chemical and biological methods is to describe the first as *linear* and the second as *cyclical*. The inputs sold to farmers by the chemical industry all come from far away. Phosphates may be taken from a mine in West Africa, nitrates from oil from the North Sea bed; pesticides, drugs and other compounds may be made synthetically from elements drawn from many places.

In most cases, these inputs are from finite supplies, sources which at some stage in the future will be exhausted. Once these substances have served their purpose on the farm, no attempt is made to retrieve them. As often as not they get swept away down a river or washed into a sewage system and in many cases wend their way to the oceans. A small fraction of them goes into our food.

Nitrates, pesticides, antibiotics – whatever the chemical aid, they have one direct effect which invariably requires a continuation: a single dose is not enough. Repeated applications become necessary, and the subsequent treatment usually has to be greater and stronger than what was previously found adequate. The more we use chemicals on our farms, the more it seems we *have* to use. As the quantities used have increased, so have the unwanted side-effects. A chemical may be targeted upon one facet of the farm but, even though it hits its target, others inescapably get affected. While nitrates stimulate the growth of wheat, for example, we are still discovering the effect they have on our water supply and in causing an imbalance in the soil which, in turn, leads to various deficiencies.

To treat agriculture as a linear exercise is to misconceive its very nature. The chemical approach sees only its narrower function of food production and holds that it is technically feasible to treat every aspect of farming as if on an assembly line. This, of course, reduces food production to a mechanical conception. The soil is treated as, and becomes, an inert substance which, as the years go by, receives a regulated supply of elements: seeds, fertilizers and water, plus some sunshine, which is not so easily regulated. But the premise is false, as we have seen, and the approach is disastrous in the long term.

Biological methods, by contrast, recognize good husbandry as cyclical. What dies will decay and disappear yet live again in some other form. This new form, too, will eventually die, and the cycle goes round again. The process of decay is itself full of life. The wind, rain, frost and sun are agents of decay; so are the millions of living creatures that transform the cabbage leaf or blade of grass into many million different micro-organisms. It is nature's law that every organic being becomes, in due course, the sustenance of another being. To the biologist this is elementary stuff, the basis on which life can be sustained indefinitely. Yet if the natural movement of the cycle is disrupted – for example, by the use on the land of large amounts of synthetic substances – it cannot be expected to function as it should and cannot be relied upon to sustain us.

It is thus a slow process to go from conventional to organic farming. The soil has to be rested, preferably by being put down to pasture for a period of time, sometimes for two or three years, and this enables it to recover its population of living creatures.

To speak of this alternative as 'farming with nature' is somewhat misleading. Any form of agriculture is an interference with nature's wilderness. The modern pig looks very different from the animal that once came from the humid forests of South-East Asia. Man has changed its conformation, colour, behaviour and, no doubt, its taste; so much so that it might well have difficulty in surviving in the habitat of its forebears. The new varieties of seed which enable wheat yields to be 4 tonnes to the acre have likewise been evolved by human hand; and to the eye of the botanist they produce a crop looking quite different from what used to be seen. The very business of keeping pigs on a farm, even as they used to be kept in sties, is not 'natural', any more than it is 'natural' to plough a field and plant seeds of wheat. There is, however, a distinction to be drawn between farming with nature in accordance with biological principles and farming regardless of any natural cycle.

I am indebted to Dr Hodges for giving me the following outline of the principles on which biological agriculture is based:

- The health of soil, plant, animal and man are linked by a common nutritional cycle.
- The health of the whole cycle will be diminished by a loss of soil fertility or by any imbalance introduced into the soil by improper husbandry.
- All living materials and waste products must be returned

to the soil for the maintenance and improvement of its fertility.

- This return is necessary for the purification of waste materials which would otherwise cause pollution and for the recycling of essential elements.
- The soil should retain an ordered structure, with decomposing material on the surface and humus-enriched soil below. This implies a minimum of soil disturbance.
- As in natural ecosystems, plants and animals should coexist, each as mixed communities. Crop rotations and mixed stocking constitute a practical expression of this principle.
- As far as possible the soil should always be covered by living and decaying material.
- The resources of an area are usually adequate for sustained growth within that area.

In the last few decades, many thousands of students have passed through the UK's agricultural colleges, and together they now command most of our acres. Should any of them read those eight principles, they will acknowledge that their college training, supplemented by all the advice they have received from ADAS, let alone from the technical representatives who call upon them from the companies servicing agriculture, has led them to do the opposite to each one of them. This underlines how difficult it will be to get farmers off the chemical treadmill, and how crucial it is for the government to set aside the resources to enable the change to be made.

GREEN FARMING FOR PROFIT

Of the small but growing number of farmers who do adhere to these eight principles, one of the best known is Barry Wookey of Upavon near Devizes in Wiltshire. What impresses visitors when they first meet him is that no one could look less of a beard-and-sandals crank. He is late middle aged. Everything about him is conventional, except his farming. His appearance is that of a successful business man; and his farm is indeed a successful business.

Mr Wookey owns 1,650 acres and rents a further 4,350. He began to go over to organic methods in 1970 by converting two fields, and each year since he has made another two or three fields change over. The process began by putting the fields down to grass, two years for grazing and one for hay. The fields are then ploughed up and left as bastard fallow, which can be an effective cleaning operation for heavy land, before being sown with winter wheat. The organically grown wheat is sold to a local mill to be made into bread-making flour. The mill, however, belongs to Mr Wookey, and as it is on the farm, transport costs are reduced to enable the wheat to be sold at a higher profit than would be obtained elsewhere; his price is usually about £200 a tonne. The backing of grass cannot give his land enough fertility, so it is supplemented by the dung from a herd of about 400 beef cattle and a stud of thirty-seven horses, mainly hunters, which he breeds. There is also a flock of sheep. No nitrates or pesticides are applied, there being no problem of weeds to affect the quality of the crop. Mr Wookey aims for a yield of 2 tonnes to the acre, about half of what an efficient conventional farmer would grow, but has achieved a yield of 2.5 tonnes.

In the mid-1980s ADAS undertook a costing, comparing this organic farmer's profits with those of conventional farms of comparable size. The result is interesting – see Table 13 (p. 260). The high yields of conventional methods are matched against the low cost of organic husbandry; and the latter wins. The cost of seeds and cultivation is more for the organic farmer, but the absence of sprays and fertilizers gives him a two-to-one advantage. Despite the considerable difference in yields, the value of the organic crop is slightly better for Mr Wookey even at ordinary organic prices. It is the margin that counts, and there appears on the face of it no doubt whose is best.

Some reservations must be made. Mr Wookey uses dung from his livestock as natural fertilizer, but the stock could lose him money, so any such loss ought to be included as a cost. Also, organic husbandry requires more skill, and the above figures make no allowance for the higher cost of

Table 13   Cost and profit comparison between conventional and organic farming, 1983 and 1984, per hectare

	Conventional	Organic
Seed	£40.60	£48.86
Cultivation	£65.38	£75.72
Harvesting	£58.00	£58.00
Fertilizer	£118.28	—
Sprays	£98.43	—
Totals	£380.69	£182.58
Years 1983 and 1984 average yield	7.4 tonnes/ha	4.4 tonnes/ha
Sold at standard price	£836.60	£528.00
Sold at organic price	—	£704.00
Sold at Rushall minimum price (£200/tonne)	—	£880.00
Margins:		
at standard price	£455.91	£345.42
at organic price	—	£521.42
at minimum price	—	£697.42

management. More important is the initial expense of conversion. Taking land out of cultivation for perhaps three years and putting it down to pasture deprives the owner of any income from growing a profitable crop. Mr Wookey lost a lot of money doing this and had to balance the books by getting his conventional farming to subsidize the cost of conversion. Not many arable farmers, their land mortgaged and with overdrafts at the bank, could afford to do the same.

Mr Wookey insists that, whereas conventional wheat growers cost the taxpayers many millions of pounds in subsidies, he costs them nothing. This is demonstrably true, as every ounce of his wheat is eaten by people willing to pay a premium price for its quality, whereas conventional farmers produce surplus wheat of poor quality that has to be dumped on the world market at a knock-down price. He is, though, a man of exceptional talent and determination. Any fool, Mr Wookey says, can farm; but to farm organically you have to be a real farmer and must put your heart in it.

When he decided to make the change-over, after reading Rachel Carson's *Silent Spring*, there was scarcely another arable farmer in the country to whom he could turn for advice, either on how to begin or on how to overcome the long catalogue of troubles which beset him. No university department of agriculture was interested. The Ministry of Agriculture scorned him, and its advisory service was useless. As for the legion of agricultural consultants, there was no money for them in telling him how to keep away from chemicals. It will probably be a long while before the majority of arable farmers are able to farm as Barry Wookey does.

Yet, despite the difficulties, biological farming is on the increase in the UK.★ Sir Julian Rose is another successful organic producer. He began to convert in 1975 and had completed the process by 1984. His 260 acres consist of 40 acres of permanent grass, with the remainder alternating between three-year leys and winter wheat, spring oats, spring barley, turnips and kale. The grassland provides for a dairy herd of 35 to 40 Guernseys, beef cattle, sheep, pigs and poultry. The herd supplies cream and about 230 bottles of milk daily – a modest yield that does not compromise the health or longevity of the stock. Sir Julian's 700 free-range hens are each kept for two years and expected to lay 200 eggs a year. Like his cattle and pigs, the poultry are fed largely on home-grown cereals; all the barley and 40 per cent of the oats and wheat are retained on the farm. He recently introduced free-range turkeys and expects his organic beef to make an increasing contribution to future profitability.

Helen Browning and Kate Hobsley farm between 80 and 90 acres of Helen's family farm organically and are in the process of converting an area twice that size. They eventually plan to make all 1,350 acres of Easterbrook Farm, beside the Wiltshire Downs, organic. Helen's father managed his livestock on a fairly extensive system without abandoning rotation, and the soil remained healthy. Conversion to biological methods has been concentrated on the dairy cattle,

★ Grateful thanks to *Living Earth*, *New Farmer and Grower* and *Organic Farming* magazines for 'case studies' of organic farmers described here.

free-range pigs and poultry and some field vegetables. The three chicken houses, each with about 200 birds, are moved around regularly to prevent the build-up of pests and to allow the hens to forage. The farm's meat produce is additive free – with the local vet treating the animals homoeopathically as far as possible – and sold in the farm's shop in a nearby town.

Like many biological farmers, Miss Browning has found that the challenges are different from those usually predicted. Pests and diseases have so far proved few. The livestock are healthy, with antibiotics used only if an animal becomes seriously unwell. The obstacles have tended to be psychological as much as economic – for example, the post-war dogma that fields must be clean, tidy and weed-free. She estimates, however, that 50 per cent more labour is needed to raise cattle organically, a cost that can be met at present only through higher prices. But poultry and pigs can in her experience be kept both extensively and economically.

One of the UK's most enterprising organic farms is Pimhill Farm in Shropshire, converted in 1949 by Sam Mayall and his son Richard and now farmed by Richard and Anne Mayall and their daughter Ginny. Pimhill has 670 acres, a 185-strong Ayrshire dairy herd, a mill and a thriving farm shop and visitors' area. The mill, established many years ago by Sam Mayall, processes the farm's 160 acres of wheat and 60 acres of oats as well as bought-in organic cereals, producing a range of stoneground flours. The Mayalls' organic pork and poultry – hygienically prepared and dressed by skilled staff on the farm – are sold, along with other produce and local craftware, in the farm's shop and crafts gallery. With its woodland trail, small-animals enclosures and picnic area for visitors, the Mayalls' farm employs seven full-time and fifteen regular part-time staff.

Will and Pam Best farm 260 acres at Godmanstone, Dorset. During the 1970s they became increasingly aware of how much fungicide, insecticide and herbicide they were using on their land. At the same time, with disorders in their cows and talk of milk surpluses, they reduced their dependence on feed concentrates, antibiotics and other drugs. They experimented with nitrogen-fixing crops, introduced sheep and pigs and started to treat their livestock homoeopathically. Conversion was completed during the mid-1980s, and all the Bests' produce – dairy, lamb, pork and wheat – is now certified organic. They raise their stock on a clover-rich ley containing a variety of grasses, legumes and herbs, grown in rotation with cereals and other forages and fed with plenty of farmyard manure. This type of organic forage has proved more drought-resistant than heavily fertilized ryegrass, more palatable and digestible and better at supplying the animals' mineral needs. While less bulk is produced, savings in fertilizer costs and premiums for organic produce compensate as sources of profitability.

The Bests use no vaccines or wormers on their sheep, and in general the provision of a good environment and a wholesome diet helps prevent disease among the stock. They use homoeopathic treatments for most routine problems and disorders, but when necessary call in the vet or apply antibiotics. Overall, they have found biological farming to be sustainable in terms of fertility and economically viable.

There are others, too – Richard Knight of Worcestershire being a leading example.

Nationwide, the Soil Association, the main body registering organic production in the UK, reports a steady rise in the number of farmers and acres of farmland registered with its certification scheme in the last few years. Registered acreage went up by 50 per cent to 25,000 acres in 1989, and the number of Soil Association symbol holders rose by 30 per cent to more than 400. Altogether there are thought to be over 2,000 registered and unregistered organic producers in the UK, farming about 50,000 acres. While this still represents less than 1 per cent of British agricultural land, Soil Association technical director Francis Blake argues that many more farmers would be prepared to convert if the market for organic produce were more secure or if the government – which is inching painfully slowly towards financial incentives for conversion – were prepared to give adequate support. The association's target of 20 per cent of British farmers to be working biologically by the year 2000 may be optimistic but would not be impossible if the government took a more active role. The means are there now that the principle of the Environmentally Sensitive Area (ESA) has been established.

For all farmers to adopt biological or organic husbandry may be a desirable ideal, but lack of training and experience, as well as the initial cost, makes it impractical for many or most in the immediate future. To speed the designation of ESAs, thus enabling public funds to assist the farmer to change direction, will be a major step forward, but a great deal of research must be undertaken before biological principles can be applied most cost-effectively.

RESEARCH AND THE FUTURE

Of the numerous reasons why research into organic farming is important, one especially should not be overlooked. A great many chemicals have been screened to make available the existing pesticides, but pathogens develop resistance to them; and as there are a finite number of compounds, it may be that most of the potentially useful chemical groupings have already been found and developed. This dilemma underscores the point that chemical farming is linear and could be coming to the end of its line in the field of pesticides.

To farm biologically one dispenses with hormones, antibiotics as growth stimulants and all the animal drugs used other than as medicines. While manure and compost are desirable and wholly practical sources of natural fertilizer on smaller farms, on larger farms the need for natural substitutes for nitrates presents a difficulty. Experiments have been carried out in Wisconsin and elsewhere using sunflowers and other plants to fix nitrogen. This approach is now being put into practice in some places, although admittedly the yields are lower than with nitrates. In years to come, however, many kinds of soil may be largely, if not entirely, fertilized by natural means without manure or compost. To expect the chemical companies or any other industry to undertake such research may be unreasonable. The case for it being done by the public sector seems to be unanswerable. The benefit to the arable farmer would be immense.

Until nitrogen can be more readily fixed by other means, there are two remedies for farmers. One is the use of the existing known natural fertilizers, which means keeping stock, as composting is scarcely practical on a large scale. The other is for the principle of the ESA to be invoked, so that farmers are compensated financially for not using nitrates at all or for applying only a limited quantity.

Getting away from the use of chemical pesticides (insecticides, fungicides, herbicides, and so on) is likely to be the most difficult step towards biological farming. However, some chemical pesticides may be consistent with biological methods; among these 'natural chemicals' are nicotine and pyrethrum, which has given us pyrethroid insecticides, and there are others which may repel insects or reduce their ability to reproduce.

In both the United States and Canada the various organizations which represent the farming community have not hesitated to express their anxieties about the general use of pesticides. The NFU of Canada, in contrast to its British counterpart, has called for a programme of biological farming, regretting that 'there's no money in it for companies that supply biological agriculture, while there is for chemical farming'. This concern on the part of farmers in North America has been reflected by official recognition of the need for research. Though much more must be done, the North Americans are at least making some advances, unlike the UK where officialdom's inertia still rules.

Research into alternative forms of pest control starts with the premise that in a state of nature, where the environment is undisturbed by man, nothing we call a pest is without its enemy. Plants may be affected by disease or destroyed by insects and may die, yet their destruction is never widespread, because the enemy that attacks the plant is itself attacked by its own enemy. The world of nature is full of parasites, predators and pathogens that are prone to attack by other parasites, predators and pathogens. If they are left to themselves, there is 'order in the jungle'. Man's agriculture inevitably disturbs this balance. The remedy, say the biologists, is to employ the parasites, predators and pathogens to redress the balance. This approach can prove cheap and effective. To brush it aside, or fail to research how biological controls can be used, is to arrogate to the chemist a power greater than nature. This opinion, which is beginning to prevail in the United States, has yet to reach the steps of our own Ministry of Agriculture.

Dr Michael Dover of the World Resources Institute, and previously of the US Environmental Protection Agency, has worked for many years on pest control methods. His report published by the WRI, *A Better Mousetrap: Improving Pest Management for Agriculture* (1985), contains an excellent summary of what has already been achieved by biological methods. These, he shows, can achieve their objective of pest control by either attacking the pest or defending the plant against it.

The three forms of attack are inoculative release (the 'classical' form of control), inundative–augmentative release and the conservation of existing populations, being the 'natural' control. As long ago as 1925 the introduction of a moth to attack a weed which destroyed 30 million acres of grazing land in Australia showed how the inoculative method can succeed. To control caterpillars, an insect pathogen – *Bacillus thuringiensis* – has been used, and it is now registered as a pesticide. This form of inundative release has also been effective against mosquitoes as well as against moths infesting forests. Altogether, according to the Washington-based Worldwatch Institute, several hundred such pest-control programmes have been set up around the world. In the view of Dr Dover, genetic engineering and tissue culture can extend the scope of this kind of control; and it is encouraging to note that the Monsanto Chemical Company is working in this area. Conservation control consists of protecting species which are the natural enemies of pests by safeguarding their habitats, withholding chemical sprays that might endanger them and affording suitable conditions for their breeding. The everyday work of the organic farmer – his crop rotations and intercropping, for example – is often a part of these natural methods.

The defensive side of biological control takes the form of breeding and evolving varieties which can withstand attack from pests. Although this has been happening for centuries, we are now better equipped with our knowledge of what plants need in the way of moisture and nutrients to advance what is called plant resistance. To be able to plant varieties that will naturally repulse the pest must be the most cost-effective kind of pest control.

At the UK's National Vegetable Research Station at Wellesbourne in Warwickshire, its director Professor John Bleasdale, Dr R. B. Maude, Dr Stanley Finch and others have made some valuable discoveries in this field. One team at the station has looked at the way oilseed rape and brassicas share certain diseases. When a crop of rape is harvested, dust spreads to adjoining fields; if they are planted with brassicas, they become infected by the fungal spores of the rape, frequently causing the crop to be lost. Research has shown that the leaf-spot and canker of the diseases are seed-borne, and when the seed is treated, the diseases are eliminated. The cost of spraying can thus be avoided. It is estimated that farmers have been saved several millions of pounds in this way, and a great deal more money has been saved by protecting adjoining crops. The research itself cost only £100,000. Many other examples could be given to show how cost-effective research into biological control can be. The Ministry of Agriculture has given little encouragement to this kind of work, and at one stage serious cuts in the expenditure of the NVRS were proposed; but now there is hope that these will not materialize.

The Agriculture and Food Research Council supervises and allocates the funds for agricultural research in the UK public sector, and it has under its wing over thirty establishments. Apart from the NVRS, some of the others are interested in biological research. The East Malling Research Station has bred a variety of gooseberry that is resistant to American gooseberry mildew and leaf-spot, two diseases to which other varieties are susceptible so that they need to be sprayed with a fungicide. Scientists at the Plant Breeding Institute have evolved new kinds of wheat and barley better capable of resisting diseases such as mildew, yellow rust, rhynchostorium, net blotch and eye-spot. The PBI has now been sold to Unilever, as part of a programme of privatization.

The total amount of money available to the Agriculture and Food Research Council is about £100 million a year.

Only a small part of this goes into research into how the farmer can get off the chemical treadmill, for most of its expenditure is still directed into increasing output. A redirection of priorities is urgently needed. Research into alternative methods of husbandry tends to be cheaper, and given the signal to change direction, agricultural scientists are in general agreement that many important advances could be made.

Perhaps the most promising area of research is in integrated pest management. IPM recognizes that pest control should strike a balance between economic and ecological factors. The financial cost of pest damage must be taken into account as well as injury to humans, plants, wildlife and the environment, so that if pest damage rises beyond a certain point, pesticides are not ruled out, but their ecological effect must also be considered. Proponents of IPM say that it combines the approaches of ecologists, soil scientists, entomologists, plant pathologists, weed scientists, agricultural engineers, agricultural economists, biochemists and ordinary chemists – indeed of anyone concerned with the growing of crops and their surroundings. Each has a part in optimizing pest control. Natural methods are preferred, but as pesticides may have a place in the scheme of management, IPM is not fully biological farming or organic husbandry. It is, however, a step off the chemical treadmill that can be taken immediately.

IS THE FARMER A BUSINESS MAN?

One of the reasons why agriculture has taken a wrong turning in the UK is that there has been no clear idea whether the farmer should be treated as a business man or as a kind of public servant. Yet the question is crucial to any discussion about a change of policy.

If we decide the farmer is a business man, a whole series of other questions get answered quite easily. A business man is there to look after himself; his business is his affair; whether it flourishes or fails is primarily his concern and to a somewhat lesser extent the concern of his employees, creditors and professional advisers. It follows that the essence of a business man is that he gets his income from his customers, and his business comes to an end if his customers do not like the price, quality or anything else about what he has for sale. As a general rule, the government does not support him with money taken away from other business men. Put in the same category, the farmer would, as we have already observed, be deemed just one in the chain of business men that brings our food to our table.

He may happen to grow what we eat, but is he any more important than the others in the chain? Tractors have been an indispensable part of the farm for a long time, so the man in Coventry who designs or helps to make them cannot be dismissed as of no consequence, nor the men who drill for the oil the tractor uses. The farm of half a century ago might have been well nigh self-sufficient, except for the blacksmith in the village and the seed merchant in the market town. Today, the farmer needs the supplies of a whole range of business men before he can begin a single day's work. The major chemical companies will send him not one but perhaps a dozen different sorts of herbicide, pesticide and fungicide, and the large fertilizer companies will send him a variety of different artificial fertilizers. Oil companies, machinery distributors, transport companies, seed merchants and others will also be at his service. Every one of them is a business, being run for a profit like any other commercial concern; and all of them depend upon other businesses to enable them to supply or service the farmer. In modern agriculture, they are all essential links in the chain that brings our food to us.

Once the farmer has done his job, and whatever he produces passes out of the farm gate, another series of people becomes no less essential before the food is on our table. Road haulage contractors, corn merchants, slaughterers, dairymen, all sorts of food processors, canners and freezers, must play a part. Again, every one of them is engaged in a straightforward commercial activity; they are business men, plain and simple.

Only the British farmer is no longer regarded as a business man whose income should come from his customers. Nor does he wish to be treated as one. At least, that is the official view of the NFU, though disquiet is growing among the farmers who have had time to reflect upon the dangerous consequences that will follow if the present policy continues. In the short term, a large number of them have gained, but the gain can be sustained only by ever higher levels of price support. How can policy-makers now justify still more taxpayers' money being given to expand production when demand is standing still? The dilemma is made more serious when the farmer realizes that the cost of everything he needs to buy for his farm will go on increasing, and those higher costs can be met only by higher farm-gate prices. His grandfather – that much-derided figure with a 'dog and stick' – had his worries, but not that one. The dog and the stick were simply got; no sales representative from a large chemical company called to take orders for them, and no overdraft was needed to pay for them. Tomorrow's survivors will be the men who can keep costs down when farm-gate prices cease to rise; but the ruthless pressures placed upon everyone who farms today make this task supremely difficult.

One way out of the dilemma is to take away any pretext that the farmer is a business man and make him a public servant. Unable to balance the books, he would, quite simply, have to be taken over by some agency of the government. This, of course, is the socialist solution, and I know one socialist who is content with the present policy, despite its social injustices, because he is certain that it will end in the land being nationalized and farming being collectivized.

The NFU wants a farmer to have the advantages of being both a business man and a public servant, without the disadvantages of either. The taxpayer who pays the bills for him can still be ordered off the land as a common trespasser. So far no very cogent reason has been advanced why this one man of the many who find us our food should have it both ways. The corn merchant, the seed salesman and the slaughterer also share in the ups and downs of harvests, the cycles and oddities of uncertain demand, so why should not they, too, receive support?

What, in any case, do we mean by support? If a dilapidated old house is said to need support, this means that it will fall down without it. If an elderly gentleman needs support as he walks along the road, this means that he will fall down unless he is given it. Society agrees to give support to certain groups of people because any income they may have is not enough to enable them to lead the kind of life the rest of society enjoys. Thus we give support to the old, the unemployed, people with disabilities and patients in mental hospitals. No clear reason seems to be given why farmers should be added to this list.

It may be said that, food being so essential to us, there is a case for its producers being subsidized. A subsidy might lower the price of food, so that everyone could be sure of having what they need at a price they could afford. If this is the argument, it would be more sensible, more cost-effective and administratively simpler to subsidize Sainsbury, Tesco and the Co-op; and, of course, we know that our present agricultural policy has not lowered the price of food in Britain but pushed it sharply up.

If there are no good reasons why we should protect farmers as business men, there are plenty of good reasons why we should not. We have already looked at some of them, but two are worth pointing out here, if only because they are so often missed.

First, when the state takes away people's opportunity to buy food from other countries, it is also doing something which is essentially reactionary. It is putting the clock back. Centuries ago, all the food our forebears ate was produced within our own shores, and usually within a narrow radius of not many miles. As methods of transport improved, so the radius widened. Spices, such as ginger and pepper, were the first to cross the seas. As each new kind of food arrived at an English port, progress was made towards letting the consumer have a wider choice, of different kinds of food or the same kind at a lower price.

With the invention of refrigerated ships, the British people gained the advantage of being able to buy, from New Zealand, lamb and butter at a cheaper price than anyone else in the world. This also enabled trade to expand between our two countries; for the more its low-cost food came here, the more New Zealand was able to import from the UK other things, notably manufactured goods.

As soon as the rules of the Common Market required the

UK to raise barriers against exports from New Zealand, the trade between the two countries plunged downwards. The barriers, being mainly in the form of tariffs, were set at such a height as to nullify the comparative advantage of lower costs, the very benefit given to us by the refrigerated ships. Why invent new ideas to reduce the price of food to consumers if the benefit is to be taken away by tariffs?

A long catalogue can be drawn up of other inventions which have given us freedom to be able to buy what we would wish to have at a price we can afford. For a government to deny its people a share in the benefit of this progress must surely be against everybody's interests. Yet this is the consequence when trade between different countries is restricted by any kind of artificial barrier imposed by a government. Only free trade is truly beneficial trade.

The second point is that protection is always an act of coercion. The British people may not realize that they are coerced against their will to eat food from France rather than Australia, or from Germany rather than New Zealand, or from our own protected and subsidized agriculture rather than from where they would prefer to buy it, but such is the case. To a tiny minority of the British people, namely a few hundred importers, this coercion is plainly visible. To make it plain to the rest of us, a few prosecutions for smuggling would be needed.

If some enterprising ship's captain were to bring a cargo of sugar from Queensland into a little port where customs officials were not on duty, what would be the outcome? The sugar, coming from a place where it is grown more cheaply than almost anywhere else in the world, would soon find a ready sale. The ship's captain could sell it at about half the price of the sugar we are allowed to eat. In fact, as the Queensland farmers are desperately trying to find a market for their sugar, the captain would perhaps have purchased the sugar at so low a price that he could afford to resell it at even less than half the price that British consumers now pay.

The smuggling sea captain would succeed in pleasing some grateful customers, but by doing so he would be committing a criminal offence. The word would get round that our captain was selling cheap sugar, and a police officer would arrest him or serve a summons. Then he would be made to stand in the dock where thieves, rapists and murderers have been. No defence to the charges could be conceived, so he would plead guilty, the court duly passing sentence upon him. A fine would be the likely punishment, higher than if he had committed an act of assault or shoplifting. Failure to pay the fine would take him to prison. Some term of imprisonment, then, is the sanction to enforce protectionism. If a threat of a fine is not an act of coercion, a period in prison must surely be one.

Yet our captain has done no more than satisfy the wishes of some people by selling them sugar at the world price. Not a single ounce would have been sold unless they had expressed a willingness to buy it, so the mischief really lies with them just as it does with the sea captain. They have exercised a momentary freedom of choice, and that is something protectionism does not permit.

The British protectionist sees the situation differently. In his eyes, Queensland is a foreign power threatening our country. The sugar is an enemy missile; it must be repulsed, and we must be protected from the danger. Listen to a protectionist speaker, and the inference to be drawn is that other countries, in exporting to us, are committing an act of hostility. This is a subtle way of justifying a penalty on anyone importing food from abroad.

Protectionism, whether with regard to food or anything else, is an intrusion upon the consumer's freedom of choice. In conditions of full and genuine free trade, when no tax or any other barrier is set up against imports, the consumer has the maximum choice. He can roam the world and buy what he wants, provided only that he can afford the price. Free trade thus becomes not only a freedom but also a right: the right to satisfy one's wants in a fair and honest way.

A socialist may demur at the word 'freedom' when used in an economic context, for he may say that it is a relative thing; only the rich have this total freedom, and for the poor it is a meaningless term. However, we are not talking about the freedom to stay at the Ritz or sojourn on the Riviera, but the one material freedom which no living man or woman can survive without: the freedom to eat. Any tax on our basic everyday food hurts the poor more than the rich. Before the British people submitted to the Common Agricultural Policy, the poorest among us were able to eat more cheaply than they can today and could spend more of their money on other things. It may be true that the proportion of their income spent on food has remained the same, but this 'fact', peddled by the protectionist lobby, holds a fallacy. Before the CAP, a majority of households in the UK could afford a Sunday joint, and Argentinian beef was regularly on the table for the poorest family. So was New Zealand butter. Tinned salmon from Canada was often followed by tinned peaches from Australia. When any kind of food from across the seas was allowed free access into our ports, it was cheaper for the poorest people of our country to have such a meal at home than it was for anyone else in the world to eat the same sort of food.

So the argument can be summed up quite simply. If the farmer is a business man, then his business is to supply people with food they choose to buy because it is better or cheaper than the available alternatives. Since protection inevitably prevents them from making this choice, it can in general have no legitimate place in a business transaction.

Two forms of protection, however, can be justified and may well be seen as necessary. We in the UK can and should protect ourselves against attempts by other countries to dump their subsidized surpluses on us. And it is right to prohibit the import of foods produced by methods that we have made illegal (because, for instance, those methods are inhumane to animals or because they lead to food being contaminated with dangerous substances or being unhealthy for some other reason).

It is in all our interests to have a system whereby farmers live in the open market. In so far as they live off protection, they are not business men but political pensioners.

HUSBANDING OUR RESOURCES

Yet, however much the farmer is seen by himself and others as a business man, he is never just a business man. What he does in the course of his work as a food producer has widespread consequences.

If a farmer buys a tractor, it does not matter very much how he decides to treat it. He may leave it out all night in the rain or the snow, because he has persuaded himself that it would be cheaper to buy a new one in a year or two than to build a shed to house it. We may think him rather foolish, but we have no right to interfere. The tractor is a mechanical thing which will one day be useless anyway, and what he chooses to do with it is his business. But what he does with his farmland may indeed be our business in all sorts of ways. The drainage of his fields, the ploughing up of footpaths, the use of certain herbicides, the burning of straw, and so on, are activities that affect other people. In twentieth-century Britain it is accepted that the public, through its legislators, can properly interfere when its interests are affected.

Unlike all the thousands of others who are links in the long chain of food supply, the farmer is in command of the countryside. A single act by him may mean life or death for much of the wildlife on his territory. In one blow he may uproot hundreds of yards of hedgerow or an ancient woodland. He may decide to swamp his land with an excess of pesticides or pollute the adjoining river with his phosphates and nitrates. Or he may treble the size of his herd and, to avoid a consequent outbreak of disease, give the animals such a dose of drugs that people eating the meat inadvertently consume something inimical to their health.

Now, many of these things are done against the better judgement of the farmer. Only an insignificant minority can derive any pleasure from laying waste their own landscape or intensifying their operations by first borrowing even more money from the bank and then having liabilities and responsibilities greater than they would wish. They are done because the farmer is on a treadmill, forced to raise output or quit.

We can avoid this dilemma only if we clearly recognize

the other function of farmers, as guardians or custodians of the countryside. Perhaps we should revive the word which used to adorn the parish registers over a century ago, when a farmer's child or marriage or death had to be recorded, and speak again of the 'husbandman'. It is of course the function, not the name, that matters; but the function matters very much indeed. It is the key to the future for Britain's farmers, food and landscape. Instead of denouncing the environmentalists, animal welfarists, doctors and the food safety lobby for giving their opinions, the agricultural establishment should seize on their concern to highlight the dilemma of the farmer. How he can survive under the present system unless he does the very things these others complain about?

The present system has its priorities the wrong way round. As a food producer, the farmer is a business man and should stand on his own feet. As a custodian of the countryside, he is something more and should be helped by the rest of us. As things are, we treat the farmer in the opposite way, and the farming establishment would rather have it this way round. In marketing the food he produces, far from the farmer being treated as a business man, they want him to be molly-coddled to a degree that no one else is. Yet in the growing of the food and the way he treats animals, the soil and the landscape, they would like the principles of *laissez-faire* to prevail. Thus agriculture has, I submit, taken a wrong turning, and it is heading for a terrible crash.

At the root of the problem is, as we have seen, the way the policy-makers and politicians have goaded the farmer to increase production to the maximum. When we end this futile and unnecessary pursuit we become free to recognize the importance of custodianship and to reward the farmer for honouring it. For reward is what the farmer needs; if he is to forego doing things that could have increased his income, then he is entitled to look for some help from the rest of us who benefit. It does not follow that he must be compensated every time he refrains from, say, felling an ancient wood or draining a marshy field, any more than a townsman is compensated when he cannot get planning permission to destroy an ancient building. But if farmers are to change their whole way of working in response to the demands of conservation, it is unreasonable to ask them to do so without help. They will have to forego some profitable activities and to undertake others that consume time and money, and many of them would be driven out of business if they were forced to do that without compensation.

The principle of financial assistance has already been established by the Field Monument Act of 1972. The farmer who has, for example, an ancient barrow in a field that he intends to plough up can receive a grant from the government to make good the pecuniary loss he suffers by protecting it. Such compensation has been extended by the Wildlife and Countryside Act of 1981 and by the Agriculture Act of 1986 (which established the principle of ESAs).

There seems to be no reason why this principle should not now be extended to the landscape generally. If a farmer believes it is necessary to cut down trees or uproot a hedgerow, fill in a pond, demolish a thatched barn or pull down a stone wall in order to maintain the profitability of his holding, it should be possible to apply for a grant by way of compensation for retaining the feature concerned and subsequently keeping it in good order.

Any scheme of this kind needs to be carefully worked out. We must, for example, avoid paying out large sums of money to landowners who threaten to destroy a valuable site just so that they can be compensated for not doing so. The general principle is nevertheless clear. Public money must in future be spent on conserving our heritage; never again must it go to encourage destruction.

The principle of these 'landscape amenity grants', or whatever other term for the idea is adopted, reinforces the status of the farmer as a business man. The public is made to recognize that he runs a business which must pay its way and give him the livelihood that is due to him. He, in turn, is assured of his independence and self-respect. He is not paid money by a resentful taxpayer to produce food in a hopelessly inefficient manner; he earns his money in the market-place because he is efficient and because his customer acknowledges it. Between the farmer, the landowner, the taxpayer and the consumer a common interest would emerge, and goodwill rather than resentment would prevail.

So the farmer ought to welcome the change, and there is little doubt that the general public would do so, too. The British people are increasingly concerned about their countryside; opinion polls show that a decisive majority of them would be willing for a small proportion of the national income – say, 1 per cent – to be spent on looking after our landscape and wildlife, on humane animal husbandry and safer food. One per cent would represent about £2,000 million, or some £10,000 for every farmer. Besides, people are today increasingly anxious about the way much of their food is grown and processed.

The net cost to the taxpayer of assistance to British farmers in their custodian role would be greatly reduced by the fact that the new system would get rid of the wild extravagances of the old one. At present, medium-sized farmers in the mountains of Wales and the hills of Scotland cost us about £50,000 a year each to support. Larger farmers cost us much more; one known to me has had an annual income of about £10,000, but the taxpayer, in one way or another, pays out £75,000 a year for him. It would be much cheaper for the taxpayer, and more beneficial to the owners and occupiers of this kind of land – apart from the environmental advantages – if a system of landscape amenity grants were set up.

People who are worried about the changing face of the British landscape, the welfare of farm animals and the way our soil is poisoned with ever larger chemical doses are sometimes horrified at the idea of farmers becoming business men, unfettered by political control. I hope I can reassure them. The political controls that I object to are the ones that flow from a price support policy. Because this policy has had the opposite effect to what was intended, farmers are driven to the very deeds the conservationists, welfarists and ecologists disapprove of. The objectives of such people (which are shared by more farmers than they may realize) will be obtained if, first, the present policy is brought to an end and, secondly, farmers are subject to the law of the land like any other business man. My point is not that farmers should be singled out for restrictions that apply only to them – only that some of their special privileges, shared by nobody else, should be cut back.

The destruction of our countryside can be stopped by applying planning restrictions to agriculture similar to those imposed upon other forms of business. Two new buildings may look identical to the passer-by; one will need planning permission, but not the other. If I put five parrots in a cage that should hold only one, I will be prosecuted, but not if I put five hens in it. I can pollute the atmosphere as a farmer, but not as a business man. My friends in the water industry tell me that they commit an offence if they ask an employee to take a hook to trim the sides of our river by himself; but I, as a farmer, can ask Billy who works for me to do exactly the same job and I am innocent of any unlawful act.

A number of new laws need to be passed to bring to an end some of the undesirable practices of modern farming. Let them be passed, but some of them will not be necessary once we have removed the root cause. Many of our present laws and much of our public money positively encourage the owners and occupiers of agricultural land to make changes that are disagreeable to the rest of us. Thatched barns get pulled down and replaced by concrete monstrosities. Rivers are dredged, and the trees on the bank cut down. Stone walls are removed. Many thousands of miles of hedges and many thousands of acres of woodland succumb to the bulldozer. In the uplands, either vast areas of dreary conifers blanket the hillside, or great stretches of beautiful high country, where the public once freely walked or rode, have miles of barbed wire and sheep fencing, serving both to keep out the public and to convert at high cost our worst-quality land into third-rate pasture.

The alternative is to encourage owners and occupiers of such land to keep it looking agreeable to the rest of us. If there are social and economic reasons why the public should be taxed to induce a minority to go on living in the more isolated and beautiful parts of the UK, there is a better way than subsidizing them to grow ultra-expensive food. A grant to keep cows, pigs and poultry in conditions that allow them to move around and breathe fresh air, instead of spending their lives in stalls or cages, would have the approval of many people. For reasons given earlier in this book, I believe that the undesirable extremes of intensive husbandry would come to an end naturally were we to change the present agricultural policy. This judgement may be over-optimistic; but surely the answer is to change the policy first, make some of the practices illegal (for example, that of keeping a sow locked inside a stall and unable to turn round for four months) and then see how the changes in animal husbandry develop.

It is important that not only farmers, but the rest of society who will have to pay the bill, reflect on why these changes are necessary. Much of the case for change has been given in this book. It should be enough to show that the intention is not to transform the farmer into a mere park-keeper, but to enable him to be both a truly efficient producer of the raw materials which form the basis of our food and also a custodian of our land.

This latter role needs to be spelled out, for it is one which many British farmers do not fully appreciate. So much has been said to them in the pages of the farming journals; so much taught them in the past in the agricultural colleges; so much advice given them by ADAS and the hundreds of sales representatives employed by the chemical companies; worst of all, so much exhortation by a succession of Ministers of Agriculture to produce ever more – that some thirty-five years of indoctrination have given too many in agriculture a 'macho' urge. In no other country in the world has there arisen such a drive to push up agricultural output as in the UK; not even in the rest of the Common Market is this orientation so pronounced. A British visitor to Norway, Austria or Switzerland is happily astonished at the state of tranquillity prevailing in the countryside. British farmers need to be reminded that such tranquillity does not necessarily mean a decline in their standard of living; indeed, the reverse may well apply.

A REVIVAL FOR SMALL FARMERS

As shown earlier in the book, the small farmer has been a major casualty of the present system. Yet he has an important part to play in the kind of farming that the UK so urgently needs. Small farmers tend to be more integrated into their local community, so an increase in their numbers will, in social terms, revitalize the countryside. With a relatively small number of acres to cultivate or animals to look after, it is easier for the small farmer to be sensitive to the needs of both. And where such farmers abound, the landscape invariably offers a more pleasant vista than where the bigger men take charge.

Just as he has been driven from the land by the policy of guaranteed prices weighted against him, so the alternative proposed in this book would enable many a small farmer to return and those who have survived to carry on with a degree of security now lacking. There are several reasons why this is so. Nearly all the existing large arable farmers have acquired their size by amalgamations in the last three decades; when owner-occupied, borrowed money has paid for the adjoining farm. High interest rates and declining farm-gate prices have, however, combined to cause a correlation between borrowers and worriers; and if the trend continues, many of these farmers will have to sell off part of their land, recreating the smaller farm.

While some of these large arable farmers may have the inclination and the temperament to go over to biological or organic methods, or to take part in an ESA scheme, they are likely to be a minority. For the record of the large-scale arable farmer shows, as a general rule, an incompatibility with the outlook needed to farm sensitively towards our landscape and wildlife. The small farmer's record is easily seen in contrast. Inevitably a less ambitious man in financial terms, his prime objective has not always been to maximize profits or to avoid taxation. He has persisted in his occupation against the odds because it was to him as much a vocation; had he mercenary motives, he would have departed years ago. In the future, the small farmer and grower will have one important advantage over his larger neighbours; if he and his wife do all the work, there are no labour costs to be paid for. Organic husbandry is harder work, and rather more labour is generally required, as well as more manual skill. The same goes for keeping animals humanely, always a labour-intensive affair.

A third reason why the small farmer will have an advantage may deserve a special mention. It has been estimated that between 5 and 10 million jobs now done in our cities and conurbations will be done at home, using information technology, within the next twenty years. Home will not then have to be within daily commuting distance of work – that is, in the suburbs – but may be 100 or more miles away. The significance of this change for our countryside is immense. Perhaps only 10 per cent of the new 'teleworkers' will take the opportunity of moving to a rural area. And perhaps only 10 per cent of them will wish to undertake some form of part-time farming by way of recreation. Judging by the upsurge in the number of people in recent years who have escaped to the countryside, however, the probability is that many more than 1 per cent of those 5 to 10 million people will, as the saying goes 'opt for the good life'.

Still, even 1 per cent of between 5 and 10 million represents a massive inflow to some kind of agriculture. They will have spare time, for the great argument in favour of this teleworking is that more leisure will follow. They will have a fully paid job, so that their part-time farming will be recreational rather than income-providing. Moreover, they will have moved to the countryside because they valued its environment and the pleasure it afforded. These factors add up to a certainty: they will become not aggro-culturists but willing recruits to simpler, gentler and more humane ways. This great legion from the cities may transform the farming scene and will undoubtedly bring reinforcements to the now beleaguered garrison of small farmers. Together they will form a powerful alliance.

LOOKING AHEAD

The farmer should be recognized as being the most important figure in our society. We can, just about, do without most occupations, but the farmer's is the one we can least afford to jettison. Assuming some modicum of truth in the saying 'we are what we eat', the human race risks disease, deformity and its demise unless the food we eat comes from an environment in which it is safe for it to be grown. Set the farmer upon this pedestal of importance, and the other principles follow. In the event of conflict between his roles as business man and a steward of the countryside, the farmer is entitled to insist that to survive and prosper he must primarily be the former. Others may disagree and assert that society has the right to forbid him to do undesirable things, just as it extends the arm of the law to inhibit other business men from behaving in a way of which it disapproves.

There is, however, a distinction between the farmer and other business men. To be a place that is cared for and agreeable to the eye, the countryside needs to be peopled; and no one is more capable of living there than the farmer himself. To have the countryside peopled by an appropriate number of farmers must remain an objective. To prohibit farmers from doing what they find necessary as business men without any compensation for loss of profit would have the certain effect of making their task well-nigh impossible, and of driving still more from the land.

Farmers, large or small, arable or livestock, on the upland hills of Scotland or the kinder vales of England, ought to ask themselves, just what is their future now? Is there one of them, anywhere or of any age, who feels confident that his son or daughter will be able to carry on two or three decades hence as he does today? In the last ten years I have spoken to farming audiences in every county in England and most of Scotland, Wales and Northern Ireland; a change has come over them, and the optimistic outlook that was once able to grasp my message has slipped away. In place of that optimism are forecasts for the future that vary from inchoate doubt to abject despair, with many degrees of foreboding in between.

There is, though, one group that is the exception: the organic farmers and growers. I have met many of them. They were the ones formerly with an uncertain future, a small minority treated with disdain. The public, however, has come to their aid. Consumer demand for organically produced food, including the products of humane animal husbandry, was negligible not so long ago but is now increasing steadily. Despite supermarkets paying – and charging – premiums of anything between 10 per cent and more than 100 per cent for organic compared with conventional produce, demand for organic food still exceeds supply. About 70 per cent of the organic food eaten in the UK has to come from France, the Netherlands, Germany, Israel and elsewhere. Spokesmen for the supermarkets insist that the demand will continue to rise.

Naturally enough, representatives of the chemical and pharmaceutical industries, along with the banks, pour cold water over this change. 'The world will starve without chemicals,' they say. And despite its murmurings of latent sympathy, the Ministry of Agriculture is no better. Its officials, who used to travel the country telling farmers at conferences to increase their production because it would be 'good for the balance of payments', are seemingly mute when precisely the same point can be made for organic food. As for the farming establishment, like the ministry it cannot change its tune without difficulty; consisting overwhelmingly, as it does, of the larger farmers – the very ones who have done so well out of the system – perhaps the establishment still believes that a little tinkering here and there ('a touch on the tiller' they call it) will put matters right for them.

All these people have let down the ordinary hard-working farmer who has no time to spare for sitting on committees in London, nor the inclination to do so, but would rather stay looking after his crops and his animals. The Venetian oligarchy set in the leadership of the farming community will continue to let it down until they too realize that they are standing on the same treadmill that has already caused half our farmers to fall off and disappear into other occupations.

Farming has a great future in the UK nevertheless. It will begin when selfish and misguided men see that there is no longer any future in deceiving the British people into believing that they should buy their food at phoney inflated prices. The alternative policy will have to be sought. For years I have challenged them to conceive an alternative other than the one set out in this book; and they have been good enough to concede that there is no third way.

Phoney prices must go. Next we must act on the knowledge that the UK has a soil, climate and terrain for many kinds of farming; but while they afford great advantages for some kinds, they make others uneconomic and some hopelessly so. British agriculture will never be truly secure until the distinction is perceived and acted upon. Our farmers will then be poised to fulfil their two roles. No longer crippled lame ducks dependent upon subsidies, they will be able to regain their self-respect as competent business men engaged in the only industry that can claim to be assuredly vital to the human race. That vital quality – in the true, literal sense – turns on farmers and growers practising methods of husbandry that can be sustained indefinitely. With that sustainability there will be a long-term future. Our food will come from a healthy soil and humane farms; and our land will be in the stewardship of good farmers.

· 11 ·

WHAT DO WE
DO NOW?

British and European agriculture is, we have seen, in a most unhealthy state. So, in may ways, is farming in most other parts of the world, including those Third World countries that have been induced to adopt some of the West's agricultural practices. (Although there are examples to the contrary, among which New Zealand is outstanding.) Very few people do not recognize that much has gone wrong, apart from those who have an interest in keeping the present system alive. And even they are coming to see that the system is already on a life-support machine and before long is bound to succumb to the growing demands to switch the wretched thing off.

It is not going to be easy to get out of this unhealthy situation into one that we can all be content to live with. Powerful commercial and political forces will try to block progress, or at least to slow it down and distort the outcome in their own favour. It is therefore very important for the rest of us to know where we want to go, to map out a practicable way of getting there and to stick firmly to it.

Fortunately there is a growing consensus about what we want to achieve, a consensus that includes far-sighted farmers as well as environmentalists and pure-food campaigners. It can be simply stated. We want an agriculture that delivers healthy and nutritious food at the lowest price available, and whose practices do not destroy our countryside or involve cruelty to animals. There is also a growing conviction that our present system of support, with all its direct and indirect subsidies, extorted from the taxpayer and consumer, works against these sensible aims and also makes life harder for most of the farmers it pretends to help.

For the future, the first step must be to end the drive to increase agricultural output at almost any price. This means ending the subsidies and protection that have, up to now, worked towards that end. Then, as suggested in Chapter 10, we must ensure that whatever public money is given to farmers goes to encourage them in their capacity as custodians of the countryside and of the animals in their charge. As real business men they must do what every real business man has to do – make their money on an honest, open and free market. And this market must be freely open to producer countries throughout the world.

To administer these changes in the United Kingdom we shall need new and better institutions than those that now serve us (or so often fail to serve). We must call in question the whole future of the Ministry of Agriculture and still more of the Common Agricultural Policy and its attendant bureaucracy.

NEW NEEDS, NEW LAWS

We must begin by passing a new Agriculture Act to embody these new principles. This new Act should make clear the supreme importance of agriculture. In doing so, it should strike a bargain for farmers as well as for the rest of us. In deciding *what* he is to produce, and in marketing it, the farmer must be left alone to do what he considers profitable; but the Act should also lay down the principles about *how* the food should be produced. The public would thus have a right to interfere when methods of farming conflict with any one of the following:

- the beauty and quality of the landscape;
- the welfare of farm animals;
- the health of the nation;
- good husbandry.

Whenever the public through the legislative process prevented the farmer pursuing his profit, there would be a prima-facie case for compensation. Obviously, not on every occasion would the public be expected to pay money to the farmer as a business man, for all manner of ingenious and whimsical schemes would be mooted to extract public money. So the details of the new policy would have to be a matter for delegated legislation in the form of Statutory Instruments to be introduced, amended or repealed with reasonable speed.

The Act would set the scene for the reconciliation of the interests of farmer, landowner, taxpayer, consumer, conservationist and welfarist. The NFU and Friends of the Earth would sit in the same canoe, both paddling in the same direction. It sounds a tall order to reconcile so many seemingly divergent interests. Yet it has to be emphasized that the present system, so long as it goes on, is forcing the farmer and the landowner further apart from the rest of the public. This must be highly dangerous for those who farm in good faith.

We already have a concept embodied in law which can make a useful starting-point for the new legislation. This is the Environmentally Sensitive Area (ESA), which was established in the Agriculture Act of 1986. The Act states:

> If it appears to the Minister that it is particularly desirable (a) to conserve and enhance the natural beauty of an area; (b) to conserve the flora and fauna or geological or physiological features of an area; or (c) to protect buildings or other objects of archaeological, architectural or historic interest in an area, and that the maintenance or adoption of particular agricultural methods is likely to facilitate such conservation, enhancement or protection, he may designate that area as an environmentally sensitive area.

Once an ESA is designated, the Minister of Agriculture may enter into an agreement with anyone with an interest in agricultural land in the area, so that he is paid to manage it in accordance with the agreement. The Act is drafted in such a way that a farmer or landowner can adopt almost any kind of agricultural practice conducive to conservation, and be paid for it out of public funds.

We need now to extend this concept by recognizing that the whole of the UK is an environmentally sensitive area; and this should be central to our new policy. To draw a line across any part of our countryside, decreeing that one side is environmentally sensitive and the other is not, is absurd. The line must travel along a lane or hedgerow, a river or canal, perhaps a railway line. However it is drawn and wherever it goes, the line will be arbitrary. Two fields will adjoin to the human eye and to the wildlife whose habitat they are; no difference will be perceptible; yet one is to be protected, while the other can submit to the engine of destruction. Even in our cities and suburbs there is a variety of wildlife worthy of protection, especially of flora. In what used to be Middlesex there are probably more wild flowers than in Hertfordshire or Bedfordshire. The idea that we can divide up our countryside into zones of protection and of destruction displays a lack of logic no less than a woeful misunderstanding of nature's realm.

How, then, would the new policy work? For any farmer to ask what it would mean to him is only natural. Equally, any farmer will agree that there is not another holding quite like his. There will be something about its size, soil, terrain and landscape, about its water courses and woodlands or about its potential to grow food or support wildlife that makes it different from any other farm. So, one blueprint to be universally applied is out of the question. We should instead draw up management agreements which farmers would be invited to sign, setting out the aims and practices to be followed on each farm. While a management agreement suitable for one holding could not be automatically appropriate for another, it has been said at the Nature Conservancy Council that seventeen standard draft agreements would be enough.

We can be clear about one principle. Whether a farmer wanted to negotiate an agreement or not would be a matter for him to decide. The land is his and, though it may be said that he holds it in trust for another generation, he can farm it as he wishes – if he wants to be a business man in competition with the most efficient farmers of the world. Because he happens to be fortunate enough to own or occupy a part of our landscape and wants to grow food on it, it does not follow that the rest of us are obliged to guarantee him a livelihood. Just as the consumer should have the freedom to choose the food he or she wishes to have, so the farmer ought to have the freedom to choose the extent to which he takes on the role of being in the food-producing chain (and therefore a business man) or the role of a steward of the countryside (and therefore a public sevant entitled to be paid accordingly).

Even when we have recognized the farmer's right to choose in this sense, it does not follow that he is free to put his choice into practice in any way he pleases, regardless of the effect on others. As was said earlier, he should, like his fellow citizens in the towns, be subject to certain restraints under the planning laws. Destroying an ancient woodland and erecting a concrete barn are no different from destroying an ancient building and erecting a concrete warehouse.

We must also protect ourselves from possible damage to our health from residues of pesticides, fertilizers, hormones and other chemicals. Careful legislation is needed here. To use artificial fertilizers or pesticides may be questionable, but it would be foolish legislation to prohibit the use of them all. Some are dangerous, and their use in the UK or elsewhere is illegal; some are safe in some circumstances, and their use has to be regulated. The law on the subject needs to be readily changed to adapt to new discoveries of science, whether of new aids for the farmer or of new dangers both to him and the rest of us.

Soil is a priceless thing. Sterilizing it and impregnating it with poisons until it can no longer grow food for us – and adversely affects the water supply on which we depend – fly in the face of common sense. The extinction of plants, trees, birds and other living creatures cannot be made good. The farmers, as caretakers of the land, are the most important people living in our country. They must be treated as such if they are to take care of it. This means active encouragement for those who farm responsibly, firm discouragement for those who would do otherwise and outright prohibition of the most harmful practices.

This prohibition should certainly cover the excesses of intensive animal rearing. There is one major advantage of being a food-importing nation, in that it can impose standards on other countries by prohibiting certain practices at home and then banning imports from others that continue with them. To our shame, the reverse is now happening. Other countries are ahead of us in this, and some are being held back by our failure to move forward. There is no doubt that Denmark, whose share of our bacon market provides a livelihood for thousands of farmers, would abolish sow stalls if we were to make them illegal and also prohibit the import of pig meat from countries which still used them. My visits to Danish farms convinced me that they have felt compelled to adopt our intensive methods simply to compete with us. So it might be said that our system has exported to Denmark a practice that every right-minded stockman would condemn as cruelty. Their laws relating to animal welfare are far ahead of ours. For example, the keeping of hens in battery cages was made illegal in Denmark long ago, though because they are in the Common Market, the Danes are not now enforcing the law.

Other improvements in animal husbandry would follow from the new approach. The great expansion of our dairy herds with over 100 cows now common has, for example, introduced the need for a high level of antibiotics, along with the possibility of hormones and continual reploughing of pastures with the consequent loss of any variety of flora. The dairy farmer has achieved little extra profit for himself and a massive problem of management. A management agreement could enable him to return to a lower output, a herd of fifty or sixty and traditional kinds of pasture with a wide mix of flora that made antibiotics no longer necessary. His income, however, would not fall, for he would be paid for his stewardship.

We would also be able to cope much more effectively with the mounting problem of nitrates. A farm in an area where the water supply indicates a dangerous level of nitrate could be made the subject of an agreement whereby no artificial fertilizers were used at all and compensation was fixed accordingly. To go further, and have the land farmed biologically, would achieve still more for the flora and fauna. Ideally, one might wish for whole areas to be so farmed; but this will be a possibility only when farmers have gained the knowledge, and agricultural research made the advances, for it to be practical.

One important type of agreement would have to cover those farmers who were planning to switch to biological or organic farming. They need help to tide them over the transition period during which their output inevitably falls, before they are able to come 'on stream' with full production of organic food at premium prices. Modified agreements would be needed for those who were not going fully organic but were aiming to reduce chemical inputs to a minimum. It is in everyone's interest to make it more financially attractive for a farm to become organic than to continue with chemical-based practices.

The encouragement of broad-leaved woodlands should be another aim embodied in farm management agreements. At present, grants are available under the 1986 Act to induce farmers to put small woods on parts of their farm set aside because of the large surpluses of European agriculture – which have begun, at last, to persuade policy-makers that there are other uses for our land apart from food production.

Despite recent fiscal changes, we still continue to put far too much of our land under conifer plantations on the plea of 'import substitution'. Economically this is largely fallacious. There is no gain, but rather a loss, in growing trees expensively in the UK when the timber could be imported from countries which can grow it more cheaply. In terms of landscape it means yet more softwoods, tediously green and already boringly lined up over so much of what was once our wilder countryside. Environmentally and ecologically they are devoid of any merit. No one can rejoice at the view; the landscape is changed for the worse, and no new opportunites for leisure and recreation are afforded. The pattern of wildlife is disturbed, and the rivers are poisoned by the acids they emit. None of this would happen unless taxpayers' money was diverted for the purpose, either through the losses of the Forestry Commission being made good by the Treasury or by grants and tax privileges given to the private investor.

The planting of more broad-leaved woodlands is, of course, another matter. Whether they should take over vast acreages, so that we have new forests of hundreds or even thousands of acres, may be doubted, though those in favour say that this would be no more than returning our landscape to what it looked like two or three centuries ago. However, there is probably general agreement that small woodlands of any size up to twenty or thirty acres would be an environmental gain. Such woodlands ought to become national candidates for management agreements. The farmer who transformed a miniature prairie of a wheat field into a broad-leaved woodland would, in the course of time, see something more pleasing to his eye and more conducive to the revival of wildlife and to people's recreation. With adequate compensation, his finanical prospects should be no less enhanced than the view from his bedroom window.

Let us consider the other schemes that should be available under the new Act. For most farms it would probably be a mixture of several, with the mixture even different on neighbouring properties. Nothing need be excluded that – in the words of the 1986 Act – 'may conserve or enhance the beauty of the area or conserve its flora and fauna'.

There is one particular problem that would need to be looked at squarely, which at present is the source of a great deal of friction between farmers and the rest of the community. This is the problem of public access to farmland. At present it is addressed only through the existence of public footpaths, and even these are by no means always kept open. Farmers naturally dislike the idea of walkers trampling over newly planted fields or leaving gates open. Non-farmers resent being told that a country walk means slogging down a tarmac road with almost all the real countryside fenced off from them, even when they would do no harm by crossing it. They feel particularly aggrieved when they consider that their taxes and the inflated prices they pay for food keep the farms going on that land.

The countryside meant little to those of our forebears who

worked sixteen hours a day in a cotton mill, six days a week, and spent most of Sunday in chapel. The transformation in the life of the British family must be recognized by this new Agriculture Act. The ordinary family now owns a car and, come the weekend, can travel many miles to escape the concrete jungle of the inner city or the lesser jungle of suburbia. Large numbers of pensioners and others made redundant or retired early can make the same journey. Although a majority of the British people once had little or no chance to see or explore the countryside, they do now. Yet the irony is that the quality, beauty and amenities of our countryside grow less as the number who seek them grows more. Farmers should catch at this irony. They should argue that they do not wish to see such a loss, but they need to be helped to keep the country beautiful; and if public access is to be increased, it must be covered by clear rules that are fair to both sides. Since not all these rules could be applied indiscriminately to all forms of countryside, they would be best embodied in farm management agreements.

Public access to a great deal of our countryside would be increased because, under the new system, it would no longer be made artificially profitable to farm all of it. Many, many acres of uplands, in particular, would be taken out of cultivation, and even the running of sheep on the wilder parts of the country would largely come to an end. We in the UK are alone in the world in harbouring an obsession about using all our available land for agriculture. No other country is so obsessed, as can be seen from Table 14 (compiled from the *Production Year Book* of the UN Food and Agriculture Organization).

Only Ireland takes a higher place in the table than the UK, but this is misleading. Ireland's soil and terrain, like those of the Netherlands, are exceptional in that scarcely a corner of the land is not suitable for some kind of farming and, by our standards, abundantly so. Nevertheless a great area of Ireland is neither farmed nor incorporated in some town, but put to no use other than recreation and leisure. France and West Germany can also afford us a lesson. Neither has conurbations encroaching as far out into the countryside as we have, and neither devotes as much of its land to farming as we do,

Table 14   Use of land for agriculture, by country

Country	Percentage of total area used for agriculture
Republic of Ireland	84
United Kingdom	77
Greece	70
Denmark	68
Spain	63
Netherlands	59
France	58
West Germany	50
Belgium and Luxembourg	48
United States	47
Portugal	44
Soviet Union	28
Japan	15
Finland	9
Sweden	9
Canada	8
Norway	3

despite the temptations of the Common Agricultural Policy. The explanation is that vast areas of both countries are either forested (in France 27 per cent, in Germany 30 per cent) or simply open spaces which the public is free to use. In neither country would areas comparable to our moorland tracts of Dartmoor, Exmoor and North Yorkshire be the habitat of tens of thousands of highly subsidized sheep.

Owners of Grades IV and V land need not be denied the right to till their ground for wheat or cover it with lambless ewes. As business men they could embark upon such folly if they wished; but, receiving no grants, subsidies or tax privileges for doing it, they would soon be within reach of Carey Street were they to try. Such land would soon be 'set aside', its owners given the opportunity of negotiating an agreement instead. Assuming that land is to be taken out of agricultural use, it should surely be those millions of acres which cannot be farmed economically yet comprise the very places where other uses can be readily found.

PAYING FOR PROGRESS

'But how could we afford it?' This is the question that is always raised whenever it is suggested that we should give farmers public money for their work as custodians rather than as an inducement to grow more food. To many people it seems that there must be a difference between subsidizing increased production of a basic need and money spent on what they see as inessentials.

The hard economic answer is that there is no difference. Money spent is money spent, the only question being what you get in return. If we can afford to pay billions of pounds a year to inflate land values and produce unwanted food, we shall be no worse off financially if we spend the same amount on conservation – and in practice we would not need to be so extravagant. All the activities we would want to promote could be made economically attractive at a lower price than we now pay to make them harder.

We saw earlier in the book the price that we now pay, in straightfoward financial terms. The figures, confirmed by the OECD and the UK Treasury, show that the present policy causes the average British family to pay £16 a week more for its food than is necessary. So it is absurd for anyone to claim that money is not available for an alternative system. As the taxes on imported food are phased out, it will be feasible to raise other forms of revenue without adding to the total tax burden on the British people. It is inconceivable that the cost of the policy proposed in this book could be even half that of the existing system.

At present we can only guess at the cost of a system of management agreements with grants geared to conservation. A reasonable first estimate would be a total of £2,000 million annually, which represents about £10,000 for every farm. Some might need next to nothing or even nothing, others ten times as much as that average. In total, this is much less than half of what the public is giving now. The public could have not a penny less than £3,000 million a year of their own money left in their pockets to spend as they wished, or the Treasury that much more to distribute on their behalf for the nation's health or education.

We should also consider the wastefulness of the present system in the way that it spends what little money is now available for conservation in trying to mitigate the destructive effects of the much larger amounts spent on pushing up output. Much of this money – the money of taxpayers and consumers, including the poorest among us – subsidizes the agribusiness man and not, in most cases, the bona-fide farmer.

One farmer in Kent has been given £100,000 not to drain marshland and so change it from good pasture to being capable of growing wheat. Another farmer in Dorset is to receive a subsidy of £20,400 a year for sixty-five years for not uprooting woodland to enable wheat and other cereals to be produced. In Norfolk, to avoid 748 acres of the Halvergate Marshes being drained for even more cereals to be grown, the four farmers concerned expect to receive £100,000 of public money every year for twenty years. It has been reported that £40 million of taxpayers' money will be needed to meet the claims being made under the 1981 Wildlife and Countryside Act by farmers and landowners who would otherwise convert marshland, woodlands and Sites of Special Scientific Interest to land fit for cereals.

The Countryside Commission and the Nature Conservancy Council and its successor bodies have a hopeless task in trying to protect our countryside against the ravages of the assault – as indeed does everybody else involved. The money available, even if it reaches the £40 million, will not be enough. Yet not a penny of it would be needed were it not for the system of subsidized output that alone makes these proposed acts of destruction pay.

A MINISTRY FOR WHAT?

If we were starting afresh to devise a new system of government control to allow agriculture to prosper and for the countryside to be protected, no one could possibly reach the conclusion that the system we have now in the UK would be the one to choose. On almost every count it would be held unsuitable.

The Ministry of Agriculture, Fisheries and Food ought to

be the guardian of both agriculture and the countryside. Farming and conservation should travel together in parallel, and anyone engaged either in their policy-making or in their everyday work in the field, far from seeing any conflict between them, should look upon them as two complementary faces of the rural scene. For forty-five years, we have had the opposite situation. A cabinet minister who goes down to the House of Commons to propose that money should be taken from the taxpayer and given to the farmer for the purpose of ripping up thousands of miles of hedgerow, destroying the habitat of a wide range of wildlife, in order to grow more surplus wheat, is hardly qualified to lead a ministry of 7,000 officials concerned with the countryside's protection. It is this ministry that has erected the treadmill, goading and cajoling farmers to go on producing more and more each year, and to get bigger and bigger, regardless of how much the farmer must overreach himself, in numerous ways, not least of all by continually borrowing more money from the bank.

The ministry's one overriding objective has been to secure ever greater increases of output from our farms. Officials whose thinking has been conditioned by this objective throughout the whole of their career in the department cannot be expected to change. It is too tall an order for anyone.

One possibility is to rename the department the Ministry of Rural Affairs, and to coax the Common Market into reshaping the CAP into a common rural affairs policy. This idea has been canvassed for several years; and on the face of it, it is a plausible step in the right direction. To be effective, such a department would have to be, in the jargon of Whitehall, the 'sponsoring ministry' in rural affairs, and other departments would become subordinate to it. In the event of a clash of opinion, the Ministry of Rural Affairs would win and the Department of the Environment lose.

Let us take some examples of what might happen. Anxiety is expressed about our water supplies, and it is shown that in many of them the nitrate level is rising too fast and well beyond the level recommended by the World Health Organization. The Department of Health claims an interest and wants the matter investigated in a formal inquiry. The Department of the Environment also says it has an interest in the subject and supports the need for an inquiry. However, the Ministry of Rural Affairs maintains that the problem rests with itself. As the 'sponsoring ministry', it would have the right to make the ultimate decision about what should be done. The ministry would also have a very good reason for not wanting an inquiry for, in its present existence as the Ministry of Agriculture, it has itself been responsible for the policy of increasing the use of nitrates and giving subsidies to farmers to encourage them to use more.

A similar dispute could arise over the law relating to pesticides. Pesticide regulation is much more lax in the UK than in the United States, Canada and Japan, where the safety and health of the general public are treated as of paramount importance – much more important than producing more food. As it is not inconceivable that at some point there will be a demand in Britain for equally strong precautions, each of the above three government departments would stake a claim to the decision-making. Health and environment both being self-evidently affected by pesticides, and both departments being likely to seek greater rather than lesser controls over their use, an obvious clash would come with the Ministry of Rural Affairs so long as it harboured officials of the old Ministry of Agriculture. To expect them to admit as being unsafe what they had for years claimed was perfectly safe is to ask too much of the nature of civil servants. Also, the very close working relationship between the Ministry of Agriculture and the representatives of the chemical industry, developed over more than forty years (and over many luncheon tables), has unfitted its senior officials for work in the world of today.

Another reason why a Ministry of Rural Affairs might not succeed is that it is scarcely possible to establish a line between what is rural and what is urban. A radius around London, for example, would have to be drawn, but where along the M4 does the line cross? Between Slough and London there are still a few pockets of rural life, not just green fields with ponies grazing, but oases of genuine countryside and an astonishing variety of wildlife.

There are, in fact, very few parts of England – though in Wales and Scotland it is different – that are now truly rural. Even Dartmoor, Exmoor and North Yorkshire derive more of their income from the tourism industry than from agriculture. A Ministry of Rural Affairs could then dabble in the affairs of something far removed from what the Ministry of Agriculture does now, and for which its officials are ill equipped.

It would be better to abolish the Ministry of Agriculture altogether. Its post-war *raison d'être* has gone. The days are over when the policy-makers were agreed that we should strive for maximum food production, so logically, the days of the ministry should be over, too. Its abolition would mark our departure from a policy that has done much damage already and, were it allowed to continue, would cause a catastrophe. Its demise would serve as a signal to us all that we had changed direction at last.

The ministry grew out of the old Board of Agriculture of Victorian times. When more than one in five of the population were engaged on the land, there was a reason for its existence; now that the farming population has fallen to one in forty, the reason is less apparent. Nor is there any evidence that the few who are left in farming are so enamoured with the ministry that they would mount the barricades in its defence. Its popularity has never been so low. Not an issue of the main farming papers is published without an attack on either its incompetence or its lack of sympathy for agriculture. If its doors closed tomorrow, no farmer in the land would sleep the worse.

Before bringing the ministry to an end, each of its functions would have to be looked at to decide whether it were needed and, if so, where it would be transferred. The ministry is currently a major spending department. In 1938, when there were approximately 500,000 farmers, well over twice as many as there are now, its expenditure added up to just under £4 million, or £8 per individual farmer. With the pound now worth about one-thirtieth of its pre-war value, this is £240 in today's money. Contrast this with the ministry's estimates for 1990–1, which, excluding EEC receipts, came to £2,508 million, representing £13,000 for the average farmer. One reason for the explosion in this expenditure is the great change in the ratio of officials to farmers. In 1938 there was one person on the staff of the ministry for every 125 farmers; today there is one for every 16.

A more important reason for this great increase in spending is the system of price support. Take it away, and one removes the heart of the ministry. In so far as agriculture is an industry, there seems no reason why its affairs should not come under the Department of Trade and Industry, like any other.

The total removal of all import levies and duties would open Britains's doors to dumping. As explained earlier in the book, there is a strong case for protecting our agriculture against food imports at prices subsidized by foreign governments, for this is a hostile act which has the effect of undermining our economy. It would be consistent with a free trade policy to keep in force the system of import levies and duties but to suspend their operation once we were satisfied that there was no element of government subsidy on the part of the exporting country. The levies and duties could be reimposed immediately if it were shown that subsidies had been reinstated. Either jointly or separately, the levies and duties would be fixed at a level which would nullify the benefits of the subsidy, but no higher than that. Their fixing and administration should be the responsibility of the Department of Customs and Excise.

With the Ministry of Agriculture abolished, what of its function with regard to food? An appreciable amount of laws, mostly in the form of statutory regulations, exist to ensure standards of food safety, and their administration is the responsibility of MAFF. Far too often, this has given rise to conflict within the ministry between officials concerned with health and others anxious to co-operate with pesticide manufacturers or the food manufacturing industries. Nor has the ministry's close working partnership with the NFU helped, for spokesmen for the farming community have usually taken the side of the chemical industry against the consumer.

There comes to mind a very obvious solution to where we should hive off the functions of watching over food safety, and that is to the Department of Health. When it was also the Department of Social Security the two wings of the ministry did not fly easily together; and now that social security is the province of a separate ministry, this leaves the door open for a new department: of Food and Health. The Secretary of State for Food and Health would preside over two departments with a common interest – to maintain a healthy nation. The cost of unhealthy eating is borne by the National Health Service; a ministry that gives the lead to healthier eating habits and ensuring that safer food comes on to the market is in unison with the doctors struggling to cope with a lengthening line of patients suffering from the many disorders and diseases which we know to be caused by what we eat.

The chemical and food manufacturing industries, both so much more loosely controlled in the UK than in other wealthy industrialized countries, would undoubtedly mount strong opposition to this change. The pharmaceutical industry, parts of which are entwined in the business of antibiotics, pesticides and nitrates, would also join them. Their opposition, however, should serve as a signal that the change ought to be beneficial to the rest of us.

The record of the Department of Health has several blemishes which ought not to be overlooked. In 1990 it published a booklet, *The NHS Reforms and You*, which included a four-page digression giving advice about healthier living. This urged us to consider eating ten kinds of food, chickens being one of them. This means broilers, the day-old birds converted into chicken weighing 5 lb within 49 days only because of the massive use of growth stimulants in the form of antibiotics. This advice demonstrates well enough the ignorance of health officials about our farming methods.

The same ministry officials proposed that it should be a criminal offence for unpasteurized milk to be sold for human consumption. Little did they realize that pasteurization also destroys the benign bacteria that prevent milk 'going off', enabling it to be safe to drink for usually a fortnight rather than a few days. Producers and distributors of raw 'green top' milk are subject to more rigorous inspection by council health officials, and no doubt rightly so, and rigorous steps to make sure it is safe to drink are taken. When the Department of Health proposed the ban on this, a campaign had to be launched to counter the charges and to show that pasteurization destroys most of milk's nutritional value. The outcome was a victory for the remaining minority of dairy producers, mostly small farmers, who supply raw milk in mainly rural areas. The department is perhaps now a little more knowledgeable about this branch of agriculture.

Some significance may be given to the role played by the Dairy Trade Association; representing the interests of the multiple dairy distributors, it has proved itself a powerful lobbying force; it knows how to operate in Whitehall and has argued consistently for the sale of pure milk to be made illegal. The fact that its members sell only pasteurized milk and the public seems to prefer untreated milk when it is available may or may not influence the association's attitude.

From these two examples a danger can be foreseen if all questions about the food crisis were transferred to the Department of Health. On the other hand, to link food and health ministerially would be an enormous encouragement to those thousands of doctors who now despair of any government highlighting the importance of food in our health. For years they have beaten a path to the Department of Health to be told that matters of food are for the Ministry of Agriculture; and, should they continue their journey there, a subordinate official may make reassuring noises, unconvincing to any medical practitioner. The complacency – or worse – in protecting the quality of our food is a serious count in the indictment against MAFF.

The new policy, then, requires MAFF to be dismembered. Its commercial functions, which include fisheries, would go to the Department of Trade and Industry. The great task of adapting agriculture to its second role of protecting the environment is for the Department of the Environment; and the no less important but hitherto suppressed functions of food safety, to a new Department of Food and Health. The Department of the Environment would also take the place of MAFF in its partnership with the Department of Education and Science in the supervision of agricultural research.

The latter would be then given the green light to advance biological farming, no matter what the chemical industry might say. It is one of the scandals of the present time that research of this kind is so underfunded. It is sensible that much of the public money available for agricultural research has been cut, as virtually all of it has been devoted to finding means of increasing agricultural output. But the need for research into how to lower the input/output ratio is urgent, and it is linked with the research into biological farming. The Ministry of Agriculture has, over the years, failed to recognize this need or to see the link between inputs and biological methods. At conferences and on farm visits, ministry officials have scoffed at organic husbandry, but at last they seem to see a place for this alternative. A modest degree of research has now been approved, although it is still left to private individuals to take the principal risks; and in this none has done more than the Prince of Wales.

Over 4,000 of the ministry's staff are in the Agricultural Development Advisory Service. These are the men – plus a few women – who go out into the field to advise the farming community. All their advice, of course, has been about how to increase output, a function no longer necessary. As a result, the Agriculture Act of 1986 has made an attempt to give them the additional role of advising the farmer on conservation. The idea is misconceived, though it may be well intentioned – despite the suggestion that its purpose is to give ADAS a new role lest public opinion is raised in protest at the taxpayers' money being spent on employing people to advise farmers how to increase the surpluses. Since its beginning, ADAS has been a nationalized service of agricultural consultants; and because it has offered its services free, other consultants, apart from the outstandingly competent, have been displaced from the profession.

Very few of the ADAS staff have either the training or the temperament for the more recent role of advising on conservation. The right course would be to denationalize the service. ADAS staff who are good at their jobs would be able to gain a living in private practice; the others could be transferred to some other branch of the Civil Service. If a farmer wants advice about how to run his business more profitably, let him go to a consultant in private practice. It is scarcely the duty of the taxpayer to pay for such advice.

So ADAS ought to be wound up. In its place there should be an Environmental Advisory Service to give free advice to farmers about how to farm with regard to every aspect of the environment. As a food producer, and therefore as a business man, the farmer should get his advice from where he likes and pay for it accordingly, like any other business man. However, the farmer is entitled to look to the taxpayer to pay for the advice he needs in his role of steward of the countryside. The work of the new Environmental Advisory Service would therefore be entirely paid for out of public funds.

To which department of state should this Environmental Advisory Service be attached? The Department of the Environment seems to be the best candidate. A major argument for the farmer is that more public money would be likely to flow in his direction were this the choice.

Lastly, we have to consider the important question of who should administer the system of farm management agreements. MAFF, even if it continues to exist, is not to be trusted with work of this kind; its whole past is in contradiction to the new spirit needed. The Countryside Commission should certainly be involved, and perhaps it should co-operate with county or district councils. Setting up an efficient and sensitive body to operate the system will be essential, but at bottom it is a question of will. Determination to achieve the principles will ensure that the details will follow naturally. Once farmers see that the new policy gives them a common interest with conservationists, and once they understand how vital this is for their own future security, the will to change must come.

THE BIGGEST BARRIER TO CHANGE – THE CAP

Changes as radical as those I propose cannot be made without having to face strong opposition from those who have been doing very nicely out of the old system. The big agribusinesses and landowners, and the suppliers of fertilizer, pesticides and machinery, will trumpet their objections. All of them will, of course, claim to be moved by a pure concern for the public welfare. The army of civil servants in MAFF and ADAS, too, are unlikely to admit very happily that almost everything they have been pressing on farmers for more than four decades has been misconceived and harmful. This sort of resistance is inevitable, but the public at large is increasingly aware of the true motives behind it, and it can be overcome.

There remains one big institutional barrier to progress, and our success in the UK will depend on how far we are able to cross it: the Common Agricultural Policy of the European Community. Enough has been said already on the damage done to ourselves, our farmers, our economy and others throughout the world by the system of protection embodied in the CAP. We now need to find answers to three questions. How much can we do within the limits the CAP imposes on us? How far can we get it to change so as to allow real progress to be made? And if it cannot be got to change far enough or fast enough, how can we escape from its restrictions?

The answer to the first question is that we could do more than we are doing even within the present CAP. Other European countries are ahead of Britain in control of pollution and in restraining the excesses of battery farming, for example. Also the ESAs which could form the basis for a new system of farm management agreements are specifically allowed by one of the CAP's regulations. When the Council of Agriculture Ministers passed Regulation 797/85 – a long piece of legislation authorizing various subsidies – articles 18 and 19 were inserted. Article 18 allows subsidies to be given in 'non-agricultural sectors and with the needs of environmental protection'. Article 19 defines 'environmentally sensitive areas' as 'of recognized importance from an ecological and landscape point of view'; it then goes on to allow the national government to give aid to farmers in such an area 'to preserve or improve the environment'. Unfortunately, article 19 adds the proviso that all prospective schemes must be submitted to the European Commission, and the Commission must decide 'on the whole aid system planned, including the application areas'. The latter is a fly in the ointment, and it severely limits the usefulness of the regulation in its present form. It does not allow us to do what we should do and declare the whole of the UK an environmentally sensitive area.

So the short answer to the first question is that we can and should do more under the exisiting CAP. But all hope of radical change depends on first changing the CAP itself.

The biggest impulse for change comes from the unsupportable surpluses that the system still generates. We already have milk quotas, and there are already schemes for persuading or compelling farmers to set aside part of their land. We are faced with the absurdity of a system that hands money to farmers to induce them to step up production to the limit on some of their acres, and then hands them more money for not growing anything at all on others. While this goes on, the CAP still spends 90 per cent of its funds on subsidizing output and only 10 per cent on promoting structural change.

So change must come, and we must ensure that it is of a kind that benefits us and encourages the kind of farming we want to see. We must recognize straight away that the interests of farmers in the UK do not always coincide with those of farmers in other European countries. For one thing, farmers form a much higher proportion of the total population in most of them; and for another, although the treadmill is going round in northern Europe, its detrimental effect is yet to catch up with what has happened here. It may be another ten years before it does – although is to be hoped that other countries will learn from our mistakes and not repeat them. In any case, we cannot expect to see any urgency among the other northern European countries for the kind of reform that is essential for the treadmill to stop turning.

Although other farmers in the EEC may be on the economic treadmill, the chemical industry has a long way to go before it persuades continental agriculture to use its products on the same scale as in the UK. The dangers listed in the first half of this book apply chiefly to Britain, and only to a minor extent in the rest of the Common Market. Apart from the Dutch, the other countries generally use nitrates no more than we did some thirty years ago. Pesticides play only

a minor part on most continental farms; and as for antibiotics, hormones, arsenic and the other aids of intensive husbandry, their use is generally limited compared with ours.
Above all, in continental Europe the system has not become
an engine of destruction, ruining wildlife and countryside,
wetlands, the downs, heaths and moors.

This means that the policy outlined in this book whereby
farmers would be compensated for not doing a list of
undesirable things would be of little, if any, appeal to them.
The policy simply would fail as a mechanism in the rest of
the Common Market to support farmers' incomes, if at the
same time guaranteed prices were taken away. To convince
the others to 'go green' and to be paid accordingly in the
place of the present CAP would be an impossible task.
Millions of them cannot change to green as they are that
already; and those who are on the chemical treadmill seem
likely to turn the wheel many times more before they tire of
the effort.

Even in those countries that are most like the UK, such as
Denmark and the Netherlands, there is no evidence that their
Ministers of Agriculture will be encouraged to support any
British proposals to change the system. While it is true that
agriculture in Denmark and the Netherlands is of a high
standard of efficiency, both nations are beneficiaries of the
CAP as it now functions. In neither is there any pressure on
the Minister of Agriculture to act in a way that would be
favourable to us. Experience in past years shows that much
the same can be said of Belgium, Luxembourg and Ireland.
As for Greece, a major argument for its joining the Common
Market was that Greek agriculture, the country's dominant
industry, would flourish with the extra support of the CAP.
The same point was put, although rather less strongly, in
favour of Spain and Portugal joining the Community.

If it turns out to be impossible to get the CAP changed in
the ways that are vital to us, then we must be prepared to
take the only other course open to us. We must announce
that we are withdrawing from it. Of course, the supporters
of the CAP tell us that any such move would be an instant
disaster. Leaving the CAP would mean leaving (or being

expelled from) the European Community, and in that terrifying event we would soon be living in impoverished isolation, unable to trade with Europe and with no other important trading partners left. It makes a good horror story for a winter night; let us take a look at the facts.

Originally, when the UK prepared to negotiate its entry into the EEC, we were firmly told by the Six that we could not expect the benefits of a wider market for our manufactured goods unless we accepted an agricultural policy that might have disadvantages for us. Those sentiments were repeated *ad nauseam* by the proponents of British entry. We are now in a position to say that, far from receiving any benefits, our manufacturing industry has suffered appallingly. We now import from the other Common Market countries manufactured goods worth thousands of millions of pounds *more* than we export to them, and economists have said that this represents about a million jobs lost. Twenty per cent of our manufacturing industry has gone, having been displaced by industry across the Channel.

There seem to be three reasons for this transfer of real wealth from our country to the others. First of all, our tariffs used to be higher against their manufactured goods than theirs were against ours, and so the removal of the tariffs gave them an immediate advantage. Secondly, there has been the creation of the 'golden triangle', mentioned in Chapter 9, between Paris, Hamburg and Milan. Millions of people have moved into this region to try to find prosperity as new industries were established (but the boundaries of the triangle cannot be exactly drawn, and many people would say it can be distorted to include the south-east of England). That there has been a pull away from the rest of the UK must be indisputable. The third reason for the transfer of wealth is the CAP itself. It put up the price of food for British wage earners and with it the level of wages. Average wages rose by no less than 75 per cent soon after our entry into the Common Market.

Any threat to expel us from the EEC if we do not continue to toe the line in the CAP is very hollow. Our partners would lose far more than we would if they tried it. Even within the CAP our leverage is greater than most people realize. Because the UK is one of its two chief paymasters, without our money it would collapse. We can afford to take a confident stance and speak up for what we know we need.

If the CAP did collapse, it would mean a lot of votes lost for some European governments, and a great many well-paid jobs lost in the bureaucracy. There would be a lot of loud shouting, but this does not mean that the EEC would be worse off in reality. With more than 60 per cent of the Community budget going on agricultural support, the resources available to help other sectors of the economy are restricted. In particular, the immense new demand for financial help and investment in the countries of Eastern Europe cannot be met if the Community continues to squander its resources on a bankrupt CAP.

The idea that the CAP is an important factor in European unity is absurd. There are natural conflicts of interest between the twelve countries. In a system of free trade they would be resolved by the market in favour of the most efficient producers of each product. In the present situation of political horse-trading they cause endless friction: lamb wars, turkey wars, fish wars, wine wars, even cauliflower wars.

It is nonsense, then, to suppose that if we withdrew from the CAP it would cause the whole EEC to collapse. Any truth in such a claim, after it has been in existence for more than thirty years, shows that it must be an edifice too flimsy to deserve to survive. It is true, however, that our withdrawal would cause the CAP itself to collapse. For without the revenue transmitted by our Treasury, there would be insufficient funds to keep it in existence, unless the other member states agreed to a most substantial increase in VAT or some other contribution.

The collapse of the CAP would then enable each member state to devise its own policy for agriculture, or for northern and southern Europe to have separate common policies. This latter idea has been canvassed in West Germany and could well be considered a practical alternative.

It goes without saying that the UK's withdrawal should be announced and carried through in the friendliest possible way. Of course, strong pressure would be applied to keep us in, but at bottom the other major countries of the EEC understand quite well why the CAP can never fit us, and they would not really be surprised by our escape.

OUT IN THE OPEN

So we in the UK can plan our way forward with precision and confidence. Here, in conclusion, is a summary of what we must do.

First, we must escape from the controls now embodied in the CAP that stop us doing what we clearly need to do. If the CAP cannot be changed, then we must leave it.

The freedom we then gain must be used to reverse our whole agricultural policy. Instead of subsidizing output, and so forcing farmers on to the high-input/high-output tread-mill, we must instead support them as custodians of the countryside, paying them for their services in this capacity and making sure that these services really are delivered.

We should do this through a system of farm management agreements, similar in many ways to those now reached in the Environmentally Sensitive Areas already designated. The status of ESA should be extended to the whole of the country.

The cost of all this is likely to be substantially below what we now spend and would be controlled by a simple principle. No public money would ever again be handed out to farmers who did not in return accept the duty to respect the landscape, the animals in their charge and the health of the community at large, in particular in its need for uncontaminated food and water.

We should open our ports to food from any country in the world that will send us what we want at prices we are ready to pay, safeguarding ourselves only against dumping and against food produced by practices that are banned in our own country. This is good ecology as well as good economics; for the cheapest food of any particular kind is generally produced in those countries that are by nature most suited to growing it, and so need less human interference in the ecosystem.

In this way we can return to what we ought never to have

abandoned: a ready supply of healthy, cheap and varied food, and the freedom to preserve our own countryside as we would wish to see it. For our farmers it means escape from the treadmill and a secure future as the business-like suppliers of what the public really wants to have from them. For all of us, it means securing the future of our two most important resources: our food and our land.

SELECT
BIBLIOGRAPHY

Astor, Viscount and Seebohm Rowntree, B., *British Agriculture*, London, Faber, 1938.

Balfour, Lady E., *The Living Soil*, London, Faber, 1944.

Body, R., *Agriculture: The Triumph and the Shame*, London, Temple Smith, 1982.

Body, R. *Farming in the Clouds*, London, Temple Smith, 1984.

Body, R., *Red or Green for Farmers?*, Saffron Walden, Broad Leys, 1987.

Brown, L. R. and Eckholm, E. P., *By Bread Alone*, Oxford, Pergamon, 1975.

Carson, R., *Silent Spring*, London, Hamish Hamilton, 1963.

Carter, V. G. and Dale, T., *Topsoil and Civilization*, Norman, University of Oklahoma Press, 1974.

Cobbett, *Rural Rides*, Harmondsworth, Penguin, 1967.

Department of the Environment Nitrate Co-ordination Group, *Nitrate in Water*, London, HMSO, 1986.

Dover, Dr M. J., *A Better Mousetrap: Improving Pest Management in Agriculture*, Washington, DC, World Resources Institute, 1985.

Druce, C., *Chicken and Egg*, London, Green Print, 1989.

Erlichman, J., *Gluttons for Punishment*, London, Penguin, 1986.

Fream, *Elements of Agriculture*, London, John Murray, 1955.

George, S., *How the Other Half Dies: The Real Reasons for World Hunger*, London, Pelican, 1986.

Green, Dr B., *Countryside Conservation*, London, Allen & Unwin, 1985.

Hodges, R. D. and Arden–Clark, C., *Soil Erosion in Britain*, Bristol, Soil Association, 1986.

Institute of Terrestrial Ecology, *Landscape Changes in Britain*, Cambridge, 1986.

Pye-Smith, C. and Hall, C. (eds), *The Countryside We Want: A Manifesto for the Year 2000*, Hartland, Green Books, 1987.

Royal Commission on Environmental Pollution, chaired by Sir. H. Kornberg, *Agriculture and Pollution*, 7th report, London, HMSO, 1979.

Russell, Sir J., *English Farming*, London, Collins, 1942.

Schumacher, Dr E. F., *Small Is Beautiful*, London, Blond & Briggs, 1973.

Whitlock, R. (ed.), *Agricultural Records AD 220–1977*, London, J. Baker, 1978.

World Resources Institute and International Institute for Environment and Development, *World Resources 1988–89*, New York, Basic Books, 1988.

INDEX

References are to the U.K. unless otherwise indicated.

INDEX

INDEX

INDEX

in organic farming 254, 259, 260, 290; phosphates 37, 46–9, 138, 232, 235, 255; potash 17, 37; price rise 199, 230–1, 232; productivity gains 42–4, 100, 142, 171, 199, 231; subsidies 17, 138, 142, 200, 235; use in EEC countries 233, 307; use in Third World 199, 200, 230–3, 245
Field Monument Act (1972) 277
fields:
  size of 18, *see also* pasture
Fiji: sugar industry 241–6 *passim*
financial institutions:
  banks' capital structure 192; investment in land 3–4, 127–8, 186, 187, 196; loans to farmers 86, 128, 148, 193–6, 216; USA 219–20
Finch, Dr Stanley 267
Finkplix 66
Finland:
  price support figures 181; restrictions on biocides 27, 28; use of land 295
First World War: effect on agriculture 131–2
fish:
  Canadian tinned salmon 204, 274; fishmeal for stock 71–2, 171; phosphate poisoning 47, 48; shellfish 36
fishing industry 97
food:
  artificial cost 2–3, 161, 178–84, 203–7, 231, 271, 284–5, 296, 309; change of eating habits 205–6, 283–4; choice restricted 202–5, 271–4; dietary needs and malnutrition 163–4, 229, 235; healthier f. needed 302–3, 311; irradiation 75; price in free market 7, 129–34 *passim*, 159–61, 311
Food and Agriculture Organization (FAO):
  food data 163, 164, 165, 168, 294; World Food Conference 167
Food and Drug Administration (USA) 56, 69, 70, 71
Food and Environment Act (1989) 31
Food and Health, Ministry of, proposed 302, 303

footpaths 293
Ford Motor Company 212
foreign exchange market 173–4
forestry:
  broad-leaf woodland 93–4, 292–3; conifer plantations 79, 279, 292; countries compared 93, 295; future demands 292; world acreage 164–5, *see also* hedgerows and trees
Forestry Commission 79, 293
France:
  afforestation 93; arable farming 134; beneficiary of CAP 5; colonial trade 233–4; eutrophication 48; horsemeat market 112, 126; manufacturing output 210; organic food 284; productivity factors 114, 135; trade balance with UK 211; use of land 294–4
Fraser, Malcolm 225–6
Fream: *Elements of Agriculture* 42, 44
free trade:
  historical 128–32, 154, 169, 217; challenge for farmers 8, 177; lack of in EEC 213–15, 221, 240, 271–4; need for in agriculture 6–7, 129, 174–6, 233, 311; route to peace 216–17; UK's need to declare 240–1, 273–4
freedom of information, *see* secrecy
Freedom of Information Act (USA) 31
Friends of the Earth 288
From Boom to Bust? (Jackson) 207
Frost, C. F.: *Research and Development in Agriculture* 14
fungicides, *see* pesticides
Funk, Dr Walter 213

gastric torsion 56
General Agreement on Tariffs and Trade (GATT) 6, 153, 203
George, Susan 167–8
Germany, West:
  arable farming 134; CAP policy 310; contributions to CAP 5; eutrophication 48; farm wages 134; manufacturing output 210; monetary policy 208; organic food 284; productivity factors 114, 135; trade

· 321 ·

INDEX

INDEX

Thames Water Authority 77
Thatcher, Margaret 180
Third World:
  demand for food 152, 157–8, 162–3,
  167–8, 229–32, 235; economic
  colonialism 158, 233–4, 241–2, 286;
  effects of EEC policies 222, 228,
  240–6; intensive farming lobby 164;
  manufacturing industry 236–7; need
  to expand agriculture 199, 200, 221,
  236–8; trade not aid 236–7; use of
  chemicals 199, 200, 230–5, 245, 255;
  use of machinery 230, 243, 245
Threlfall Dr, 60
Thring, C. F. (Peter) 142, 147
Times quoted 70
Topsoil and Civilization (Carter and
  Dale) 11
trace elements *see* chemicals
Trade and Industry, Dept of 301, 303
Treasury, The:
  curbs on grants 141; price support
  figures admitted 179, 180, 206, 296
trees *see* forestry; hedgerows and trees
trimethroprim 59, 60
Trinidad: sugar 241–6 *passim*
Tull, Jethro 85
Turkey:
  alluvial soil 12; restrictions on
  biocides 27, 28
turkeys *see* poultry farming
Twelftree, Mr and Mrs 73
2, 4, 5-T herbicide 28, 147

unemployment 3, 113, 208–12, 216
Unilever 103, 192, 248, 252, 267
Union of Banana Exporting Countries
  159
United Brands company 159
United Nations *see* Food and
  Agriculture Organization; World
  Health Organization
United States of America:
  biocide testing and restrictions 27,
  28, 30, 31, 32, 265, 266, 299; cancer
  experiments 46; cereal exports 79, 99;
  dairy farming 69, 221–2; drug
  research and restrictions 55–6, 61,
  64, 69–71; eutrophication 47, 48, 49;

farming crisis 219–22, 240; free trade
  with UK tradition 99, 217, 220;
  freedom of information 31; grain
  production 24, 110–11, 130, 132,
  152–3, 217–20; land availability and
  use 23, 165, 218, 233, 295; price
  support figures 181; soil destruction 9,
  23, 233; surplus milk 69; trade deficit
  221, 222; use of pigs in research 53;
  wartime support for Britain 169
universities: research 189
Uruguay: land usage 167

vancomycin 57
VAT: CA financed by 178
veal *see* calf rearing
Veterinary Record quoted 53, 74
veterinary service:
  data on drug variance 35;
  dilemma of factory farms 60–1;
  homoeopathic 262, 263;
  pressure from drug companies 60
Vietnam: Agent Orange 28
Villiers, C. P. 148
vitamain E deficiency 56
vivisection 33, 190
Volac system of calf rearing 63
Voluntary Committee on Overseas Aid
  and Development 165

wages *see* farmworkers; income
Wales:
  19th C. farming 131; hill farm
  support 278; loss of moorland 92;
  unemployment 208
Walker, Peter 126, 127, 182, 207
War on Want 165
Warwickshire:
  conservation of hedgerows 87;
  loss of trees 94
Washington Post quoted 70
water:
  acid pollution 292;
  antibiotics contamination 63–4; EEC
  directive (1985) 44, 46;
  eutrophication 47–9; nitrate
  contamination 8, 38, 44–6, 79, 256,
  290, 291, 298–9; slurry hazards 75–6;
  Third World needs 230; w. table
  77–8